SUNY SERIES IN THE SOCIOLOGY OF WORK
Judith R. Blau, Editor

*Organization in a
Changing Environment*

Russell K. Schutt

Organization In a Changing Environment

Unionization of Welfare Employees

State University of New York Press

To Beth

Published by
State University of New York Press, Albany

© 1986 State University of New York

All rights reserved

Printed in the United States of America

For information, address State University of New York
Press, State University Plaza, Albany, N.Y., 12246

Library of Congress Cataloging in Publication Data

Schutt, Russell K.
  Organization in a changing environment.

  Bibliography: p.
    1. Trade-unions—Social workers—United States.
  2. Organizational change—United States. 3. Social work
  administration—United States. I. Title.
  HV46.2.U6S38 1985   362.88'113613'0973   84-26787
  ISBN 0-88706-044-7
  ISBN 0-88706-045-5 (pbk.)

10 9 8 7 6 5 4 3 2 1

Contents

Figures

Tables

Preface

The 1960s and 1970s were years of turbulence and change in government social services. A rapid expansion in the size of government social service agencies was followed by vigorous efforts to limit their growth. Organized protests by recipients, sharp debate by legislators, and widespread unionization of government employees indicated the strains associated with these changes.

Conflict and change in organizations have long been a central concern of sociologists. Since the 1960s, however, new approaches have been used to explain these phenomena. An emphasis on the internal logic of organizational characteristics has been replaced by concern with the impact of the environment. A presumption of organizational cohesion has given way to recognition of the frequency of conflict. *Organization in a Changing Environment* draws on such insights of recent research and theory to elaborate an integrated theory of the emergence and change of voluntary organizations.

The union of welfare employees selected for analysis utilizing this theory shared many characteristics with other government employee unions emerging in the 1960s. In the years after its emergence, leaders and members of the union confronted many of the same problems that their counterparts in other voluntary organizations must resolve. Seemingly self-destructive features of democracy, difficulty in maintaining supportive relations with other organizations, and membership apathy were recurrent concerns. Periods of union impact alternated with periods of ineffectiveness. By contributing to the understanding of these phenomena, the book may at least partially repay some of the many employees, union members and leaders, and agency officials who contributed their time to the research on which this book is based.

I conducted research on the Illinois Union of Social Service Employees in several stages for a period of ten years. In this time, many people contributed to the project. Some of their contributions have been noted in my previous reports and papers. Nonetheless, I must again acknowledge my indebtedness to the members and leaders of the Illinois Union of Social Service Employees, to several officials in public aid in Cook County and the State of Illinois, and to many non-union employees for their willingness to participate in portions of the research. I am especially grateful to those former and current union activists who submitted to interviews of an hour or more. Although a pledge of confidentiality prevents me from acknowledging their specific contributions, their remarks were critical for the effort to convert the fruits of earlier more limited research into a book.

Many sociologists have helped at various times in the research on which this book is based. My first debt is to Mildred A. Schwartz, who facilitated my dissertation efforts, encouraged me to begin additional research in this area after completing the dissertation, and provided frequent advice on the book. My colleague Robert A. Dentler contributed many insightful comments and sound criticisms. Judith R. Blau, editor of SUNY's series in the sociology of work also gave excellent advice. Howard Aldrich, Leonard Blumberg, John Johnstone, Richard Weatherley and Gordon Zahn made many helpful suggestions. Helen R. Miller and William P. Bridges also made important contributions to much earlier stages of the research. During the final stages of manuscript preparation, I have become deeply indebted to Malcolm Willison, of the SUNY Press staff.

The work of my research assistants in this project has been exemplary. I am grateful to Platon Coutsoukis, Doreen Drury, Francois Louis, Jeannie Rich, and Elfriede Wedam for their dedication. Roberta Baskerville, Anne Foxx, and Cheryl Morrisson each earned my gratitude for typing portions of the manuscript. The Computing Services staff at the University of Massachusetts at Boston provided help on various occasions. Several Faculty Development Grants from the University of Massachusetts at Boston provided financial support for the later stages of the research. Throughout this work, my wife, Elizabeth Schneider Schutt has provided encouragement, support, and understanding.

CHAPTER ONE

Introduction

ORGANIZATIONAL EMERGENCE

Public Sector Unionism

In 1960, public employees were one of the largest blocs of unorganized white-collar workers (Hart, 1964), and white-collar workers in general seemed uninterested in labor unions (Strauss, 1954). The reasons "Why White-Collar Workers Can't Be Organized" were said to include allegiance to their employer, identification with professionals, aversion to collective action, and a nonunion tradition (Bruner, 1957; Burns and Solomon, 1963). Surveys of white-collar government employees found that informal social relations functioned in harmony with organizational goals, and that the authority of supervisors was relatively high (Blau, 1963; Francis and Stone, 1956).

This pattern of employee adaptation was ruptured within the next five years. The number of federal employee collective bargaining agreements rose from twenty-six in 1961 to 600 in 1967. The number of such agreements in municipal government climbed from forty-seven in 1943 to 512 in 1965 (Posey, 1968). Membership in the American Federation of Government Employees (A.F.G.E.) grew from 60,000 in 1959 to 115,000 in 1963, and to 255,000 in 1980. Membership in the American Federation of State, County, and Municipal Employees (A.F.S.C.M.E.) expanded by five hundred thousand from 1964 to 1976, and had reached 1,098,000 by 1980 (*Business Week*, 1963; U.S. Bureau of the Census, 1984:440; Wurf, 1976:175). By the mid-1970s, 51 percent of state and local government employees had joined unions, even while the proportion of employees unionized in private industry remained stagnant at 29 percent (Wurf, 1976:175).

Repeated outbursts of militancy accompanied public employee unionization. Teachers' strikes captured headlines in New York in 1960, 1962, and, for six and a half weeks, in 1967; in San Francisco in 1968; and in many other cities in the 1960s (Rosenthal, 1969). In 1964, police walked out on strike in Detroit, and thousands of New

1

York City post office employees participated in a demonstration for higher pay (Posey, 1968). The National Education Association, involved in only twenty-two strikes from 1946 to 1965, found itself with eleven strikes by its members in 1966 alone (Rosenthal, 1969). The average number of public employees involved in strikes each year rose from 3,900 before 1966 to 176,000 during 1966 to 1974 (Lewin, 1976:148–51). In less than a decade, views of professional associations as just "learned societies" (Strauss, 1963), of union bargaining as anathema to the spirit of professionalism (Kleingartner, 1967), and of white-collar employees as imbued with a middle-class status orientation had been largely outdated (Lewin, 1976:150). Labor relations in the public sector had forsaken accommodation for conflict.

Although it was often strikes by teachers and police that captured headlines, unionization and rising levels of conflict also extended to public welfare agencies. From New York City to Gary, Indiana, to Los Angeles, welfare workers turned to unions in increasing numbers. New York City caseworkers walked off their jobs for six weeks in 1967 (Posey, 1968:112). In Chicago, welfare workers began an independent union in 1965, and within the next two years conducted two strikes against the Cook County Department of Public Aid. Membership rose to fifteen hundred within one year, and protests and grievance actions became commonplace within the agency. Not content with the structure and goals of existing labor unions, several of the new welfare employee unions formed their own national federation and pledged to expand collective bargaining to new groups of welfare workers.

Why did large numbers of social service and other government employees turn to unions in the 1960s? To many of the participants, the explanation was simple: "Long-standing pay inequities, wage freezes, and a helter-skelter method of compensating welfare workers," the president of the new Chicago union of welfare employees explained. "They are very young, just out of school. They're green and gullible," the head of the Cook County Department of Public Aid argued (*Sun-Times*, May 12, 1966:39). "Concerned human beings who want only decent working conditions and pay scales and the freedom to work in a professional way with those who look to us for help," proclaimed the union's "Manifesto for a More Humane Welfare System" (*West Side Torch*, May 19, 1966:4). In a decade in which riots by the poor, student protests, soaring welfare rolls, and fiscal crises followed each other in rapid succession, no explanation of employee behavior seemed too simple, too broad, or too obviously incorrect.

However, the reality of public welfare work was sufficiently complex to strain the credibility of simple explanations. While pay levels, work pressures, and frustrated professional aspirations each appeared to be possible bases for unionism, the relative a priori importance of these and other factors is not so obvious. Public welfare casework involved some of the features of private social work, but in a bureaucratically constrained setting. Caseworkers visited clients during "district days," but spent most of their time in the office completing forms and talking with current and prospective clients. They had some discretionary authority in making decisions about clients, but were closely supervised by supervisory caseworkers. Although required to have a bachelor's degree, few caseworkers had any graduate training in social work. Clerks in public welfare worked in units apart from caseworkers, often on different floors of the public aid buildings. They maintained files and financial records on clients, and procured these for caseworkers as needed. Most clerks in the Cook County Department of Public Aid lacked education beyond high school, and in spite of relatively low pay, tended to remain in the agency for years. Where among these features of public aid work and public aid employees were the sources of unionization?

Theories of Organizational Emergence

Sociological theory cannot in itself resolve debate over the sources of organized protest and union emergence. What such theory can do is to highlight the key questions that must be asked, and suggest the types of answers that may be obtained. Theory can be used to guide the investigation in the most productive direction.

Traditional social movement theory sought to explain the emergence of protest with the grievances felt by protesters (Smelser, 1962). While grievance-based theories have differed in the extent to which they emphasize rational or less rational bases for grievances and an absolute or relative analytical conception of them, these theories share an emphasis on the motivations of the participants themselves. In this respect, grievance-based explanations parallel the justifications that union organizers themselves routinely use in their campaigns (Billings and Greenya, 1974). In spite of their intrinsic appeal, however, grievance-based explanations of protest have been weakened by a substantial body of empirical evidence that finds the level of grievances in a population cannot in itself be expected to produce organized protest (McCarthy and Zald, 1973; 1977).

In recent years, sociologists seeking explanations for the emergence of protest and associated organizations have increasingly focused on the level of resources available to potential participants (Tierney, 1982). Mobilization of farm workers, for example, could not be explained by grievances alone. These had been at high levels long before the formation of the United Farm Workers. Protest organization emerged when associational structures and political alliances generated substantial resources for organizing (Walsh, 1978; see also Aminzade, 1984).

Crisis and change were the hallmarks of public welfare during the 1960s, and potential sources for grievances and for resources were abundant. By the mid- to late 1960s, welfare agencies throughout the country were in a state of crisis. Increases in fiscal support had not kept pace with a rapid expansion in the welfare rolls, even while the level of demands made by welfare clients had risen. Into this environment came new caseworkers recently exposed to protest on the nation's college campuses. Often skilled in organizing, and willing to devote time and effort to collective action, they provided a rich resource for unionization.

These bases for unionization are identified and discussed in more detail in this book. The effort begins with a more detailed analysis of the types of grievances that have been engendered by public welfare agencies and expressed by their employees since the beginning of modern public welfare in the 1930s. Grievances expressed by employees during the period of unionization in the 1960s are then discussed, and the resources available to employees are identified. Factors are noted which had once constrained union organization but which were relaxed in the 1960s.

ORGANIZATIONAL CHANGE

If the characteristics of organizations remained constant throughout their history, the study of organizations could conclude with analysis of the conditions that shape their emergence. Such is not the case. Change, not stability, is the normal sequel to organizational emergence. As a result, characteristics of organizations upon emerging are often no longer evident in subsequent years. The second goal of this book is to identify the factors that shape change in unions and other voluntary organizations.

Change in the Independent Union of Public Aid Employees (I.U.P.A.E.)

Within its first fifteen years, the welfare employee union, first named the Independent Union of Public Aid Employees (I.U.P.A.E.), changed dramatically. Organized in 1965 without direction from established unions, the I.U.P.A.E. first operated as a participatory democracy that relied on members' voluntary contributions of time and skills. Proclaiming its goals to include nothing less than reform of the welfare system itself, the union often rejected traditional means for goal achievement in favor of direct militant actions. However, the union gradually adopted a more traditional bureaucratic structure. Its name was changed to the Illinois Union of Social Service Employees (I.U.S.S.E.). Member involvement declined, official union goals were limited, and less abrasive tactics became the norm.

These changes began within the first year of the union's development. The union's first Constitutional Convention lessened the role of the membership in decision making, and reduced the collective nature of the union's leadership structure. Four years later, a second Constitutional Convention further increased the power of the union's leadership, and retreated from the initial commitment to welfare reform. During the first four years, the union led two strikes, but never again attempted a full-scale challenge to the agency. In subsequent years, the union affiliated with a large national labor union, expanded its paid staff, and acquired more of the trappings of a bureaucracy. The frequent replacement of union leaders in yearly elections gave way to a twelve-year term by one president. Frequent work actions initiated by members in their own offices largely became a thing of the past.

Union development between the first years of democracy and discord and the later period of bureaucracy and bargaining was not, however, a process of gradual or seemingly inexorable expansion of leadership power. Recurrent bouts of factional conflict, periods of confrontation followed by quiescence, and spurts of membership growth followed by stagnation alternated throughout the union's history. Each change in the union was accompanied by virulent internal conflict, and few changes occurred until factors beyond the union's control had altered the environment in which it functioned.

Figure 1 records the associated fluctuations in the union's rate of expansion, and indicates the dynamic nature of its history. In its first two years (1965–1967) the union grew rapidly, and member involvement was high. With the end of the second strike, however, it entered a four-year period of stagnation. In 1972, as it affiliated with a national union, expanded statewide, and secured collective bargaining rights, the union's growth rate again turned upward and membership activity increased. Shortly after negotiation of its first contract (1977), however, membership growth plummeted. A gradual recovery began in 1979.

Theories of Organizational Change

What explains change from a more participatory, democratic, protest-oriented style of organization to a more bureaucratic form? In

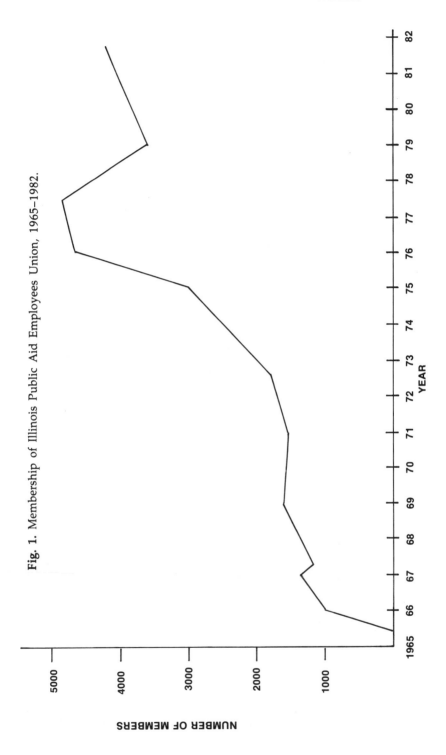

Fig. 1. Membership of Illinois Public Aid Employees Union, 1965–1982.

the Cook County welfare employees' union, activists observing particular changes accounted for them in the vivid language characteristic of sharp political conflict. The union was "becoming staid," joining up with "big labor," its leaders "selling out" its early commitments. Or, as seen by the proponents of change, "responsible leaders" were trying to prevent the union's domination by "ultra-leftists" and "crazies." Lost in the rhetoric was an explanation for the changes and a description of them that encompassed more than the issues in any particular conflict.

Sociologists have often invoked Robert Michels' "iron law of oligarchy" as both description and explanation of this type of organizational change. Based on his observation of and disillusionment with the German Social Democratic Party in the early twentieth century, Michels' *Political Parties* presented a powerful argument for the inevitability of bureaucratic, even "oligarchic," rule in initially democratic organizations. While organizational emergence was "absolutely essential" for the political struggle of the masses, Michels (1962:62) warned, "We escape Scylla only to dash ourselves on Charybdis."

> Thus the appearance of oligarchical phenomena in the very bosom of the revolutionary parties is a conclusive proof of the existence of immanent oligarchical tendencies in every kind of human organization which strives for the attainment of definite ends (Michels, 1962:50).

As description, the "iron law" summarizes the experience of a wide variety of voluntary organizations, including trade unions. Historical investigations of union politics frequently reveal declining levels of member influence (Lester, 1958; Lipset, Trow, and Coleman, 1962; Stein, 1963). In contrast to the democratic rhetoric of the early years in most unions, most union leaders are elected without opposition (Applebaum and Blaine, 1975; Taft, 1944), and few members bother to attend local membership meetings (Sayles and Strauss, 1953). In other organizations, from the National Welfare Rights Organization (Piven and Cloward, 1977) to the Tennessee Valley Authority (Selznick, 1966), increased leadership control has been the outcome of organizational change.

At the core of Michels' explanation was the belief that the emergence of oligarchy was an inherent concomitant of organization—that it was "immanent" in organization itself (1962:50). Expert, specialized leaders were required to coordinate the activities of large organizations, Michels (1962:63–77) argued. As organizations grew in size, the need for leader expertise would increase, and in consequence the power of leaders and the gap between leaders and members would grow (Michels, 1962:65–73). Members would become ever more dependent on, but less able to monitor, their leaders, and their "adoration of the chiefs," would increase (Michels, 1962:65–73, 95). From being the democratic servant of their members, organizations would become their membership's oligarchic masters.

Sociologists since Michels have frequently explained organizational change in terms of the internal needs he highlighted, even when they have not relied explicitly on his "iron law" formulation (Blau and Scott, 1972:169; cf. Meyer and Brown, 1977). Selznick (1943:49) highlighted the internal logic of goal change in the Tennessee Valley Authority:

> The day-to-day behavior of the group becomes centered around specific problems and proximate goals which have primarily an internal relevance. Then, since these activities come to constitute an increasing proportion of the time and thoughts of the participants, they are—from the point of view of actual behavior—*substituted* for the professed goals.

The "ways in which structure tends to create equal competitors for leadership," Edelstein and Warner (1975:62–63) presumed, can be understood without reference to the larger context of organizational action. While eschewing internally centered theory used to explain other aspects of organizational behavior, Aldrich (1979:204–11) emphasized Michels' internal factors when accounting for organizational transformation.

In spite of its frequent citation, however, Michels' pessimistic prognosis for organizational change has not received the universal confirmation he seemed to expect. The International Typographical Union was perhaps the most notable exception. For over one hundred years, the I.T.U. maintained a vigorous democratic internal life, complete with hotly contested elections and an intensely involved membership (Lipset, Trow, and Coleman, 1962). Although no other American unions have been so exceptionally democratic for so long a period, the extent of member influence is often much greater than that connoted by Michels' imagery (Seidman, et al., 1958), and democratic politics have sometimes reemerged after a long period of the "iron law" (Clark, 1981). In other organizations as diverse as the Foundation for Infantile Paralysis (Sills, 1957) and the Townsend Movement (Messinger, 1955), organizational continuance has not meant oligarchic control.

Issues in Developing Theory

The weakness of Michels' "iron law" as a description of organizational change is complemented by its incompleteness as an explanation of that change. Although some of the inadequacies of Michels' approach have been recognized (Schwartz, Rosenthal, and Schwartz, 1981; Zald and Ash, 1966), a comprehensive alternative to it has not been developed. In order to construct such an alternative, the major tenets of Michels' theory and their limitations must be the initial focus of attention.

Michels' primary oversight was his failure to consider systematically the impact of the external environment. Organizations do not exist in a vacuum. They function in an environment composed of other organizations and individuals, and their success and failure, their growth and contraction cannot be understood apart from that environment. A publicity campaign may enhance recruitment efforts in a receptive environment, yet mobilize opposition in a hostile environment. The militant union strike that leads to substantial gains during a period of economic expansion is likely to do no more than bankrupt the union treasury during a recession. It seems unlikely that the path of organizational development can be understood without knowing the medium through which that path is traced (Pfeffer and Salancik, 1978:1).[1] The application of organization–environment perspectives to other facets of organizational behavior provides the basis for a theory that takes the organization's environment into account (Blau and Scott, 1972:173; Meyer, 1978:22).

Michels' explanation of organizational change was also weakened by his cursory treatment of the bases of organizational emergence. He assumed that organizations were necessary to press the grievances of those who lacked other means of resolving their problems. However, Michels neglected to analyze the consequences of variation in stages, levels, and types of grievances for the likelihood of organizational emergence. Instead, he characterized all members, even those in emerging organizations, as "indifferent," "not easily stirred," "immobile and passive," "used to being ruled," and "incompetent" (1962:88–90, 105, 111–12, 172, 205, 227, 364). As a result, Michels neglected to consider systematically the continuing influence of the pressures involved in organizational emergence. These pressures do not cease when a new organization forms, although they are then expressed within an organized context. Within the organization, these pressures may become the bases for factionalism or for exit from the organization. The processes of organizational emergence and change are intertwined in a continuous pattern, and neither can be fully understood without consideration of the other.

Besides neglecting systematic consideration of the characteristics of organizational environments and the bases of organizational emergence, Michels' "iron law" also focused attention on structural change without systematic treatment of other organizational dimensions. Yet the process of organizational change involves more than simply movement between democratic and oligarchic structures. Organizational goals vary, the tactics that the organization uses change, and levels of members' involvement can rise and fall. The characteristics of the organization in terms of each of these dimensions may influence its characteristics in terms of the others. Membership involvement may increase when organizations adopt broad goals (Craig and Gross, 1970:23), or when organizations use democratic structures (Knoke, 1981). Tactical militancy is likely to decline with structural bureaucratization (Roomkin, 1976). Without identification of the key dimensions of variation within organizations and attention to their interrelations, explanations of organizational change necessarily will be incomplete.

The theoretical framework used in this volume will attempt to overcome each of these limitations in Michels' approach. The major features of organizational environments will be explicitly modeled, and the impact of these features will be assessed. The explanation of organizational emergence developed early in the book will be used throughout to enhance understanding of the process of organizational change. Organizations will be conceived as having four key dimensions: goals, involvement, structure, and tactics. This multidimensional conception of organizations, from its acronym termed the GIST model of organizations, will allow identification of the interrelations between the different aspects of organizational change.

If the characteristics of organizations vary with the characteristics of their environments, there can be no "iron laws" of organizational development. In different or changing environments, the developmental paths followed by organizations should diverge. The sociological understanding of organizational transformation is thus at a critical stage. While the rhetoric of Michels, backed by persuasive evidence, still suffuses explanations of organizational development, awareness of the importance of organizational environments—of the other organizations and individuals that interact with an organization—suggests that new directions in theory must be charted.

RESEARCH METHODS

The analysis of the emergence and development of the public aid employees' union combines both qualitative and quantitative methods. Intensive interviews with current and former union activists, inspection of union documents, and observation at union meetings provide the data for the historical analysis. Surveys conducted among employees in 1973 are used to test propositions concerning the union's early history, while another survey of union members in 1976 is used to study members' attitudes on the eve of negotiating the union's first contract. A quantitative content analysis of union documents allows some statistical tests of changes in the union over its entire fifteen-year history. Table 1 presents key features of these data.

The methods used in data collection are described in more detail in the Appendix. Some general comments about them are useful at this point. The use of several sets of data expands the range of issues that can be addressed in the study. Data on individual orientations and organizational characteristics gathered at several points in time facilitate a qualitative overview of the union's history, as well as quantitative examination of members' orientations (Denzin, 1970). The analysis is thus able to bridge the gap between the historian's traditional ideographic explanations, based on claims of unique prior influences, and the social scientists' nomothetic mode of causal explanation, which focuses on probabilistic tests of relationships between variables (Stinchcombe, 1978). The analysis does not "obliterate and destroy" historical detail (Moore, 1978:xvi) in the course of developing and testing general propositions.

The narrative of the union's history is broken into four periods. The first begins with the union's formation in 1965 and extends to its second strike, conducted in 1967. As indicated in Figure 1, this was a period of rapid growth as well as of major conflict. The second period encompasses the five years in which union growth stagnated

Table 1. Characteristics of Data Sources

Study	Population	Sampling	Number of Cases	Method
Interviews	Union activists	Purposive sample	40	Intensive interviews
Documents	All leaflets to union members & union newspapers	Stratified random sample of leaflets & all newspapers	362	Content analysis
Offices	All unionized offices, Cook County Dept. of Public Aid	Entire population	29	Coding of union voting in 1976; aggregation of union member characteristics (from survey responses)
Employees	All employees, Cook County Dept. of Public Aid 1973	Entire population	1,218	Self-administered questionnaires
Contract survey	Professional & Paraprofessional union members in Illinois 1976	Stratified random sample	544	Mailed questionnaires

after the second strike. The election of a new president in 1972 occurred just prior to takeover of the Cook County Department of Public Aid (C.C.D.P.A.) by the state agency and demarcates the start of the third period. During this period, collective bargaining began, the union affiliated with the American Federation of State, County, and Municipal Employees (A.F.S.C.M.E.), and union growth accelerated. The fourth period begins with the end of this rapid growth, and corresponds to the emergence of a new type of conflict within the union, and to renewed problems in securing gains from the agency.

Current and former union activists were purposively selected for intensive interviews so as to represent each period in the union's history and each faction active in each of these periods. In addition, each president was interviewed, with one exception. Although some of the leading earlier activists were not available for interview, coverage was sufficient to allow construction of the detailed chronology of events in each period, and representation of opposing views on those events. These views are presented in the quotes from union activists throughout the book.

Data on employee orientations were obtained in two surveys. A survey of all C.C.D.P.A. employees in 1973 is used for statistical analyses of the bases of union membership and the sources of factional conflict at that time. The results are incorporated into a study of the period of union stagnation which immediately preceded the survey. A survey was conducted again in 1976, but only of union members in the professional and paraprofessional bargaining units. Questionnaires were mailed to a stratified random sample of union members throughout Illinois in both the Department of Public Aid and the Division of Vocational Rehabilitation. Occurring just prior to negotiation of the union's first collective bargaining contract, the survey facilitates assessment of member orientations and their sources in the period of renewed union growth.

A content analysis was done on union documents distributed throughout the years studied. Based on a stratified random sample of official union leaflets and all issues of the union newspapers, this analysis provides a summary of changes in the union's characteristics and the issues important to it. Excerpts from union documents are also used throughout the book to supplement descriptions of events and to illustrate alternative orientations within the union.

ORGANIZATION OF THE BOOK

Organization in a Changing Environment uses an externally-centered theory of organizational emergence and change to explain the development of a public welfare employee union. The conceptual framework and major tenets of this theory are developed in chapter 2, and then applied throughout the book. In the concluding chapter of the book, chapter 11, the theory is specified and evaluated. Within these theoretical boundaries, the history of the emergence and changes of the Illinois public aid employees' union is presented. This history is divided into two major sections. The first section encompasses the union's initial emergence and its first two strikes (chapters 4 and 5), and the subsequent period of limited growth (chapter 6). This section is preceded by a discussion of public welfare work in the 1960s (chapter 3), and followed by a description of the reorganization of Chicago public welfare work in the early 1970s (chapter 7). The consequences of this reorganization are investigated through study of the union's subsequent history in chapter 8, and in chapter 9 through analysis of survey data. The most recent stage of the union's history is presented in chapter 10.

CHAPTER TWO

Organizations and
Their Environments

Resolving the issues in organizational theory identified in chapter 1 serves both as the goal for the analysis in this book, and as the basis for linking the analysis to the larger body of research and theory on organizations. As we relate the union's history to these questions, its history takes on a larger significance. The analysis in the book will then contribute to the development of more general organizational theory applicable to the study of organizations of other types, at other times, and in other places.

How can this goal be achieved? The history of organizations provides the foundation for understanding social processes within them. Without knowledge of the ebb and flow of activity in an organization over time, of the events that are preserved in the memories of participants and that have shaped organizational development, analyses of organizations are necessarily limited and may be misleading. However, the historical record in itself is insufficient. *Explanation* of organizational processes—identification of the bases for organizational emergence and change—requires a broader conceptual framework. A map is needed of the terrain through which the analysis will proceed, as well as a plan for proceeding through that terrain toward the ultimate goal.

This chapter will first present a general explanation of organizational emergence. The variables with which the analysis of the emergence of voluntary organizations must be concerned will be identified, and the sources of their variation will be discussed. Conceptual models of organizations and their environments will then be presented to sensitize the analysis to important social processes within and between organizations and their environments. The result should be a more comprehensive and consistent description of organizations and their environments than would emerge from simply recounting organizational history. The chapter will conclude by presenting an external theory of organizational change. This theory draws on current theory, and serves as a guide and point of reference for the analysis of union history.

EXPLAINING ORGANIZATIONAL EMERGENCE

Organizations provide a means for accomplishing tasks that single individuals or large undifferentiated groups cannot (Aldrich, 1979:3; Olson, 1971:7; Sills, 1957). Through organization, individuals' time, money, knowledge, and other resources are combined and directed toward achievement of a goal (Michels, 1962; Perrow, 1970:107–11). Whether that goal is to influence government policies, wage scales, or school prayer laws, whether the organization is a political party, a trade union, or a religious group, the multiplication of individual resources through organization increases the likelihood of the individuals' and groups' goal attainment (Michels, 1962:61).

New organizations are unlikely to emerge when existing institutional arrangements satisfy the needs of individuals and social groups. It is when the needs of individuals or groups are *not* satisfied by existing organizations that the emergence of a new organization becomes more likely. However, the presence of unmet needs is not in itself a sufficient condition for organizational emergence. If neither individuals nor existing organizations have time, money, talent, or other resources to contribute, new organizations cannot emerge. In other words, a new organization requires resources to develop its ability to satisfy previously unmet needs. The emergence of new organizations thus connotes both a gap between the needs of individuals and extant organizations and the availability of sufficient resources to fill that gap (Walsh, 1981; cf. Hannan and Freeman, 1977).

Without a minimal level of both needs and resources, the emergence of new organization will be stymied. South African workers have experienced high levels of grievance, for example, but their low pay, little leisure time, few family contacts, and limited access to meeting halls and other potential resources have made it difficult for them to organize (Daniel, 1978; Johnstone, 1976:168–200). In the mid-1960s, the level of discontent among college students was relatively low (Lipset, 1972:40–49; Trimberger, 1973), even though the amount of time, ability, money, and other resources available for student organizers was relatively high (Lipset, 1972:36–37). As a result, protest organization did not grow rapidly. The failure of unionism among the resource-rich faculty in elite schools can be attributed similarly to a lack of substantial grievances (Ladd and Lipset, 1973).

Beyond a necessary threshold level of both grievances and resources, the likelihood of organizational emergence will increase with the level of unmet needs and of untapped resources.[1] The rapid growth of industrial unionism during the 1930s occurred during a time of high levels of grievances among the laboring population, but the effect of these grievances was complemented by the resources contributed by radical groups and new labor legislation (Fine, 1958; Prickett, 1968; Ross, 1963; Seidler, 1961). It was after the level of discontent among college students increased, with continuation of the Vietnam War and government efforts to quell limited protests against it, that the student movement swelled in size (Lipset, 1972:44–45; Trimberger, 1973:43). Local anti-nuclear power activists in the aftermath of the Three Mile Island accident had higher levels of discontent, but also higher socioeconomic status and more solidary ties to others than those who did not actively participate (Walsh and Warland, 1983).

In addition to grievances and resources, the explanation of organizational emergence must be sensitive to the role of external constraints. Social control efforts directed at potential movement participants may decrease the likelihood of organizational emergence (McCarthy and Zald, 1973:25–28). Values, reference groups, expectations, past experiences, and relations with target groups may also constrain or enhance the growth of new organizations (Freeman, 1979:176–82). Explanations for the rise of social movements and new organizations must thus be sensitive to the levels of grievances, resources, and constraints in the potentially organizable population (Oberschall, 1973).

The importance of resources and grievances, as well as of constraints, has been recognized in the theories of social movements and organizational emergence, but the necessity of examining their joint occurrence is often neglected. Traditional social movement theory has emphasized the importance of grievances in producing social movements, with little attention to the level of available resources (McCarthy and Zald, 1973:10; Messinger, 1955:9; Moore, 1978; Smelser, 1962:18, 47). Resource mobilization theory focuses instead on variation in the level of resources to explain the emergence of social movement organizations (McCarthy and Zald, 1973:1–2), but slights variation in the level of grievances (McCarthy and Zald, 1977:1215).[2] Neither perspective can adequately explain the ebb and flow of social movements and protest organizations. It is when grievances increase *and* resources are available that protest and protest organizations emerge (Aminzade, 1984; Walsh and Warland, 1983).

Grievances

Employees may develop grievances concerning the economic rewards they receive from their work as well as about the intrinsic quality of their work. However, these grievances are a product of the interaction of employee orientations with the level of extrinsic and intrinsic rewards actually received, rather than a simple expression of the absolute level of rewards. The complex determination of grievances among employees has continued to generate both controversy in sociological theory and discrepancies in interpretation of research results.

Many studies of both blue- and white-collar workers have linked their orientations to their social backgrounds (Zurcher, Meadow, and Zurcher, 1965). The economic orientations of blue-collar employees may be due in part to a cultural background emphasizing central life interests outside of the work place (Blauner, 1964:29; also see Dubin, 1956:134–41). Blue-collar workers tend to have an "instrumental orientation" that accounts for their concerns with economic rewards (Goldthorpe, et al., 1968:38–39; 1969:77–78). On the other hand, advanced education is associated with desires for work autonomy, treatment as a professional, and ability to serve clients (Hall, 1969; Scott, 1966; Taylor, 1968). In the bureaucratized semiprofessions, these desires are likely to conflict with job requirements and bureaucratic, hierarchical control (Blau and Scott, 1962; Hall, 1968:102; Hall, 1969:108–13). Not surprisingly, advanced education and a professional orientation among semiprofessionals have been associated with dissatisfaction and support for employee militancy (Alutto and Belasco, 1974; Corwin, 1970:172–200; Etzioni, 1969:96–97; Fox and Wince, 1976:56; Hall, 1969:108–12; Katzell, Korman, and Levine, 1971:62–74; Kleingartner, 1967:7; Lipset and Schwartz, 1966:307–10; Prottas, 1979:118–19; Scott, 1969:91).

The explanation for the types of grievance likely to be experienced among employees as rooted in their social backgrounds can be traced to the work of Emile Durkheim (Gruenberg, 1980). Durkheim (1951:249) regarded individual orientations and behavior as malleable, shaped by culture to comport with the needs of society. Individuals socialized in different cultures would thus tend to have different expectations. While employees schooled to expect intrinsically interesting work would feel aggrieved in jobs involving routine work, employees interested only in economic rewards would not be bothered by routine jobs.

A different perspective on the origins of employee grievances is rooted in the work of Karl Marx. Marx (1978:168) emphasized the importance of social class, and identified economic needs as the center of workers' class interests, regardless of their social background. The maintenance of wages was "the first aim of resistance" by combinations of workers (Marx, 1978:168). As predicted from this perspective, militancy among college faculty varies inversely with pay level (Feuille and Blandin, 1976; Ladd and Lipset, 1973), and union membership is higher among teachers in the lower grades who are dissatisfied with their income (Nagi and Pugh, 1973).

Marx (1964:124–28) did not neglect intrinsic rewards, but felt that, as with economic rewards, interest in them was generated in the work place itself. People have a need to develop their capacities regardless of their education or other attributes, Marx (1961:98) asserted in his early writings. To the extent that a job frustrates this need, dissatisfaction should result (Shepard, 1973), while to the extent that intrinsic rewards are increased, satisfaction should rise (Kahn, 1972:179). In public welfare, intrinsic rewards were reduced by excessive caseloads, inadequate resources, and indeterminate objectives (Jacobs, 1969:417–18; Katzell, Korman, and Levine, 1971:62–74; Lipsky, 1980:15–16; Prottas, 1979:18, 91–101). Frustration is produced because "the job is impossible to do in ideal terms," not because of high levels of employee education (Lipsky, 1980:79–80; Toren, 1969:158).

Resources

The potential bases of resources for the emerging organization are as diverse as the sources of grievances. Both individuals and extant organizations may provide resources that aid in the emergence of new organizations. Populations with more communal ties, higher levels of organizational membership, previous activism, and integration as a community are more likely to participate in social movements (Oberschall, 1973). Resources available from individuals in such populations include material and other tangible goods, personal skills in organizing, and their time and commitment (Aveni, 1978; Freeman, 1979; Perrow, 1970).

The likelihood of individuals contributing resources to an emerging organization varies with both their social background and their occupational position. Political participation increases with education and age (Hagburg and Blaine, 1967; Verba and Nie, 1972:8–92, 138–73). Higher social status is associated with positive civic attitudes and these in turn with higher rates of political participation (Verba and Nie, 1972:126, 149–73; Lipset, 1963:208). As a result, blacks are found to participate politically more than whites, when social class differences are controlled. Higher status in the work place is also associated with higher rates of political participation in general and participation in unions in particular (Salisbury, 1975:326; Verba and Nie, 1972). Union activists tend to have more skilled jobs, greater prestige, and higher pay than nonactivists (Alutto and Belasco, 1974; Dean, 1954; Perline and Lorenz, 1970; Sayles and Strauss,

1953:197–207; Spinrad, 1960). Job satisfaction, identification with the occupation, and seniority are also directly associated with frequency of union participation (Hagburg, 1966; Hagburg and Blaine, 1967; Perline and Lorenz, 1970; Spinrad, 1960). The likelihood of organizational emergence thus varies systematically across different populations of potential members. In general, higher-status populations have higher rates of organizational emergence, due to generally higher levels of resources and willingness to contribute them to organizations.

Potential members are not the only source of resources for the emerging organization. The "multiorganizational field" may also provide resources through networks connecting organizations and through ties connecting individuals to other organizations (DiMaggio and Powell, 1983). For example, the emergence of the United Farm Workers has been explained as a product of César Chavez's success in developing associational structures among farm workers, and in using extant family units for organizing (Walsh, 1978). The rise of social movements in the 1960s has been explained as a product of the resources created by media publicity and provided by "conscience constituents" to a small number of full-time activists (McCarthy and Zald, 1973:17–23; Oberschall, 1978).

Constraints

Grievances and resources are not the only determinants of organizational emergence. Levels of both may be relatively high, yet the conversion of them into a new organization may be inhibited by structural or attitudinal barriers to collective action. Legislation, for example, could make the costs of collective action intolerably high, in spite of high levels of grievances and ample resources. Employees could be very discontented with pay levels, have spare time to organize, and still fail to launch protest due to attitudinal inhibitions against collective action. "Constraints," then, act as a filter between grievances, resources and organizational emergence (cf., Freeman, 1979:176–82; Pfeffer and Salancik, 1978:14).

A variety of structural and attitudinal factors have been treated as constraints in explanations of organizational emergence. Freeman (1979:176–82) referred to values, past experiences, reference groups, expectations (which may be a function of past experiences and reference groups), and relations with target groups as constraints. Aldrich (1979:183–88) identified work force characteristics, market characteristics and economic concentration, and government regulation as constraints on the viability of new forms. In this book, constraints will be considered to be those factors that influence the expression of grievances and the usage of resources, without directly affecting the level of grievances or resources themselves.

A MODEL OF ORGANIZATIONAL ENVIRONMENTS

Once an organization emerges, analysis of social processes within it must consider more than just the grievances individuals have brought to it, the resources they and other organizations can contribute, and the constraints on their actions. Although grievances and resources are still important, they are now expressed and utilized within an organizational context, and can no longer be interpreted apart from that context. Individuals' grievances are converted into organizational goals, and their resources are utilized within an organizational structure. In this process of transposition from individuals to the organization, changes occur. From an array of individual grievances, only some are expressed, and fewer emphasized, as organizational goals. From a variety of individual resources, only some are contributed to the organization. Maintenance of the organization itself—leaders and staff, office and files, paper, pen, and phone—requires resources. This requirement in turn establishes an organizational goal that is independent of the original purpose of the members' combining. An expanded framework is therefore required to understand organizational processes.

Conceptual models of both organizations and their environments are developed here to facilitate understanding of interaction between them. These models identify the connections between organizations and environments, and also encompass the grievances and resources that were identified as important in explaining organizational emergence. First, a conceptual model of organizational environments having these properties is presented. Then, a model of organizations that is compatible with the environmental model is discussed.

From the point of view of an organization, the environment has two fundamental dimensions. An organization's environment consists of the "entire system of interconnected individuals and organizations related to one another and [to] a focal organization through the organization's transactions" (Pfeffer and Salancik, 1978:63–69). In other words, each individual or organization that affects an organization, no matter how remote in space or time, is part of the organization's environment (Pfeffer and Salancik, 1978:12). However, some important distinctions can be made among features of the environment (Aldrich, 1979:63–70; Dill, 1958). For the analysis of change in voluntary organizations, a conception of their environments as having two dimensions—level and relevance—will be most useful.

The organizational environment has two levels (Curtis and Zurcher, 1973:53). The matrix of individuals in and around an organization comprises the social level of its environment (Pfeffer and Salancik, 1978:29–30). At the social level of a work organization's environment, for example, are its employees, their families and friends, its stockholders and customers. The social environment of a social movement organization would include movement beneficiaries and its "conscience constituents" (Zald and Ash, 1966).

The network of organizations in which a given organization functions comprises the institutional level of its environment. The institutional level includes other organizations that are the object of attempts at influence, as well as those organizations from which resources are sought (Knoke and Wood, 1981:165). These organizations constitute, in the aggregate, "a recognized area of institutional life" (DiMaggio and Powell, 1983:148). Bargaining between unions and employers, attempts by political groups at influencing the government, mergers and coalitions between organizations, all are processes in the institutional environment. The ability of organizations to achieve their goals is most directly a product of their actions at the institutional level (Zald and Ash, 1966:329, 336).

Environmental features also vary in terms of their relevance to the organization. Those individuals or organizations with which the organization is in direct and frequent contact are of primary relevance to it. It is from these individuals and organizations that most resources are gathered, to which most influence attempts are directed, and upon which there is most dependence (Pfeffer and Salancik, 1978:43–54). Individual members of an organization, its constituents, comprise an organization's primary environment at the social level. At the institutional level the primary environment of an organization would include, for example, the company with which a union negotiates, the other firms from which a company buys materials or to which it sells products, and the governmental body which sets a school's policy.[3]

Organizations and individuals of secondary relevance to the organization are those that are in direct interaction with others in its primary environment, but which are not normally sources for resource acquisition or objects of influence attempts. For unions, this would include employees who are not union members, consumer groups, its employer's competitors and customers, and the government. For work organizations, the secondary environment would include their competitors, customers, trade associations and the government. Tertiary and more distant features of the environment can also be identified. McCarthy and Zald (1977:1221–23), for example, distinguish "bystander publics" from those with a more direct connection to a social movement organization. These more distant features of the environment will not be explicitly considered in this book.

Figure 2 represents the two dimensions of organizational environments in a fourfold table. In the cells of the table, major features of a union's environment are simultaneously classified in terms of their level and relevance. A union's membership is its primary social environment, for example, while customers of the unionized firm would comprise part of the union's secondary social environment. Other types of organizations may have other features in the primary and secondary columns at one or both levels. The primary social environment of firms, for example, would include both their customers and their employees, while their primary institutional environment would include unions, suppliers of materials, and distributors of their products.

THE GIST MODEL OF ORGANIZATIONS

Organizations are goal-directed social structures.[4] The ends which the organization seeks to achieve are its goals, while the means employed to reach these ends are the organization's tactics. These two characteristics make the organization "goal-directed." The organization is social in that it is the involvement of individuals—voting, attending meetings, entering and leaving the organization—that enable it to act. The organization's structure is the pattern of relations between members as expressed in the written documents, verbal agreements, and social conventions that shape activities of individuals in the organization. Thus, the organization is a "social structure." Taken together, the goals, involvement, structure, and tactics of the organization comprise the GIST model.

Fig. 2. Environment of Unions.

| LEVEL | RELEVANCE | |
	Primary	Secondary
Social	Members	Other employees, customers
Institutional	Firm	Other unions, Other firms, government

Goals

An organizational goal is a valued state which the organization seeks to achieve or maintain. Goals may be classified as either external or internal. External goals are new advantages that the organization seeks to realize for its beneficiaries (Gamson, 1975). These are often the official, public goals of the organization (Perrow, 1961). Winning an election may be an external goal of a political party, for example, while improving student abilities may be an external goal of a school. An external goal of a community group might be the maintenance of rent controls or the passage of a law allowing school prayer. An organization may have more than one external goal, and external goals may vary in their importance to the organization.

External goals represent, by definition, the needs of members of the organization (in membership-centric voluntary organizations). However, members within the organization may differ in their needs. As in the generation of grievances, these differences in needs may be rooted in either the work situation itself, or in social background. A particular promotional policy may advantage employees in one occupation more than employees in another, for example.[5] The promotional policy thus is in the immediate self-interest of the advantaged employees, but not of those who are not advantaged by it. In addition, feelings of solidarity or group identification may lead to felt needs on the basis of shared experiences or feelings of common fate, rather than on the basis of immediate self-interest (Fireman and Gamson, 1979).

Establishment of a given need as an organizational goal, and efforts to achieve that goal, can be expected to be supported most by those groups for whom such needs are greatest. The goals actually adopted and pursued by an organization are likely to be those preferred by the greatest number of members (Firey, 1948). Groups that are able to contribute more resources to the organization, because of larger size or greater propensity to participate or higher levels of skill are more likely to have their needs expressed and pursued as goals (Gamson, 1968). However, an organization may pursue several goals in an attempt to meet the needs of several groups within it (Zald and Ash, 1966:337). A union, for example, might seek to increase both wages and worker participation in management, but wage gains may be its "bottom line" at the bargaining table because they are desired by a greater proportion of the membership.

Disparities in needs, and thus in preferred organizational goals between subgroups within an organization may lead to the emergence of factions. The greater the disparities in goal preferences, the greater the likelihood of factional conflict (Firey, 1948:20–21). If particular subgroups are disadvantaged with respect to many of the goals sought by an organization, factional conflict becomes more likely, while its probability decreases when the organization seeks some goals expressing the needs of each of the subgroups within it (Zald and Ash, 1966:337).

Internal goals represent the organization's concerns with enhancing its strength and ability (Gamson, 1975; Zald and Ash, 1966). Also termed "organizational" and "organizational maintenance" goals, these are often the operative goals of the organization (Perrow, 1961). They express "needs" that did not exist prior to the organization's emergence, and thus are rooted in the organization itself, rather than in its environment. While external goals vary widely between organizations, internal goals are in their nature largely similar between organizations. The maintenance or enhancement of leader and staff salaries, expansion of physical facilities, improved recruitment procedures, as well as better internal communication, all represent possible internal goals.

Structure

Structure binds an organization together (Aldrich, 1979) and provides a framework within which goals may be achieved (Sills, 1957:11). The rules that shape relations between members, the organization's written constitution, and the distribution of power in the organization are all components of its structure (Kanter, 1977; Sills, 1957:11, 66). To the outsider, an organization's structure is its most visible manifestation. For the member, the structure largely defines his or her organizational role.

Organizational structures vary most significantly in terms of the relative importance of leaders and members in organizational decision-making.[6] An oligarchic structure gives sets of leaders exclusive power to make organizational decisions. Oligarchies are characterized by "undemocratic control of government vested in relatively few individuals and exercised in their own interests by virtue of their firm grip on high organizational posts" (Edelstein and Warner, 1975:32).[7] In an oligarchy, leaders are likely to serve for long periods, without formal opportunities for their removal by members. Members may be expected to contribute substantial resources to the organization, but these contributions are not rewarded with a role in organizational decision-making.

Michels (1962) used the terms "oligarchy" and "bureaucracy" interchangeably, and his forecast of the growth of oligarchy in voluntary organizations has often been characterized as the process of "bureaucratization." However, this usage blurs important differences between bureaucracies and other organizational types (Weber, 1947). Specialization of participants' duties, formalization of procedures, limitation of rewards to officeholders, and the availability of paths for career advancement set bureaucratic structures apart from oligarchies (Aldrich, 1979; Hage, 1965). Although bureaucratic structures are hierarchically organized, these other characteristics each limit the power of organizational leaders. Leaders cannot exercise power over all aspects of participants' behavior: They must follow standard procedures in their actions, they are remunerated according to established rules, and they and/or their staff may be replaced as those below them advance in the hierarchy.

While bureaucratic structures preserve a distance between the organization and its social environment, democratic structures reduce that distance. Democratic structures provide for the appointment and replacement of organizational leaders by decision of the membership, and presume membership input into organizational decision-making. In a democracy, membership involvement in the organization's affairs is high enough to serve as an effective means of two-way communication between leaders and members. Involvement also provides resources to the organization and to factions within it, and thus diminishes the need for reliance on elites or outside groups for resources. The experience of participation serves to educate members about civic responsibilities, and thus encourages continued participation (Pateman, 1970). Because organizational politics are not shaped by disproportionate contributions of resources from organizational elites or outside groups, cleavages in the membership will be reflected in organizational politics. Cleavage in turn stimulates membership activism, generates alternative ideas and plans, and impedes concentration of power among the organization's leaders.[8]

Two major types of democratic structure can be distinguished. The particular feature of *representative* democracies is the competitive election of organizational leaders (Schumpeter, 1976:269). Usually linked to a continuing bi- or multiparty system, the existence of competitive elections makes it difficult for leaders to persist in unpopular policies for an extended period, and thus severely constrains their exercise of power. Nonetheless, ongoing decision-making in the organization is handled by elected leaders, rather than by members themselves.

In *participatory* democratic structures, members do participate in the ongoing process of decision-making. The participatory democratic organization minimizes the gap between leaders and members, and increases the power of members relative to leaders (Pateman, 1970). Rather than largely confining member influence to the electoral process, participatory democratic organizations involve members in the committees or boards that make executive decisions, and discourage single leaders from making final decisions on their own (Rothschild-Whitt, 1979).

These four types of organizational structure can be arranged along a continuum in terms of the extent to which they concentrate power in the hands of the organization's leadership. Oligarchies concentrate the most power in the leadership, while participatory democracies do so the least. Leaders have less power in bureaucracies than in oligarchies, but more than in representative democracies. Of course, the actual structures of organizations often mix characteristics from different types, but the major distinctive features of these structures enable their separate description and empirical identification.

The formal structure of an organization influences the impact of resources available to it from the social level of its environment (Pfeffer and Salancik, 1978). A one-person, one-vote democratic electoral system, for example, distributes resources according to the relative numbers of group supporters, while a system that weights individual votes according to region, occupation, or other criteria alters group resources accordingly. In nonelectoral politics, structures that facilitate membership participation maximize the resources of groups with more active supporters, while hierarchical structures increase the relative resource advantage of those higher in the hierarchy (Pfeffer and Salancik, 1978:46–50).

Within the formal structure of any organization, informal social processes alter the relations of members to each other and to their leaders (Blau and Scott, 1962). In participatory democratic organizations, the intense involvement of members in the leadership of the organization minimizes the gap between the formal and informal structures. Patterns of social relations between members become aspects of the formal structure itself. The more hierarchical the organization's structure, however, the greater the possibility of difference between the organization's formal structure and the informal social processes within it.

Due to the informal structure, the actual distribution of power within an organization may be affected by social ties and relations that are not accounted for within the formal structure (Kanter, 1977). These informal social processes can be understood through examination of patterns of involvement in the organization.

Involvement

Whenever the actions of an individual contribute to the resources of an organization, the individual is involved in the organization. Types of involvement range from joining an organization, contributing to a fund drive, or signing a petition, to voting in an election, serving on a committee, or running for elected office. Through such acts, involvement supplies an organization with such resources as money, time, manpower, expertise, and status (Freeman, 1979; Perrow, 1970:65; see also Aldrich, 1979:16–17). Particular resources may be contributed by individuals throughout the primary and secondary social environment of the organization, although involvement would usually be greater among members than nonmembers (McCarthy and Zald, 1977).

The variation among types of organizational members in propensity to participate may have important consequences. When differences in goal preferences among the membership are closely correlated with differences in propensity to participate in organizational affairs, the organization is more likely to focus its efforts on achievement of the goals preferred by the more involved category.

The involvement of individuals in the organization is the primary link between the organization and its social environment. Members' attitudes and behaviors are shaped by their experiences in other organizations and in the rest of their lives, as well as by experiences occurring due to their membership itself. Organizations try to increase member commitment to collective interests through encouraging the internalization of norms (Knoke and Wood, 1981:11). However, this attempt to constrain member behavior is countered by attitudes and behaviors that are rooted in the external environment and brought into the organization by the members. Individuals "track all kinds of mud from the rest of their lives with them into the organization, and they have all kinds of interests that are independent of the organization" (Perrow, 1979:4; Pfeffer and Salancik, 1978). Membership involvement is thus a two-edged sword for an organization— at once providing a source of resources and a host of unexpected demands.

Tactics

Tactics are the means used to achieve organizational goals. Such action as negotiation, informal discussion with authorities, petitions, demonstrations, and strikes are each a type of organizational tactic.[9] They can be laid out in terms of the degree of conflict they involve (Tannenbaum, 1965:725–29). Cooperative tactics include negotiations, arbitration, and informal discussion, while militant tactics include demonstrations, strikes, picketing, marches, and work slowdowns.

Support for particular tactics varies with members' social background and job situation. Militancy among industrial process workers increased, in one study, with their prior exposure to a homogeneous working class culture (Cotgrove and Vamplew, 1972:169–85). Black workers in Detroit displayed higher levels of class consciousness and militancy than white workers (Leggett, 1968). Militancy is greater among men than women, and decreases with age (Cole, 1969; Fox and Wince, 1976; Hellriegel, French, and Peterson, 1970; Ladd and Lipset, 1973). Pay level may also influence militancy, at least among college faculty (Feuille and Blandin, 1976; Ladd and Lipset, 1973).

It is through the response to its tactics that the organization receives feedback from its institutional environment (Thompson and McEwan, 1972). The extent of resistance to a union strike, for example, provides the union with information on the orientation of management toward it. Based on this information, the organization may increase its own militancy, adopt new tactics, or decide to shift its efforts toward the achievement of other goals. In any institutional environment, some tactics will be accepted as legitimate by those organizations toward which they are directed. An organization can be said to be *institutionalized* when it is able to use accepted tactics to achieve most of its goals. A union is institutionalized, for example, when it achieves collective bargaining rights for its members (Kaufman, 1982:482).

The tactics used by an organization will thus be determined not only by the preferences of its membership, but also by the response of other organizations to those tactics. An institutionalized union can achieve many goals through processing grievances and in contract negotiations. Strikes may be accepted by the employer as legitimate when contract negotiations break down. Prior to institutionalization, however, a union is likely to use tactics that are more conflictful, in an attempt to force the employer to react to union demands (Gouldner, 1965; Moore, 1978; Snyder, 1975). When the demands of particular subgroups are not achieved by the organization with tactics legitimated by institutionalization, noninstitutionalized tactics may be attempted (Ragin, Coverman, and Hayward, 1982).

The GIST model and the associated two-dimensional model of organizational environments provide a framework for the description of voluntary organizations and their relations with their environment, and thus a foundation upon which to develop an external theory of organizational change. As an aid to description, the GIST framework encourages systematic attention to each of the major components of organizations, rather than to a more limited portion of them (cf. Edelstein and Warner, 1975). The transformation of voluntary organizations that Michels (1962) described with his "iron law of oligarchy" can be described in GIST terminology as a change from a democratic to an oligarchic structure, from an emphasis on external to an emphasis on internal goals, from high to low levels of involvement, and from militant to cooperative tactics.

An External Theory of Organizational Change

In spite of their value as descriptive tools, neither the GIST model nor the associated two-dimensional model of organizational environments provides an *explanation* for organizational change. While they can be used to characterize organizations and their environments at multiple points in time, they do not have a dynamic element that could account for change in these characteristics. Only recently has environment-centered theory provided a basis for incorporating such a dynamic element into a theory of organizational change (Meyer, 1978:22).[10] This dynamic element is based in the need of organizations for resources, or "generalized means, . . . facilities, that are potentially controllable . . . and usable—however indirectly—in relationships between the organization and its environment" (Yuchtman and Seashore, 1967:900).

The Initial Configuration

When they first emerge, new membership-based voluntary organizations have close ties to their social environment (Meyer and Brown, 1977:383).[11] Many of the grievances that led to the formation of a new organization are translated into organizational goals, and the individual resources tapped in the process of organizational emergence remain critical for organizational functioning. This necessary dependence on the social environment is associated with high levels of membership involvement, since it is through involvement that members' resources are contributed to and member grievances are expressed by the organization. Also due to the dependence of the new organization on its social environment, tactics employed by the organization to achieve its goals usually reflect those preferred by the membership. Reactions to the organization's tactics from its institutional environment have less impact as long as the organization can obtain sufficient resources from its social environment.

The dependence of the emergent voluntary organization on its social environment results in an initial GIST configuration that has been labeled "collectivist." The collectivist organization relies on the logic of substantive rationality, motivated in its actions by values held for their own sake (Rothschild-Whitt, 1979:509–10). The collectivist organization rejects the commitment to formal or instrumental rationality that characterizes the ideal-typical bureaucracy. Decisions are made through a process of developing consensus that eschews the formal procedures of representative democracy as well as the hierarchical controls of bureaucracy.

Rothschild-Whitt's (1979) study of five alternative types of work organization confirms the existence of a collectivist GIST configuration. The relationships among the GIST dimensions in a variety of studies of voluntary organizations suggest also the coherence of the collectivist type. A democratic structure has been associated with high levels of member involvement (Freeman, 1979; Knoke, 1981) and with support for general social goals (Tannenbaum, 1968). Similarly, organizations that have diverse goals, that is, fulfill various functions for their membership, are also likely to have higher levels of involvement (Craig and Gross, 1970:23). The restraint in organizational tactics that is necessary when the organization is institutionalized is not likely to be achievable in a highly democratic structure (Gamson, 1975).

Pressures for Change

Given the complementary nature of these initial characteristics, some other factors are needed to explain organizational change. These factors can be located in both of the levels of the organization's environment. The environment can create organizational change through making available or withholding resources (Aldrich, 1979:22, 61, 74). The acquisition of resources from the social level of organizational environments can be impaired by factionalism (Bendix, 1947:493–95). Due to differences in their backgrounds or situations outside the organization, subgroups of members may differ in their perceived needs, and thus in their support for particular organizational goals (Fireman and Gamson, 1979; Perrow, 1979; Schwartz, Rosenthal, and Schwartz, 1981). For example, differences in occupational status, ethnicity, and orientation in national politics all contributed to factional division in Kenyan unions (Sandbrook, 1975), while social background differences were associated with political party affiliation in the International Typographical Union (Lipset, Trow, and Coleman, 1962).

The emergence of factional activity is a natural accompaniment of organizations with democratic structures (Zald and Ash, 1966). Human populations in whatever combination differ in terms of a wide range of characteristics and attitudes, and can be expected to differ in terms of grievances (Schwartz, Rosenthal, and Schwartz, 1981:24). While this tendency toward factionalism increases with the heterogeneity of the organizational membership (Rothschild-Whitt, 1979:520–21), the high probability of its emergence is indicated by the emergence and persistence of political conflict (in the form of organized political parties) within the status-homogeneous membership of the International Typographical Union (Lipset, Trow, and Coleman, 1962). Factional activity in turn draws member resources away from the organization's leadership and may impair organizational goal achievement (Blau, 1963:265; Gamson, 1975). The dependence of the collectivist organization on consensual decision-making and its expectation of high levels of member involvement make factional conflict difficult to absorb (Rothschild-Whitt, 1979:521). There is thus pressure to suppress factionalism and to eliminate those structural characteristics that facilitate its expression.

As long as the organization is dependent on its social environment for resources, it is unlikely to be able to suppress factionalism. However, organizations are not solely dependent on one source of resources (Aldrich, 1979:20–21, 61). The institutional environment affords amother source for resource acquisition, and thus enables the organization to reduce its dependence on the social environment. An organization can, therefore, substitute resources derived from its institutional environment for some of those unavailable from its social environment (Piven and Cloward, 1977).[12]

Due to this substitutability of resources, a decline in the resources available from one level of an organization's environment will not necessarily lead to its collapse. The leaders of the nineteenth-century Southern Farmers' Alliance, for example, were largely plantation owners. Their ties to other organizations enabled them to pursue policies opposed by most of their more impoverished membership (Schwartz, Rosenthal, and Schwartz, 1981). Member participation was not related to goal attainment among the "professional" social influence associations in Knoke and Wood's (1981:190) sample, while there was a positive relationship between these variables for the "amateur" social influence associations.

Since the organization attempts to achieve its goals in the institutional environment, there is a tendency to seek institutionalization even apart from the desire to lessen dependence on member resources. However, substitution of resources available in the institutional environment for those previously obtained in the social environment has important structural consequences. To maximize resource acquisition from the institutional environment, structural changes must occur (Rothschild-Whitt, 1979:522–23). Hierarchical structures facilitate interorganizational relationships by allowing one or a few leaders to represent the organization (DiMaggio and Powell, 1983:151). Managements pressure unions to exercise "responsible leadership," for example, as a condition for granting them recognition (Lipset, 1960:217; McPherson, 1940). In general, a "web of institutional controls" impedes efforts to maintain GIST configurations that are highly discrepant with those of other organizations (McCarthy and Zald, 1973:26).

The Transformation

A comprehensive explanation of organizational transformation can now be presented. Resource substitution allows an organization to change its initial GIST configuration in response to the internal pressure of factionalism and the external pressure for conformity. Bureaucratization provides a means for lessening factionalism and clarifying lines of intraorganizational authority. By specifying organizational boundaries and drawing a sharp distinction between those behaviors within and outside of the organization's purview, bureaucratic organizations segment the roles that individuals play into intra- and extraorganizational components (Aldrich, 1979:13). As a result, the tendency for factionalism rooted in individual backgrounds and situations outside of the organization is reduced. The NAACP's bureaucratic structure, for example, enabled it to resist pressure from radical members more effectively than the less centralized CORE (Rudwick and Meier, 1970).

Since bureaucratization decreases the organization's attachment to its social environment, this change in itself decreases available resources. As organizational structures become less democratic, the organization becomes less susceptible to membership control, and levels of member commitment fall (Blau, 1956:69; Freeman, 1979; Knoke, 1981; Sills, 1957). The substitutability of resources allows the solution of this problem of deficient resources. The acceptance of an organization into a network of relations with other organizations, its institutionalization, restores the flow of resources by changing its source from the social to the institutional levels of the environment (McCarthy and Zald, 1973:18–20). Although less militant tactics are associated with greater institutional dependence, resource acquisition from the institutional level is likely to increase (Piven and Cloward, 1977; Roomkin, 1976; Selznick, 1966). Strikes by British unions, for example, won more gains as the unions became members, rather than challengers, of existing political institutions (Ragin, Coverman, and Hayward, 1982). Publicity in outside media and interorganizational ties that accrued to those leaders of the German Social Democratic Party who also served in the Reichstag strengthened their internal power in the party (Michels, 1962:153–66). Leaders of the Tennessee Valley Authority focused their activities on securing external funding (Selznick, 1966).

The likelihood and direction of organizational change is, of course, no more fixed than the environments in which organizations function. The persistence of a democratic structure in the International Typographical Union, for example, can be attributed to the high level of resources available from its membership (Lipset, Trow, and Coleman, 1962). A variety of features of the union's environment contributed to the high level of resources among the organization's membership, and its relatively equal distribution. Income and status homogeneity of the middle-class membership equalized resources across subgroups. The autonomy of the chapel, or shop, from the union's administration increased the ability of chapel leaders to mobilize resources from the social environment, without control or supervision of their efforts by the top administration. The legitimacy of the opposition aided the survival chances of internal factions by decreasing the resource advantage of organizational leaders, by preventing the expulsion of dissidents, and by providing the opposition with access to meetings and media. The existence of an "occupational community" was reflected in a high level of informal relations between members, which provided resources for factions and/or the organization's leaders. The job security of members also increased their willingness to contribute resources to the union.

CONCLUSIONS

The change in an organization's GIST configuration, which has been termed the organizational transformation, thus begins outside of the organization itself, in the constraints and opportunities of the social and institutional environments. According to this external theory, an internal perspective cannot provide an adequate explanation of organizational change. The processes described by Michels' "iron law" can be no more certain than organizational environments are constant. Implicit in the GIST model is a view of organizations as permeated by their environments through members' involvement and organizational tactics. Variation in the external environment thus *must* influence the organization, while internal variation in the organization inevitably affects its relations with the environment (Pfeffer and Salancik, 1978:38; Sills, 1957:1–2).

As it identifies the connections between organizations and their environments, the resource substitution theory developed from these models also draws attention to the importance of *both* the institutional and social levels of the environment. Previous research has often focused on only one level. Lipset, Trow, and Coleman (1962) carefully analyzed the characteristics of printers, but gave little attention to other organizations with which the printers' union interacted. Recent externally centered theories of organizational behavior have emphasized the importance of other organizations rather than member individuals (DiMaggio and Powell, 1983). The resource substitution theory of organizational transformation suggests the hazards of limiting attention to one environmental level. Since the role of these levels of the environment will vary with their ability to provide resources to a given organization, organizational development cannot be understood without analysis of interaction with both environmental levels.

The dynamic theory of organizational emergence and change that can be developed within the GIST framework suggests a means for explaining variation in organizational histories. Rather than appealing to an "iron law," this resource substitution theory highlights the need for consideration of multiple factors. The theory will be evaluated and refined with an intensive analysis of the emergence and change of one voluntary organization. By specifying the important features of organizations, their environments, and their possible relationships, the theory should help this analysis reap the maximum possible benefit from such a case study. Since the theory is based on the insights of more general organizational theories, this analysis can be related to numerous other studies. It is to the analysis of the history of the Independent Union of Public Aid Employees that this book now turns.

CHAPTER THREE

Public Welfare and the Roots of Employee Discontent

Unionization of public welfare agencies cannot be understood apart from the institutional strains generated in the United States during the 1960s. Violent outbursts of the poor in America's central cities threatened the cohesion of American society, and demanded an immediate response. The numbers of people supported by public welfare soared, and the numbers of employees in public welfare agencies also increased.

It was this environment of rapid change and unexpected strain that spawned welfare employee unionism, and it is in this environment that the explanation of union emergence will begin. However, public welfare in the 1960s cannot be understood apart from its prior history, nor can the actions of caseworkers in the 1960s be understood apart from their occupational heritage. Explanation of an episode of collective protest in terms of "the way things are" is hazardous until this is compared with "the way things were." History provides a basis both for understanding formative influences on current events and for identifying differences between the past and the present (Meyer and Brown, 1977).

THE DEVELOPMENT OF SOCIAL WORK

Social work emerged as a distinct occupation in the last half of the nineteenth century. For much of the next century, social work in private agencies gradually adopted more professional characteristics and attempted to establish an exclusive claim to the work of ministering to the needy. The Depression of the 1930s transformed the government into the primary provider of relief, and permanently changed the social work field.

The Process of Professionalization

Professional occupations use a distinctive style of organization of work and of orientation to work. The resulting characteristics include use of theoretically based knowledge, self-control, and internalized ethics, a primary orientation to the community, and emphasis on intrinsic work rewards (Barber, 1963; see also Hughes, 1963). These characteristics do not describe the situation or orientations of all professionals, of course. Rather, there is a range of variation around these characteristics, and workers in occupations not normally classified as professions may have some "professional" characteristics. Nonetheless, these characteristics create a "morally praiseworthy" image that helps to justify professional privileges (Becker, 1962), as well as a standard by which professional performance can be judged. Attempts to professionalize are thus common in occupations that already possess a reasonable measure of these characteristics (Larson, 1977).

In order to professionalize, occupations must develop an altruistic image and "the capacity to control esoteric and identifiable skills—that is, to create and control a cognitive and technical basis" (Larson, 1977:180). As necessary parts of this attempt, professionalization also requires the creation of a distinctive educational program tied to universities and the development of an occupational association (Larson, 1977:50–51).

The Origins of Social Work

United States welfare policy during most of the nineteenth century continued the tradition of the English Poor Law of 1601. The basic tenets of the Poor Law were that relief was a public responsibility, except when support could be obtained from relatives, and was limited to permanent residents of the providing locality. The plight of the poor was generally regarded as evidence of their own moral weakness, to be eradicated by severe administration of relief (Bruno, 1957:27). Lay boards of managers controlled the administration of relief to insulate it from political corruption (Leiby, 1978:173–79), and local volunteers were the primary relief workers (Leiby, 1978:182).

After the Civil War, the provision of social services began to expand and organize. The Massachusetts Board of Charities, founded in 1863, was the first state board to supervise public social services. In 1877, charity volunteers in Buffalo formed the first local Charity Organization Society, and in 1888 the settlement house movement began in New York (Morales and Sheafor, 1977:17–39). While each of these new social service organizations precipitated the establishment of many similar organizations elsewhere, it was the Buffalo Charity Organization Society that proved to be the precursor of the profession of social work. Settlement houses continued to be staffed primarily by lay persons, and public social services were largely confined to institutional care well into the twentieth century (Bruno, 1957:112).

Charity organization societies dominated the provision of private social services in the late nineteenth and early twentieth centuries. Describing their work as "scientific philanthropy," the charity societies sought to distinguish their approach from that of routine public charity and more casual, sporadic private relief efforts. Applicants for charity were investigated by a paid secretary and then referred to an appropriate society. After a case conference, a volunteer was sent to visit the new recipient. Volunteers were expected to take an objective approach to the recipient's situation and to emphasize the value of working (Leiby, 1978:344–47; Lubove, 1965:6–12).

While the Charity Organization Society approach helped social work take on more characteristics of a traditional occupation, it stopped far short of the attributes of a profession. Most important, neither a unique set of skills nor a related body of knowledge were identified. Volunteers were termed "friendly visitors," and were expected to use personal skills and moral insight to encourage the poor to change their ways (Lubove, 1965:13–17). A speech by Abraham Flexner to the National Conference of Charities and Corrections in 1915 highlighted the gap between the characteristics of social work and those of established professions. Since social work lacked a special body of knowledge, Flexner announced, it could not be considered a profession (Bruno, 1957:138–43; Morales and Sheafor, 1977:39–41).

Professionalization of Social Work

(1) Development of a unique skill. Even as Flexner's assessment of the nature of social work was being formulated, the characteristics of social work were changing (Lubove, 1965:18–21, 49–51). Most important, a new conception of the role of the social worker was emerging. Mary Richmond, a Buffalo social work leader, proposed that social workers should no longer just provide moral guidance and emotional support. Rather, social workers were to collect and interpret social evidence in order to effectively engage in "casework": "those processes which develop personality through adjustments consciously effected, individual by individual, between men and their social environment" (Steiner, 1966:181).

Focusing on casework as the primary social work concern was consistent with the earlier charity organization emphasis on objectivity in relations with recipients. Nonetheless, identification of a special method as the core of social work represented a sharp break with the earlier volunteer approach (Lubove, 1965:119). Effective casework required "insight into individuality," "insight into the social environment," "direct action of mind upon mind," and "indirect action through the social environment" (Mary Richmond, 1917, quoted in Lubove, 1965:48). Advanced education was needed to develop these skills, and volunteers could not be expected to possess them.

Mary Richmond's *Social Diagnosis* (1917) elaborated the principles of case work. Its instant popularity among social workers reflected the value of the casework focus for the emerging profession, and the compatibility of that focus with practices in new social work specialties in hospitals and schools. Growing recognition of Freud and development of psychiatric social work in the 1920s shifted the focus of many social workers even more toward clients' personalities (Lubove, 1965:104–17). Richmond's view of social workers as "technicians with a responsibility to their cases" who draw upon a specialized body of knowledge was ensconced in the profession of social work (Trattner, 1979:212–19). Thirty years later, caseworkers could still be said to:

> absorb, synthesize, and apply the best psychoanalytic knowledge that is available, just as they make use of the best relevant sociological, medical, or cultural knowledge. They apply this knowledge for their own professional ends, using their own professional methods under the supervision of skilled casework supervisors. (Garrett, 1949:224.)

(2) Education for social work. Development of special schools of social work both contributed to and was furthered by identification of a unique body of knowledge underlying professional practice. Proponents of the casework approach recognized the need for professional schools as early as 1897. The first social work school was established in 1898. By 1917, seventeen schools of social work had opened, and the American Association of Professional Schools of Social Work was founded (Bruno, 1957:138–43). Two years of graduate professional school was accepted as the standard for the Master's of Social Work degree in 1939. By 1962, fifty-six social work schools enrolled 6,039 students in MSW programs (Leiby, 1978:340–41). The standard curriculum in these schools consisted of courses in psychiatry, casework philosophy and method, interviewing, and community resources (Garrett, 1949:225).

Education for professional social work was not supposed to end with receipt of the MSW. Close supervision on the job was to continue a process of practical education begun through field placements while in school.

Through supervision, the values, norms, and performance standards of the profession were conveyed to neophytes, and reinforced in the case of experienced workers (Lubove, 1965:167–68).

As social workers helped their clients to improve their functioning, so supervisory social workers were to help social workers improve their performance (Lubove, 1965:155–69).

(3) Professional associations. Development of professional associations facilitated efforts to define a unique focus and to establish special schools for social workers. The first organization to bring social workers together at the national level was the National Conference of Charities and Corrections, formed in 1879 (its name was changed in 1917 to the National Conference of Social Work). However, the National Conference focused on the functioning of state charity boards, rather than on social work in general (Bruno, 1957:4–9, 42).

Founded in 1917, the National Social Workers' Exchange initially sought to provide vocational counseling for social workers. Rooted in local social worker clubs that had emerged in large cities in the early twentieth century, the Exchange had no formal criteria for membership. In 1921, members changed its name to the American Association of Social Workers, and required new members to have professional experience and education (Bruno, 1957:145–51). Committed to the professionalization of social work, the A.A.S.W. sought to develop standards for the education and employment of social workers, to cultivate a public image of social workers as professionals, and to form a code of ethics to guide professional conduct (Lubove, 1965:131).

The process of professionalization continued with the founding of the National Association of Social Workers in 1957. The N.A.S.W. brought social workers from seven specialized groups into one association and superseded the A.A.S.W. (Bruno, 1957:409). A Masters in Social Work from an accredited school was required for N.A.S.W. membership. However, in 1961, the N.A.S.W. formed the Academy of Certified Social Workers for social service employees who could not satisfy this requirement. Certification was added as a prerequisite for many social work jobs not requiring the MSW (Morales and Sheafor, 1977:42). In 1957, Ernest Greenwood, an analyst of the history of social work, finally reversed the judgment made in Abraham Flexner's 1915 address to the Conference on Education for Social Work. Social work, Greenwood concluded, had become a profession (Morales and Sheafor, 1977:43).

THE PUBLIC SECTOR

Growth of Public Assistance

While private social work continued its "professional project" through much of the twentieth century, that effort included fewer and fewer of those workers engaged in direct social service. Since the Depression of the 1930s, the growth of public sector social work has eclipsed the progress of professionalization in the private sector.

Prior to the 1930s, federal and state governments had played a minimal role in the provision of relief outside of institutional settings. In the nineteenth century, lay boards of managers had managed charity and correction agencies in order to maintain their independence from government control. As of 1890, the federal government itself made almost no contribution to total national welfare expenditures, even though these expenditures accounted for one-tenth of the national income (Trattner, 1979:244). It was not until the Progressive movement's emphasis on the positive functions of government that states reorganized their welfare services into executive departments (Leiby, 1978:173–79). These state services still included little relief outside of institutions. In 1929, only three percent of state welfare budgets were for noninstitutional care (Lubove, 1965:52–54).

The federal government's first entry into the provision of social services came in 1912. The concern of social workers and others with the consequences of poverty and long hours of work for children led to establishment of the U.S. Children's Bureau in 1912. Authorized to "investigate and report" on matters pertaining to child welfare, the Children's Bureau encouraged efforts to establish child health centers and widows' pensions. The Children's Bureau skirted the problem of child labor, and President Hoover discontinued the child and maternal health centers in 1929 (Trattner, 1979:177–88). Nonetheless, the Bureau established a precedent for direct federal involvement in welfare (Bruno, 1957:154; Trattner, 1979:177–88).

With the mass unemployment of the Depression, even Herbert Hoover's commitment to free enterprise gave way to a limited loan program to enhance state relief efforts (Salamon, 1978:71–72). After Franklin Delano Roosevelt's inauguration, the government began to develop a more comprehensive federal welfare system. First came the Federal Emergency Relief Act. In the early years of the new administration, the F.E.R.A. distributed unemployment relief through a special agency. Then, in 1935, the Social Security Act established the framework for the modern public welfare system. For those who were employable, the Act launched a social insurance system as protection against old age and unemployment. To support those who were unemployable, the aged, the blind, and dependent children, the Act provided for federal "grants in aid" to states. Since states had to have centrally administered relief programs in order to receive these grants, public assistance offices were established in all of the more than three thousand counties in the United States by 1937 (Leiby, 1978:225–32; Salamon, 1978:15–16, 74–78).

Welfare expenditures became a major item in the federal budget. By 1940, the federal government provided 41 percent of total expenditures on public welfare, which now represented 8 percent ($6 billion) of national income (Trattner, 1979:236–44). Federal welfare grant coverage was expanded to include the disabled in 1950, the medically indigent aged in 1960, and the children of unemployed fathers in 1961. Private philanthropies increasingly provided counseling services for those not entirely destitute, rather than income support to those who were (Salamon, 1978:15–16; Steiner, 1966:6–17).

Social Work in the Public Sector

The rapid expansion of positions in social service far exceeded the ability of trained social workers to fill them. As early as 1934, one survey of government social workers in rural counties found that 92 percent had no prior courses or paid experience in social work. In spite of hastily prepared institutes and shortened programs in schools (as well as staff reductions when many recipients were sent to Works Progress Administration projects after 1935), this lack of professional training among government social service employees persisted. In 1950, only four percent of social workers in public aid agencies had the MSW (Leiby, 1978:279). By the 1960s, only 11 percent of public welfare workers in direct service had had just one year of graduate work, and only one percent had completed two or more years (Steiner, 1966:183).

The work of the new public caseworkers was not much more professional than their educational backgrounds. Most employees determined or reviewed eligibility. This work was largely routine, although the complexity of the eligibility rules required caseworkers to exercise some discretion, and interaction with recipients demanded some interpersonal skills (Leiby, 1978:241). At best, the caseworker in the public sector was, and remained, a

> jack-of-all-trades, . . . an accountant, investigator, secretary, file clerk, house-hunter, moving expert, used furniture dealer—and occasionally, a social worker (Illinois Department of Public Aid, 1972:6).

Clients tended to view public caseworkers as "investigators," rather than as "professional helpers" (Scott, 1969:129–30; Gottlieb, 1974:27).

Rather than self-regulation, caseworkers were subject to a hierarchical authority system (Scott, 1969:82–85), and received little positive sanction from the larger society (Ritzer, 1972; Toren, 1964).

The new public employees in social work did not readily identify themselves with professional social work. During the Depression, a radical "Rank and File Movement" spread through large city relief agencies (Leiby, 1978:242–43). Members focused on traditional union concerns: standardized salaries, improved working conditions, and adequate grievance procedures. While the Rank and Filers also demanded increased relief benefits, the motivation for these demands was more a sense of identification with unemployed clients than a commitment to professional advocacy (Brown, 1940:295–97).

Many leaders in private social work looked askance at their counterparts in the public sector. Although professional social workers were often hired as supervisors and administrators in public welfare agencies during the 1930s,

> the vast expansion of public assistance functions and expenditures beginning in the 1930s was superimposed upon a long tradition of disdain totally incongruous with the political and economic power assumed by the public welfare sector (Lubove, 1965:54).

Lacking specialized training, public welfare workers were barred from admission to the National Association of Social Workers, and were not invited to its founding convention in 1955 (Steiner, 1966:196–97). The editors of *Social Work*, an organ for the profession, called for removing "the albatross of 'relief' . . . from the neck of social service" so that social workers could concentrate on "professional casework" (Steiner, 1966:185).

SOCIAL REFORM

In addition to stimulating the growth of public welfare, the 1930s Depression also focused many social workers' attention on the economic bases of client problems.

> The futility of the case-by-case method of dealing with the problem is increasingly obvious. The flood must be stopped at its source, not mopped up by the bucketful, however scientifically modelled the bucket. (Quoted in Trattner, 1979:224.)

In 1933, the American Association of Social Workers called for labor standards legislation, taxes on wealth rather than on consumers, public works, and more relief (Bruno, 1957:346–47). The Rank and

File Movement in Social Work allied itself with groups of the unemployed to press for social change (Brown, 1940:295–97).

Unlike the rise of public welfare, interest in social reform was not
new to the field of social work. Exposure to the environment of the
poor had turned some social workers toward social reform activity
even before the turn of the century. Edward T. Devine, a proponent
of government action to raise living standards, became the head of
the New York Charity Organization Society in 1896. In 1919, John
Fitch, at the New York School of Social Work, wrote that "the interest
of the social worker in social action is a test of his integrity" (Bruno,
1957:137–38). Throughout the history of social work and in both its
private and public sectors, interest in social reform periodically drew
some social workers' attention away from the dominant focus on
casework with the individual recipient (Leiby, 1978:352).

PROFESSIONALS IN PUBLIC WELFARE

The growth of public welfare did not cease with the end of the
Depression. Although legislators had assumed that an expanding
economy and a growing social insurance system would eliminate the
need for large-scale public welfare, the new relief system continued
to expand after World War II (Salamon, 1978:81). Congress turned
to a group of social work professionals for advice (Trattner, 1979:255).

In their "Report to the Secretary of Health, Education, and Welfare,"
the Ad Hoc Committee on Public Welfare (1961:13) reached a predictable conclusion:

> Financial assistance . . . is not enough . . . . The very
> essence of a vital program should be full use of all
> rehabilitative services, . . . strengthening all their own
> resources. Achieving this requires the special knowledge and
> skill of social workers with graduate training and [of] other
> well-trained specialists.

The 1962 Public Welfare Amendments to the Social Security Act
represented a tentative step toward the professionalization of public
welfare. The Amendments reflected a belief in the individual casework
method of treatment, an emphasis on rehabilitation services, and a
commitment to a limit of sixty clients to be served by any one
caseworker (Salamon, 1978:85–88; Steiner, 1971:36–37; Street, Martin, and Gordon, 1979:109–11). As the "War on Poverty" began,
federal support for casework increased further (Hilliard, 1964:8; Trattner, 1979:255).

PUBLIC WELFARE IN ILLINOIS AND COOK COUNTY

Public welfare in Illinois had become a center of controversy in the early 1960s. Administration by a bipartisan Public Aid Commission tended to cast each decision about welfare in a political light.

> There was the long fight over birth control services, . . . there were investigations of relief recipients by Hilliard's forces [the director of the Cook County Department of Public Aid], and investigations of the investigators by Maremont's forces [the state director of public aid, ousted by the State Senate after he accused Senators of racial prejudice], there was the long fight over ceilings, with thousands of welfare recipients going without money and food while the legislators made speeches. (*Renewal*, March, 1964.)

Nonetheless, the federal attempt to professionalize public welfare was felt in Illinois. A private consulting firm evaluated the Commission's work in 1960, and urged a greater emphasis on service provision (Steiner, 1966:208–10). In 1962, the Commission was given funds to hire 300 new caseworkers (*From the State Capitals*, August 20, 1962).

The Cook County Department of Public Aid (C.C.D.P.A.), serving Chicago and surrounding suburbs, had substantial administrative authority, its own Director, and 55 percent of the welfare recipients in Illinois (McKelvey, 1967). It too sought a "professional" solution to the rising welfare rolls. A C.C.D.P.A. study early in the 1960s found the main cause of increase in the general assistance caseload was the increasing numbers of uneducated manual workers left unemployed by the process of automation, and made unemployable by rising educational requirements (Steiner, 1966:216). Concluding that "neutral and passive financial support by society is no longer sufficient," Cook County's Public Aid Director, Raymond Hilliard, began a mass literacy campaign to "bring the individual closer to society and closer to a realization of what he must do if he is to become a full member of that society" (Brooks, 1963:11, 14).

> Our splendid but faltering economic machine [will not] wreck itself [if the Department receives] an adequate supply of troops, caseworkers who *with sufficient time to devote* can work miracles of restoring dependent persons to self-support. (Hilliard, 1964:8, 9, emphasis added.)

During this period, some of the caseworkers who would later become militant opponents of agency policies reacted favorably to their work.

There [had been] a lot of pressure, high case loads, and much turmoil. The Illinois General Assembly had cut off appropriations [for several weeks]. There was no decline in case loads until H.E.W. got in the picture.

This [experimental] office was run to show the effectiveness of small case loads . . . . Being a caseworker was not bad, although the pay was poor. . . . I spent two weeks [working] with a sixteen-year-old who had a stillbirth. I was involved in social work with clients, and was able to make visits to clients.[1]

In 1964 to 1965, case loads in the agency were small. H.E.W. [the U.S. Department of Health, Education and Welfare] philosophy was . . . that this would lead to reducing the rolls. Caseworkers had time to do everything for clients.

The ideology of professionalism had gained acceptance in welfare services, the need for low case loads had been recognized by welfare administrators, and many staff had had the experience of working with low case loads.

The Welfare Explosion and Its Consequences

The effort to upgrade the level of services to clients was short-lived. By 1964, public welfare rolls were exploding, and the goal of giving caseworkers low case loads and sufficient time for rehabilitation of clients appeared increasingly unrealistic (Street, Martin, and Gordon, 1979:111). During the 1950s, only one hundred ten thousand (110,000) families had been added to the welfare rolls nationwide (a 17% increase). By February, 1969, another eight hundred thousand (800,000) families had been added (a 107% increase). Seventy-one percent of this dramatic increase occurred after 1964 (Piven and Cloward, 1971:183, 186). Figure 3 presents the corresponding figures for individuals on AFDC (and see Trattner, 1979:250).

This explosion of the welfare case load resulted in part from the migration northward of many former Southern tenant farmers. The violent outbreaks in American cities in the 1960s and the increasing assertiveness of the poor brought increasing numbers into welfare offices. The resulting pressures for increasing the numbers of welfare recipients were great[2] (see Figure 4). A study published by The National Advisory Commission on Civil Disorders, the so-called Kerner Commission, pointed out the connection:

Public welfare agencies are important points of contact between the residents of the ghetto and the larger white

Fig. 3. Individuals on Aid to Families with Dependent Children (AFDC) United States, 1950–1971.

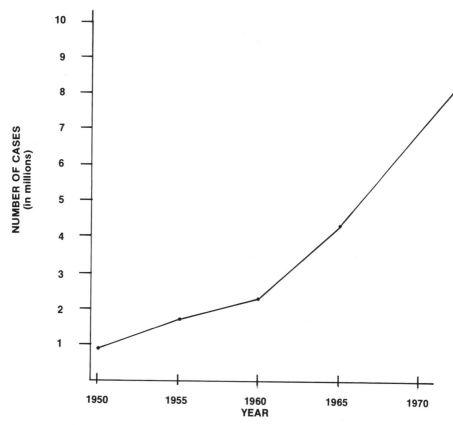

Source: Salamon, 1978:83–84.

community. . . . Within the ghetto, public welfare has been widely criticized. On the one hand, the agencies are criticized for not doing enough for poor Negroes. On the other hand, they are attacked for being a manifestation of white welfare colonialism interfering in the life of the ghetto. (Berk, 1968:139.)

Public welfare in Illinois was exposed to some of the same pressures occurring at the national level. Chicago was rocked by a violent riot of ghetto residents, and recipients marched on public welfare offices demanding their rights. The number of recipients in Illinois spiraled upward in the latter years of the decade. The number of Aid to Families with Dependent Children (A.F.D.C.) cases in Illinois rose

Fig. 4. Approved AFDC Applications of Families United States, 1960–1968.

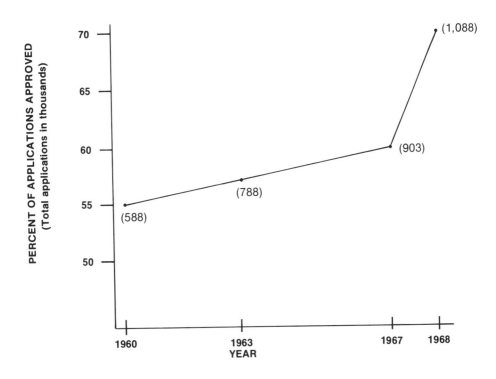

Source: Piven and Cloward, 1977:273–74.

from 71,000 to 115,000 in two years (1969–1971), while the number of general assistance cases, primarily in Chicago, grew from 29,000 to 40,000 in just one year (1970) (*From the State Capitals*, January 18, 1971). The expansion of Chicago's case load was more gradual than in many cities, but the trend was still dramatically upward (Piven and Cloward, 1971:218, 336.)

The expansion of the welfare rolls, a response to the problems of the poor, in turn led to a political counterreaction. The fiscal consequences of relief, rather than its causes, demanded immediate attention. From 1965 to 1975, the cost of A.F.D.C. rose 300 percent, while at the state level welfare expenditures grew 40 percent faster than the overall state spending rise (Salamon, 1978:17–30; Trattner, 1979:244–50). Attempts were now made to limit eligibility for welfare, and to exert tighter control over the welfare system. The 1967

Amendments to the Social Security Act deemphasized casework and adopted a work/training requirement for A.F.D.C. recipients (Trattner, 1979:259–60; Salamon, 1978:88). In Illinois, state legislators attacked the size of the welfare rolls, refused to confirm the appointment of a reform-oriented director, and cut the public aid budget by one million dollars per month (Steiner, 1966:222–36; *From the State Capitals*, November 1, 1963).

CASEWORKER REACTIONS

Increasing numbers of recipients and decreasing fiscal resources translated into fewer resources per client and greater pressures on caseworkers. The consequences for caseworker reactions to their work were profound. Except for those who had participated in the attempt to lower case loads in the mid-1960s, reactions to work in public aid had not been generally positive.

> The necessity to adapt to the bureaucratic procedures of complex welfare organizations creates obstacles for service, partly by diverting energies to learning the official regulations and administering them, partly by engendering anxieties and rigidities, and partly by the limitations imposed by internalized bureaucratic constraints. (Blau, 1960:358; also see Hall, 1968:102; Jacobs, 1969:415–16; Saucier, 1971:185–86; Scott, 1966:266–68.)

Before the explosion of the welfare case load, several adaptive mechanisms held negative reactions to casework in check. With increasing years of service, many caseworkers learned how to adapt to agency regulations. Although their attitudes toward clients "hardened," their ability to serve clients improved (Blau, 1960; Street, 1979:50–53; Tissue, 1970). One study found that the percentage of caseworkers who both worried about cases after working hours and felt it was important to be liked by clients fell from fifty-seven to thirty-three after one year of employment (Blau, 1960:347–49). Supervisory caseworkers aided in this socialization process by transmitting a psychological perspective on clients' problems (Scott, 1969:125–29). An "equilibrium" of sorts had been achieved between the low level of professionalization in public aid and its degree of bureaucratization (Hall, 1968:104).

This equilibrium was shattered by the increase in the welfare rolls. As new staff were hired to meet the demands of the expanded case load, the average length of employment declined. Professional aspirations, high among many college graduates, tended to be associated with frustration with, criticism of, and deviance from agency policies

(Blau and Scott, 1962:73–74; Etzioni, 1969:96; Hall, 1969:108–12; Kleingartner, 1967:7; Lipset and Schwartz, 1966:307–10; Scott, 1969:91). The Kerner Commission's survey of caseworkers in fifteen cities found frequent complaints with agency operations.

> Three kinds of problems stand out as serious in the minds of the social workers: 'lack of money for clients', 'lack of time', and 'hampering rules and regulations'. Approximately eighty percent of the social workers believed that these top three were at least somewhat serious, indicating the high degree to which this occupational group felt there were grave deficiencies in the welfare system as presently run. (Berk, 1968:142).

New caseworkers in some Cook County offices quickly detected the turmoil in public assistance.

> The whole thing was quite overwhelming—not only all the forms that had to be filled out and the incredible mess of the bureaucracy and all the rules changes. One of the things that really drove me crazy about the job was it seemed like we would get three to four bulletins a day, changing the policy of the agency in one area or another, and, because there was such a turnover, few people had all the current regulations. It was a real problem, knowing what the current policy of the agency was.

Not all offices experienced the same case load pressure by the middle of the decade, but even in these offices, "People . . . were bored and overqualified. A hell of a lot were independent-minded. . . . The job was extremely frustrating." Interest in civil rights issues was pronounced among public welfare employees, and encouraged thoughts of social reform efforts (Berk, 1968:140). The level of employee grievances was increasing throughout the agency, and the appeal of unionism was rising with it.

CONCLUSIONS

The middle years of the 1960s represented a unique period of intensified strain in public welfare. The continuing evolution of public welfare agencies and of the social work field, the contradictory pressures experienced in both public welfare and the profession of social work, and aspects of the turmoil of the 1960s interacted in a way that intensified rather than ameliorated conflict in public welfare.

A tension between the desire for amelioration of the problems of the poor and the logic of fiscal restraint had shaped the development of public welfare since its inception. The need for substantial resources to facilitate amelioration was asserted in public welfare policy early in the 1960s. However, the welfare explosion short-circuited the attempt to alter the conditions of welfare delivery. Instead, the rising case loads soon threatened government fiscal policy. Responding to insufficient funds, welfare agencies increased the number of cases handled per caseworker.

Private social workers were professionalizing their occupation, and had come to shun the public welfare caseworkers who lacked most of the characteristics associated with professional work. Nonetheless, professionalism was held out as an ideal for public caseworkers, and this was encouraged during the experiment with reduced case loads in the mid-1960s. When public welfare agencies were no longer able to support the style of work associated with achievement of this ideal, the potential base of dissatisfied caseworkers soared.

The history of social work also illustrated the potential salience of an alternative orientation. In the Depression, many social workers had rejected professional ideology in favor of attempts to achieve social reforms. Resurgence of social movement activity in the 1960s as well as renewed recognition of the persistence of poverty were both pronounced on the nation's college campuses, and thus quickly appeared among public welfare caseworkers. Rather than gradual resocialization to a more bureaucratic conception of work, new caseworkers were now quick to turn from professional aspirations to social reform efforts.

CHAPTER FOUR

Union Emergence

The Cook County Department of Public Aid was rapidly and permanently transformed during the mid-1960s. In the early years of the decade, Director Hilliard's proselytizing on behalf of the poor frequently captured media attention. By the middle of the decade, these headlines had been replaced by stories of protests and strikes by welfare employees. Frustrations with the conditions of service in welfare had found an outlet in unionization. Director Hilliard, said by some to have been deeply dismayed by the turmoil in his Department, had died.

THE BACKGROUND TO UNIONIZATION

Chicago's public aid workers had first formed a union during the Depression of the 1930s. Organized independently, the union soon affiliated with the United Public Workers (U.P.W.) of the Congress of Industrial Organizations. The union expanded during the 1940s, and by 1949 fifty percent of the Department's employees had joined. However, in the early years of the McCarthy period, the U.P.W. was expelled from the C.I.O. for alleged Communist Party ties. After years of regular negotiations, the Director of Public Aid stopped dealing with the local union at that point (McKelvey, 1967).

The U.P.W. local was soon replaced by another. Claiming to speak for some former U.P.W. members, Local 73 of the Building Service Employees International Union (B.S.E.I.U.) obtained informal recognition in 1951. Although no formal agreement was signed, the Cook County Board of Commissioners and the agency's Director granted Local 73 the right to use bulletin boards in public aid offices and the right to distribute literature, and agreed to meet with the union about pay and other concerns. In February, 1964, these rights were expanded to include a formal grievance procedure through which complaints could be appealed up to the Director (McKelvey, 1967).

When the frustrations of caseworkers began to mount in the 1960s, some new employees began to think of collective organization. In the spring of 1965, it took only a relatively minor problem to send caseworkers on a mission to secure assistance from the B.S.E.I.U. local.

> It started with a silly incident. The agency was going to transfer two employees to another office (they were incompetents). They discovered there was no grievance procedure, and no way to make their case. . . . At the Western [District] Office, after the incident, people got together (it was a friendly office) when the plight of the sad sacks got known. The gossip was that there was to be a salary reduction [for all employees].

For some caseworkers, the absence of any right to a hearing symbolized a general lack of agency responsiveness to employees. The attempted transfer quickly became a focus for worker discontent. Activists at the Western District Office devoted their extra time to an organizing effort focused on the lack of disciplinary hearings.

A dense matrix of informal social relations had already developed in the Western office prior to the disciplinary incident. Not experiencing the same case load pressures of many offices, Western District Office employees played games during lunch breaks, and, after work, bowled and played bridge, softball, and volleyball together. Many new caseworkers enjoyed the experience of working "among peers" having similar social background and college experience. These social ties provided a critical resource for those caseworkers seeking to organize around the issue of disciplinary transfers. As one of them recalled, "Unionists were just an informal group that got bigger."

The "informal group" brought the problem of the disciplinary transfers to a Local 73 meeting. However, their pleas for action were met with delay. The activists were told that the union's district council would have to approve any action, and some recalled being referred to as "crazy hotheads." Social workers, the militants were told, would not be attracted to militant action.

> [Local 73's leaders] didn't appreciate that Department of Public Aid caseworkers were not social workers. Caseworkers had no loyalties to their work situation as such—No more than due to being just basically liberals. They were not wedded to that work. The times were that way. There was much [political] activity.

Securely tied to Chicago's Democratic machine, drawing most of its resources from a large membership of manual service workers, and lacking official recognition in public aid, Local 73's leadership found it difficult to respond sympathetically, much less aggressively, to the complaints of the Western office activists.

INITIAL GOALS AND TACTICS

The conditions for new organization were now fulfilled. The needs of individuals could not be met within the existing institutional environment, substantial resources were available for new organization, and constraints on organizing were at the same low level apparent during most of the 1960s. In short order, these unmet needs were converted to goals for a new organization, and the untapped resources were channeled into that organization's structure.

Seventeen public aid employees met to plan the new union on May 23, 1965. Although they came from several district offices, the early activists shared a common sense of frustration with work in the agency, and an interest in collectively organizing against it. Many had only recently begun work as caseworkers. In other respects, their backgrounds were more varied. One who had begun work in the Department that spring had been "just kicking around" after working in a family business and driving a cab. "Public aid sounded interesting, and I needed a job." After being reprimanded for attempting to organize a welfare mothers' group after work hours, he had decided that a union could be used to accomplish the goals of community organizations. Another caseworker activist had spent two years in Europe after completing college. After "bumming around," "I ended up in casework, because you could always get that job." Another had spent time in the Marine Corps after high school, worked at several jobs, and then gone to college. "The reason why I picked public aid was because at that point in time it was my opinion that there was a lot of money being spent on public aid at that time, plus I was kind of a bleeding heart."

The few black early union activists tended to have had somewhat longer experience in public aid work. One black caseworker had joined the agency in 1963 and had experienced frequent pressure due to case loads as high as 300 in a southside office. A clerk who had begun in 1961 found that the problems of work in public aid activated an old family interest in union organizing.

In several intense meetings, the "Seventeen Founding Members" drafted a statement of "Goals and Principles" (Independent Union of Public Aid Employees, 1965). Claiming to represent "the massed voice of dedicated welfare workers," the statement was an impassioned indictment of agency practices:

For years the department has not been sufficiently meeting the
needs of the society and especially those least fortunate in the
society whom it is supposed to be serving. . . .

The Welfare Department is not preventing dependency,
despondency, or human misery. It is not retruning [sic] its
clients to self-care, self-support, or improved functioning. . . .

We believe that a stable, experienced and trained staff,
operating under conditions which permit them to exercize [sic]
their competence, is prerequisite to the ability of the
department to accomplish its stated purpose. Should this be
the end result of our efforts, we will have witnessed the
creation of a new weapon in the increasing struggle for the
common weal.

In conclusion, the statement promised,

We can lower the turnover and raise morale, we can hold on
to sensitive and interested workers who quit from the
frustrations met in a job where it is presently impossible for a
worker to meet the most basic needs of his clients. We can
prevent experienced workers from deserting at their first
opportunity. We can do these things, but only if we receive
the right of collective bargaining. . . . Our basic demand is a
democratic election to determine who shall bargain for public
aid employees.

Calling themselves the Independent Union of Public Aid Employees
(I.U.P.A.E.), the activists sought first to achieve formal recognition
from the Department. A demand for an election to allow employees
to choose their collective bargaining agent (either the new union or
Local 73) headed a list of nineteen demands approved at a September,
1965 membership meeting. In a letter to the Department's Director,
the union presented its rationale for the demand.

There is a long-standing need for adequate representation of
employee interests and for a meaningful channel of
communication. We have come into being in order to fulfill
this need. . . . Our purpose is to improve the working
conditions of the employees. . . . We are certain that our
goals reflect your own aspirations.[1]

The union requested permission to hold meetings in district offices
during lunch periods, to distribute literature in district offices except
during working hours, and to use a bulletin board for union an-
nouncements.

Director Hilliard did not share the enthusiasm of the I.U.P.A.E.'s membership for a role in the Department. Although he agreed to hear union leader's complaints, Hilliard quickly cancelled the meeting when he found that union publicity conveyed the "erroneous impression . . . that the proposed meeting was to be regarded as some form of recognition of some group which you claim to represent." The union asked employees, "Isn't This Obviously an Attempt to Deny Your Right of Free Speech, by Rendering You Ignorant of the Facts?", but Hilliard still refused to negotiate. Neither additional charges of agency harassment, nor a petition "as evidence of an employee mandate for recognition [from] 1600 employees [who] have chosen the IUPAE to lead and mobilize them in a real struggle for decent salaries and working conditions" changed the Director's mind (see also McKelvey, 1967:464).

The union seized on a new agency pay plan to demonstrate that, as it claimed in a leaflet, "there is only one union in the agency with enough cartilage in its backbone to stand up to the Administration and the state legislature on the issue of wages and working conditions in the manner that employees have a right to demand of their union." Proposed when the pay freeze was lifted in November 1965, the new salary plan was to lower the minimum starting pay, emphasize merit as a basis for raises, and restrict the definition of merit itself. In spite of union rallies and picketing outside of the agency's Central Administrative Office, however, these "inequities" were not altered. Agency recalcitrance, leaders admitted, had again diminished "our power as a militant union."

Failing to achieve its main goals, the union turned to its secondary environment for additional resources. Emphasizing its concern with the needs of the underprivileged, the I.U.P.A.E.'s leaders sent letters of support and requests for assistance to groups concerned with increasing social security payments, improving conditions among farm workers, solving problems of aging, and raising benefit levels for welfare recipients. In these letters, they announced that:

> The new union intends to take the side of public aid
> recipients in fighting for increased allowances, changes in
> administrative policies and state laws to benefit the client, and
> education of the client to know exactly what his rights and
> responsibilities are with respect to state law and administrative
> policies. Furthermore, the new union is seeking several job
> improvements which will materially better the lot of the
> recipient. . . . In order to achieve these goals the new union
> is soliciting community-wide support.

Community and civil rights groups, the Senior Citizens' Council of Chicago, and the Chicago chapter of the National Association of Social Workers all responded with affirmations of support for the new union.

I.U.P.A.E. leaders also made contact with other new unions of welfare employees. Together with New York City's caseworker union, the Illinois union organized a conference for welfare employee unionists for December 1965. Spurred by a recent twenty-seven-day strike by New York City caseworkers, and rebuffed by "the growing conservative attitude of large do-nothing unions," the conference participants decided they would have to rely on each other for support. The result was the formation of the National Federation of Social Service Employees, and a declaration that the common problems of their members were, in the words of a leaflet, "high work loads and turnover and low wages and morale, . . . the poor image of the welfare worker, and his dependence upon legislative foibles."

In less than one year, the new union had begun to express the concerns of many employees, secure untapped resources from them, and extend its base of support to other organizations in its secondary institutional environment. Its most basic appeal was to employees dissatisfied with the conditions of their work in the Department and seeking a collective response. Linking the poor conditions of work in the Department to the problems experienced by welfare recipients, the union also sought to appeal directly to those employees particularly concerned with client problems.

STRUCTURE AND INVOLVEMENT

The union's initial structure reflected its origins in the informal social relations between employees, and provided for a practice of collective decision making resembling the natural process of decision making in informal groups. The five people "doing the most talking" were elected to an Executive Committee, subject to recall by a majority vote of the stewards and members. No formal distinctions were made among Executive Committee members, and their decisions had to be made collectively. No president or other officers were recognized, and even the powers of the Executive Committee as a whole were limited. The Executive Committee met weekly with delegates from public aid offices, and was bound by the decisions of the Delegates' Assembly. Meetings frequently continued into the early morning hours, and important decisions were made at other times with conference calls among Executive Committee members.

The stress of long meetings, continual debate, and hectic conference calls eventually took its toll, even on the youthful union activists.

Some began to express their dissatisfaction with the group decision-making process by seeking a more traditional union structure.

> One of the problems was, by having thinking people . . . it's very hard to come to any consensus. We would have meetings that would go until three in the morning over— whatever it is—could be something big, could be something little—. . . the price you pay for dealing with intelligent people.

Debates were remembered over the color of paper to be used in leaflets, the size of paper orders, the type of duplicating machine to be used. "Everything became a major issue and a major problem." By the time the union's first constitutional convention was convened, this structure had become the focus of debate.

The Constitutional Convention

Thirty union members debated heatedly in the union's first "ConCon," beginning in August 1965 and continuing for about six weeks. Recalled by some participants as "a big to-do about nothing" that was dominated by aspiring Thomas Jeffersons arguing as if over the Federalist Papers, the ConCon nonetheless resulted in the first important changes in union structure. The participatory, collective style of governance in the union was replaced by a somewhat more traditional representative style, and differences among union members congealed into sharply delineated factions.

Three factions emerged in the ConCon. Two of them argued for a structure that would continue the initial emphasis on member participation and collective leadership. The model constitution they proposed included provisions that "the Executive Committee shall in all instances preserve absolute democracy and complete freedom of expression in its deliberations," and that "all attempts will be made to conduct meetings in an open and democratic way and in a spirit of free discussion." (Proposed Constitution of the I.U.P.A.E.) Direct membership policy making was to be encouraged through provisions for direct referenda, membership meetings every two weeks, and approval of all basic policy decisions by majority vote of the membership. The powers of leaders were to be limited by yearly elections of Executive Committee members, with only twenty-five signatures required for nomination, and by allowing immediate recall of Executive Committee members upon majority vote of the membership. Emphasizing a concern with members' financial situation rather than with the union's funds, dues were to be limited to one dollar per month.

> We weren't far enough along to decide who should be
> leaders. People had never seen power before. The idea
> fascinated them. The times fostered grand ideas in young
> people. . . . [The proposed constitution] provided for the
> maximum possible democracy. You were dealing with a group
> of real firebrands who didn't want to be dominated by a small
> group. . . . People [leaders] had to be on their toes to keep
> their constituency. . . . We even got away from Delegates'
> Assembly control. Members would vote on key issues
> themselves.

In spite of arguments that the participatory proposal would force
leaders to learn "what's going on" with the membership, and require
factions to work together, opposition to this proposal was strong.
Even leaders of the radical factions recognized that many members
favored a more traditional structure.

> Members were uncomfortable with [the lack of a traditional
> structure] in the main, because people attach themselves to
> things they are familiar with. "Who will take us seriously
> with such an unusual structure?" Most members, except for
> the hard, radical core, *wanted* a leader.

Supporters of a more traditional structure cited the time wasted by
the competition between Executive Committee members for media
exposure, and the general inconvenience of collective leadership. "We
were pushing for a strong Presidency, a strong executive. . . . However, it was so controversial. . . ."

The two factions supporting the participatory model disagreed over
an affirmative action proposal. One faction sought to reserve a position
on the Executive Committee for a clerk, while making no other
distinctions among other Executive Committee members. The presidential candidate of this faction, a black caseworker with ties to the
largely black clerical staff, argued that the special position would
increase clerical involvement in a union still dominated by caseworkers.

> [His] proposal called for an Executive Committee with at least
> one position reserved for a clerical. Just about everyone
> objected to it. The proposal would mean there would be at
> least one black woman on the Executive Committee. The
> Constitutional Convention turned into a racial thing. . . . [The
> leader of the faction] had invited Al Raby [a local civil rights
> leader] to talk to the union, then disinvited him due to
> Executive Committee opposition. But he came anyway. Many
> people were convinced [that the faction's leader] was trying to

turn the union into a civil rights organization. . . . I was appalled that others would object to the union's being associated with the civil rights movement. . . . I thought it was racism. Some said to hold a position for a clerk would be reverse discrimination—it would be setting a quota. . . . [The faction's leader] definitely wanted a quota.

The Constitution finally adopted was a compromise between the major alternatives (I.U.P.A.E., 1966). Some of the key provisions of the participatory proposal were retained. Officers were to be elected for one-year terms subject to immediate membership recall, and members retained the right to initiate binding referenda. However, the power of the union leadership was increased by several provisions incorporated from the representative proposal. A more traditional Executive Board was created, with a president, four vice-presidents (in charge of organizing, publicity, caseworker affairs, and clerical affairs), a treasurer, and a secretary. Election to these offices would require only a majority of those voting, rather than a majority of the entire membership, and the president was authorized to speak for the entire union. The decision to have both a clerical and a caseworker vice-president resolved the affirmative action dispute. Offices were allotted representatives to the Delegates' Assembly in proportion to the size of their membership, and general membership meetings were to be held only quarterly.

The First Election

The three factions that had evolved in the ConCon emerged as alternative slates in the union's first formal election in April 1966. Although supporters of all three slates emphasized the importance of gaining collective bargaining rights, they diverged in their orientation toward other goals and the union's structure. One slate, headed by Allen Kaplan, took what others termed a "traditional labor union position." Its supporters viewed strong leadership as essential for success, and eschewed the past practice of "ultra-democracy." The union goals they emphasized were those expressing traditional "bread and butter" concerns.

I myself always thought, and still do, that the philosophy of the union should be one to really get bread and butter for the employee, and get [better] working conditions and a grievance procedure for the employee. When I say bread and butter, I include benefits. . . . I thought the union should be doing more to support the employee. . . . I viewed the union as an employee organization, rather than as a social organization.
. . .

The other two slates in the first election represented more radical alternatives to the traditional position. Both favored a participatory democratic structure that provided for direct membership control over key decisions as well as a collective leadership. Goals favored by these two slates differed. One slate focused on public aid policy.

> We were not interested in a traditional union. We were for bread and butter, but this was not a major focus. [The leader of the faction] was into the possibility of organizing on a nationwide basis to control the structure of public aid. Unions were to sweep the country in combination with welfare rights organizations and community groups, to control the policy underlying the whole welfare system. . . . [The faction's leader] was tactically militant too. Some rank and file members saw militant actions as everything, but [he] felt they were just a portion of our work, to help unions develop.

The other radical slate continued to argue for special efforts to ensure clerical representation in the union's leadership, and its presidential candidate proposed making ties to local civil rights organizations.

The election campaign tapped divisions deep within the agency's work force.

> In the early days, you had the people that really came from a trade union standpoint, dealing with trade union principles, you had idealists, elitists, realists, and the really professional social work types. . . . You had all this mixture.

A clerical activist recalled two schools of thought in the union,

> You had mostly young white males and females freshly out of college, having always been home with mommy and daddy and maybe another brother and sister and a dog and a cat. . . . For the most part some had never had to work their way through college, and on the other spectrum, you had a lot of either early or middle-aged . . . black women, who were working, most of them single heads of households. . . . We went into organizing the union with a natural distrust and dislike [of caseworkers] that had been built-in many years before.

Support for the three presidential candidates was evenly distributed among the union's membership. Out of 776 votes cast, only thirty-one separated the top and bottom candidates. As a result, a runoff election was conducted for the presidency and three of the seven other Executive positions. The leader of the "civil rights" slate led in the initial voting, but lost to the "traditional labor" candidate in the runoff by sixty-five votes (out of 861 cast). Three other candidates of the traditional slate were also victorious.

After the election, charges of illicit campaign practices were widespread, and left the union bitterly divided.

[The losing presidential candidate] felt we stole the election. We had not done anything illicit, but hard campaigning. We labeled [the other candidate] as a radical who wanted to get the union into a strike but didn't know what he wanted. . . .

. . . how to deal with a certain ultra-leftist element. . . . the only way that they really could have been dealt with would have been to be thrown out of the local, which we did not do, we did not even attempt to do. . . .

[The winning candidate] was never liked by the Delegates' Assembly. He had a reputation with delegates for being out for himself, and using the union as a stepping stone. The delegates opposed everything he tried to do.

The primary problem confronting the new union leaders had become the lessening of internal conflict within the union itself.

CONCLUSIONS

Emergence of a new union of public aid employees in Cook County was a product of mounting levels of unresolved grievances, accumulation of substantial untapped resources, and lessening of traditional constraints against collective action. Rising case loads and an apparent inability of the agency to resolve the problems of its clients contributed to a perception among new caseworkers of agency unresponsiveness to their needs and those of their clients. The pay freeze among state employees aggravated grievances among those not concerned with the intrinsic drawbacks of their work. Unable to cope satisfactorily with these problems itself, the agency could not resolve the rising grievances against it.

Expansion of the public welfare work force and a high rate of caseworker turnover brought many new caseworkers to the agency directly after completion of their college degrees. Many had developed organizing skills through participation in activist student political groups. These resources were consumed neither, in some agency offices, by work nor by the existing union in the agency. Those caseworkers lacking other family or career responsibilities were able to contribute substantial resources to a new organization.

Some of the factors that increased the levels of grievance and resources among public aid employees also contributed to a lessening of constraints against organizing. On-the-job socialization traditionally had helped caseworkers learn to cope with bureaucratic rules, and to adopt a psychological perspective on clients (Blau, 1960). Rapid increases in the numbers of new staff reduced the effectiveness of such socialization, and exposure to the civil rights movement helped to lessen acceptance of psychological explanations of client problems. The social movements of the 1960s generally increased acceptance of the legitimacy of social protest, and reduced confidence in the ability of government institutions to resolve the problems toward which protest was directed. At the same time, other organizations that grew out of these social movements provided a valuable source of resources for new protest efforts.

The new union's initial goals and structure reflected its interaction with the social environment. The grievances of employees were translated directly into union goals, while the intense social relations between employees in some offices were reproduced in the participatory democracy of the union. Even in the union's formative period, however, translation of the grievances and resources of individuals into organizational form in turn led to further changes. When the agency refused to bargain with the union, recognition became its primary goal, and achievement of a contract came to be seen as the prerequisite for organizational effectiveness. Symbolizing the agency's general unresponsiveness, recognition was a demand that all union activists could support. In effect, the demand for recognition quickly began to displace the initial focus on the frustrations of public aid work.

The union's initial participatory structure represented the "classical" conception of democracy found in the work of Rousseau and other eighteenth-century philosophers: "that institutional arrangement for arriving at political decisions which realizes the common good by making the people itself decide issues through the election of individuals who are to assemble in order to carry out its will" (Schumpeter, 1976:250). Such a structure minimizes the vertical distance between leaders and members, and maximally disperses decision making (Pateman, 1970:22–25). In the first year of the I.U.P.A.E., this style of organization allowed maximum use of the abundant resources of individual members, their continuing socialization to the collective ethos of the union, and member confidence that the "will of the membership" would not be subverted by union leaders (Pateman, 1970:42–43).

As the process of decision making through informal meetings of activists was converted into a formal organizational structure, problems in the participatory model began to surface. The "common will" that Rousseau had presumed did not emerge from discussion among individuals with different grievances. Differences in race and occupation were associated with support for different goals. Social reform goals received more support from white caseworkers, while the largely black clerical staff exhibited more support for economic goals. Structural preferences also varied along race and occupational lines. Supporters of social reform goals argued for a participatory structure, while those preferring an emphasis on economic goals were more often supporters of the representative type of structure. In spite of these differences, however, shared concerns with work loads, and a common interest in securing union recognition provided a strong basis for united union action.

The more representative form of democracy adopted by the union's first Constitutional Convention lessened problems from the participatory style. Emphasis was placed on the competition of leaders for membership votes in free elections, and on the membership participation required for successful elections (Schumpeter, 1976). Between elections, the elected leaders were given more responsibility for decision making. Although the new constitution shed far fewer of the key features of a participatory democracy than do the constitutions of most democracies, its adoption represented a significant development for the union.

The results of the union's first election indicated that the participatory style of organizational structure and an emphasis on broad social reform goals still appealed to a substantial segment of the union's membership. As long as the union had to rely primarily on its social environment for resources, those who participated the most in union affairs exerted an influence on it beyond their numbers. The supporters of social reform goals and a participatory structure tended to be those with the highest level of participation in the union. More significant changes in the union's environment would be required to lessen internal conflict over its direction.

Chapter Five

Two Strikes

The union's emergence infected members with a sense of power and optimism. Previously untapped resources were now multiplied by the union. High levels of involvement required by the union's participatory structure were readily generated from the intense commitment of its members. Other organizations stood ready to contribute resources. The only factor missing from the equation was union impact. At best, the agency administration viewed the new union as no more legitimate than somnolent Local 73, and refused to recognize the I.U.P.A.E. as the representative of agency employees. Internally, the union's resources were already beginning to dissipate in factional conflict. Both members and leaders sensed that the time had come to channel some of the union's resources into a bid for greater power.

An Extended Coffee Break

What came to be the union's first strike began as an "early coffee break" by union members. Allen Kaplan, the union's newly elected president, proposed a one-hour work stoppage at an emergency meeting of the Delegates' Assembly shortly after his election in 1966 (*Sun-Times*, May 27, 1966:12).

> After we had labeled [the opposition candidate] as a radical and ourselves as responsible unionists, we called for the most militant action the union had ever conducted. . . . We needed to do something to get the union moving and heal the split.

Militant sentiment was high among the Delegates, who eagerly approved the plan. Four demands were adopted as the goals of the work action, and were publicized in a leaflet to employees:

1. a uniform and systematic salary schedule based on automatic yearly increases;
2. a representation election date for employees to select their sole collective bargaining agent;

3. organizing privileges in the agency district offices;
4. dues check-off for I.U.P.A.E. members.

Union leaders began to encourage employees "to express dramatically and decisively your discontent to the administration." They argued that action beyond the series of demonstrations already conducted after work would be necessary to obtain collective bargaining, and declined to modify their plans after employees were granted a retroactive pay adjustment. Local labor leaders were brought to speak at a pre-stoppage membership rally, and pro-stoppage sentiment mounted.

On May 4 and 5, 1966, 71 percent of the union membership approved the work stoppage planned for May 11. When 376 employees participated in the stoppage, however, the agency did not approve. All were sent home with fifteen-day suspensions.

> We all went into work, and then we all got our suspension
> letters around. . . . Well, everybody almost had their
> suspension letters by noon. So the rest of the day was chaos.

Terming the suspended workers "dissidents and misfits" (*Daily News,* May 12, 1966:6), Director Hilliard explained that they were "very young, just out of school . . . green and gullible" (*Sun-Times,* May 12, 1966:39).

Differences between union factions were set aside as five hundred members called for a strike at a highly charged emergency meeting (*Daily News,* May 12, 1966:6; *Sun-Times,* May 27, 1966:12).

> At the rally after the suspensions, I was caught up in
> emotions. The administration had played into the union's
> hands with the suspensions.

Retaining the original four demands of the work stoppage, the strike call also added a demand for no reprisals against participants in the work action.

The strike began the morning after the meeting. Within five days, employee absences rose to between 1,035 (Hilliard) and 2,043 (I.U.P.A.E.) out of a work force of about 4800 (McKelvey, 1967:464).

> I think that we stung the agency so because they never
> dreamed . . . ; they really thought Hilliard had the employees
> under control, and that we would just take our suspensions
> and we wouldn't get any backing.

On the picket lines, strikers displayed a high level of enthusiasm, and used the occasion to build social ties. "We had a picket line all day, and went drinking afterwards." Statements of support, financial contributions, and additional picketers arrived from leaders of such organizations as the United Auto Workers, the American Federation of Teachers, the Cook County College Teachers' Union, the Precision Electronics Industrial Workers Union, the Chicago Symphony Orchestra Members Committee, the Englewood Civic Organization, Dr. Martin Luther King, Jr., and his Southern Christian Leadership Conference, and the West Side Organizations. Even some nonstriking agency employees issued statements of support.

The original demands of the strike were modified as it continued. The demand for a systematic salary schedule was dropped as a "basic demand," and union recognition soon became the key objective (*Daily News*, May 13, 1966). A demand for service improvements was also added. A minister employed as a caseworker, Doug Cater, moved by the strike, had authored "A Manifesto for a More Humane Welfare System." Attacking the Department's treatment of clients, the manifesto charged that "conscientious college graduates who are sincerely dedicated to the aim of helping the needy [were turned] into police agents and clerical workers. . . ." In a dramatic appeal for support from those public aid employees not on strike, Cater's manifesto argued that "our fight is in the best interests of the community," and pledged that:

> We will not rest until we have succeeded in making some significant changes in our welfare system. And we will remain on strike until the head of our agency agrees to recognize us as concerned human beings who want only decent working conditions and pay scales and the freedom to work in a professional way with those who look to us to help. (*West Side Torch*, May 19, 1966:4.)

Cater's appeal led to his election as union president within the year.

Publication of the Manifesto had a galvanizing effect. Organizations in the union's secondary institutional environment came to its support. *Chicago's American* editorialized that "good or bad, the complaints should at least be listened to" (May 13, 1966). The American Federation of State, County and Municipal Employees asserted that the strike was "completely justified." Community and civil rights organizations joined with the union "to fight a common enemy."

> If recipients can help the caseworkers get lower case loads, more pay, and a better training session, then recipients will be able to expect better treatment (*West Side Torch*, May 19, 1966:5).

At first, Director Hilliard had presumed the strike would have little impact on the agency.

It's a little beyond me how suspended workers can strike. They are picketing because they have time off and nothing else to do. There has been no interference with the operation of the department so far. (*Daily News*, May 12, 1966:1.)

As at least one thousand employees remained on strike, however, pressure to negotiate a settlement mounted (*Daily News*, May 21, 1966).

Director Hilliard offered to allow eighty-five workers already suspended for strike activity return to work with no reprisals. Union leaders were not placated by this offer, but negotiations began by the strike's seventh day. Involving the union and a special committee of the Cook County Board of Commissioners, they did not move quickly (*Sun-Times*, May 12, 1966:39; May 20, 1966:27). The agency threatened to fire the "hard core" strikers (*Sun-Times*, May 21, 1966:2), and a County Commissioner threatened to request an injunction against them (*Sun-Times*, May 22, 1966). Nonetheless, the union's president remained convinced that "our three basic demands are so reasonable the County Board can't deny them" (*Daily News*, May 21, 1966). Union leaders and five hundred voting members rejected a proposed settlement that failed to guarantee organizing privileges for the union, and gave the B.S.E.I.U.'s Local 73 too large a role in a fact-finding board (*Sun-Times*, May 23, 1966:2,8; *Chicago Tribune*, May 23, 1966:1,2; *Daily News*, May 23, 1966).

Two features of Chicago's politics at the time of the strike worked in the union's favor. The Cook County Democratic Party was allied with "old-guard" labor leaders, and would not support the public aid strike. However, Seymour Simon, the Cook County Board's President, had recently been "dumped" by the Democratic machine. Formerly a "rising star," he had not been slated for reelection and had become unwilling to toe the party line (Weber, 1969:326; *Sun-Times*, May 27, 1966:12; *Chicago Tribune*, May 23, 1966). In addition, a chance meeting between Chicago's powerful Mayor Daley and I.U.P.A.E. President Kaplan apparently convinced Daley to back a settlement (*Sun-Times*, May 25, 1966; May 27, 1966:12; *Chicago Tribune*, May 23, 1966:1,2).

The negotiations were going round and round—getting nowhere. We stopped in to see Daley during a break. He had been briefed on the issues. The strike was in the news and the Democrats looked bad. . . . A nod from Daley [to Cook County Board President Dunne] did it.

Fourteen days after the strike had begun, union leaders were ready to present a revised settlement agreement to the membership for approval. The proposed settlement provided for no reprisals against strikers, full organizing privileges, a dues check-off, and formation of a fact-finding board to study the feasibility of a collective bargaining election. Although the early demands for a salary schedule and a collective bargaining election were omitted, the settlement still represented a major advance in the union's role in the Department. Membership approval of the settlement was also facilitated by the appointment of three apparently pro-labor individuals to the fact-finding board. Cook County Board President Simon eliminated one reason for rejecting the settlement by vetoing a plan to insert letters of commendation in the personnel files of nonstrikers (*Sun-Times,* May 25, 1966; May 26, 1966:3; *Chicago Tribune,* May 24, 1966:1,2; May 26, 1966:1,2). The President of the New York welfare workers' union urged the strikers to compromise their demand for a guaranteed collective bargaining election (*Sun-Times,* May 27, 1966:12). Eight hundred union members finally gave close to unanimous approval to the agreement.

The strike settlement only provided a structure for further union efforts to organize and negotiate, but the union also pledged to the community that "co-operatively, employees and clients will eradicate the deprivation and degradation of poverty." The settlement's emphasis on collective bargaining was justified as "only a means to an end, . . . improvements in the lot of all public aid recipients." "Diligent and militant unionism [would] force administrators to improve the overall working conditions toward the aim of greater efficiency [and] enforce the maintenance and improvement of the quality of the services." Inefficiency and lack of organization in public aid were held to be the "real reasons for lower salaries." Special appeals were also made to underprivileged groups in the agency. Public aid Homemakers were urged to join the union "to work for more pay and better working conditions," and clerks were told that the union would take action to get "*immediate* pay raises for all clerks." A credit union was begun by the union to aid members with financial difficulties. Community groups (*West Side Torch,* June 3, 1966:4) and columnists (Jack Mably, *Chicago's American,* May 27, 1966; cf., *Daily News,* May 27, 1966:14) publicly applauded the "aims professional social workers have" (*Daily News,* June 4, 1966).

Director Hilliard reported to a press conference (*Chicago's American,* May 27, 1966) that he had come to consider the strikers a "likable, agreeable bunch."

> I am willing to listen to their recommendations on policy changes in the administration of welfare rolls. I think their views on policies—because they are the ones who ultimately

administer them—are of the greatest importance. . . . This doesn't mean that we adopt policies on the basis of referendum.

Others were not so pleased with the union's avowed intent to work to change the welfare system. Calling these ideas "delusions of grandeur," the *Daily News* (May 27, 1966:14) editorialized:

[President Kaplan] evidently mistook what was essentially a labor dispute settlement as a mandate for the union to dictate policy for the welfare agency. This is a false and dangerous premise. Public policy originates with the people. . . . Hilliard and the city board should make sure that the union confines itself strictly to labor issues and not questions of public policy.

Public policy had yet to be set down in writing, however.

NEGOTIATING A CONTRACT?

Director Hilliard died shortly after acceding the right of his employees to bargain collectively. His temporary successor, John Ballew, did not change the agency's stance. "The right of employees to join, or not to join, a labor union is the basic principle of good employee relations and sound collective bargaining," he told the Fact-Finding Board. Union leaders were enthusiastic about the prospect of securing a contract.

Now we are girding to win a greater victory, a collective bargaining election and contract which will secure our demands (*IUPAE News*, July 6, 1966:2).

Not until these gains [pay raises] and others are achieved at the bargaining table and guaranteed by a signed contract will the abuse and misuse of CCDPA employees cease (*IUPAE News*, September 6, 1966:2).

Nonetheless, the fact finders had still not issued their report by October 5, 1966. Rapidly losing faith in the process, the union Delegates' Assembly proposed to strike for the proposed contract if an election had not been scheduled by October 21. After members ratified the proposal, a demonstration was held at the County Board Building "to prove our strength." On the same day, the Fact-Finding Board issued its report.

Collective bargaining provides a channel for communication, not only for the employees anxious to improve their conditions of service, but also for the public employer. By collective bargaining it is enabled to gain understanding of the true aspirations of its employees, and awareness of problem areas which impede most effective public service. (McKelvey, 1967:474.)

In spite of the glowing language, the County Board promptly tabled the report. It was not until the strike threat had been renewed and another meeting between Mayor Daley and President Kaplan had occurred that the first collective bargaining election for county employees in its 135-year history was scheduled (*Daily News*, October 22, 1966; *Sun-Times*, October 22, 1966).

The contest between the new union and the old Local 73 was bitter, if unbalanced. Local 73 declined to appear on the election ballot and instead simply urged a "NO" vote.

> Local 73 contends that this election is a fraud and a misrepresentation to the employees of the Department. It *cannot* lead to genuine collective bargaining [since it is with the County and not State government]. (Local 73 *Union Newsletter*, n.d.)

> Say NO to *amateur unionism!!!*
> Say NO to *confusion like that* existing in *N. Y. City!!!*
> Say NO to *misrepresentation* and *false hopes* regarding *Collective bargaining!!!*
> Say NO to a *rebel union* barely able to hold *rebellious factions* and *rebellious "leaders"* in check!!!
> Say NO to *delayed adolescents* who are *destroying* YOUR *good image* in the *public eye!!!* (leaflet)

> A "YES" vote means that you want collective bargaining; that you want controls and guarantees over the conditions under which you work; that you want first class citizenship; that you want to be free (*IUPAE News*, December 1966:1–2).

> The Good Shepherd leads his flocks to the Green Pastures.
> The Bad Shepherd leads his flocks to the Barren Hills.
> As it is with the sheep, so it is with the employees of the Cook County Department of Public Aid. (Local 73 *Union Newsletter*, December 8, 1966.)

On December 14, 1966, public aid employees voted to be represented by the Illinois Union of Public Aid Employees by 2,677 to 1,056. At the conclusion of the election, President Kaplan resigned to run for public office. The conflict with the union's Delegates' Assembly had taken its toll.

As the union prepared for negotiations to begin in January 1967 under the leadership of its new president, Vice-president Saul Rosen, a major personnel change in the agency abruptly halted progress. Seymour Simon was replaced by a Republican, Richard Ogilvie, as President of the Board of County Commissioners. Ogilvie, in turn, appointed a new director of the Cook County Department of Public Aid. Although a Republican, William H. Robinson had also been a professional social worker, a welfare rights activist, and one of the few black legislators in Illinois. He was recommended for the Directorship of Public Aid by three community organizations as "the only man who really understands poverty enough." Aware that he had testified on the union's behalf before the Fact-Finding Board, the I.U.P.A.E. itself welcomed Robinson as the new Director.

After waiting a month for negotiations to begin, however, the union was again threatening to strike. The formal negotiations that finally began on March 15, 1967, themselves lasted only one month. The agency, the union complained, had "rejected every substantive proposal the union has sought to make." Union attempts to secure the right to distribute handbooks on welfare policy to clients in public aid offices and to change procedures governing emergency disbursement of checks were both rejected as outside the scope of bargaining. The agency, on the other hand, claimed that the union was attempting to infringe on the ultimate authority of the Commissioners, the Department of Public Aid, and other political bodies.

THE SECOND ELECTION

The election of union executive officers interrupted efforts to secure a contract. Saul Rosen, temporary president of the union, declined to run. Members who had supported former President Kaplan then convinced the author of the "Manifesto," the Reverend Doug Cater, to attempt to "give the strong, mature, responsible leadership which the union needs."

Doug Cater had not been interested primarily in welfare employee unionism. He had come to the University of Chicago for some courses, and then had started public aid work just as "a job." However, he developed a deep interest in the welfare of his clients. Finding the new union "a little suspicious" at first, Cater

> went to a meeting, and decided the union was interested in
> welfare improvements, not just in union (economic) issues.
> . . . [He] had the feeling that the union leaders were
> interested in reforms of less humane aspects of the agency,
> and became a member.

In spite of his lack of union experience, his backers felt that Cater's maturity, political connections, and extensive knowledge of welfare policy issues could gain the union "a national reputation as a forceful pioneer in the fight to improve the lot of public employees and that of welfare recipients."

The opposition slate, continuing the tradition of the radical opposition in the union's first election, called for a more democratic structure. The past Executive Board was accused of "totalitarian" practices, and members were informed that "a creative enlightened force for good can succeed *only* by sticking rigidly to the democratic system." Supporters of the union's leadership felt that there was a more negative side to the opposition's appeal.

> The fundamental tactic that the ultraleftists used was to attack those of us in office for not being left enough. It was a tactic which had been used in the first election also, but didn't succeed in the first election. The slate . . . was accused of being the conservative slate. . . . In the real world of functioning, you can't, you do have to be more temperate in your behavior, many times, than where you actually would like to be ultimately, because the forces aligned against you are powerful enough that you have to be cautious in dealing with them.

The opposition's arguments appeared to have some appeal to many members. In the election, the four "creative" vice-presidential candidates were victorious, but Cater's "responsible leadership" was also endorsed by 725 to 679. The union was now about to begin its longest strike, with a divided Executive Board and a President whose initial aim was only "to work for a more humane welfare system."

The Second Strike

Shortly after the union elections, negotiations with the agency broke down. Even relatively mild union proposals for advisory arbitration and a "management rights clause" were being rejected by the agency's negotiators. The Delegates' Assembly promptly decided to call for a strike. The first strike had sanctified the logic of militant action, and union leaders began to realize that they would have to sanction another strike to maintain credibility with the membership.

> ———tried to dissuade members from striking. He was booed out of the room. . . . Employees were looking for another strike. The previous experience had been successful, and the civil rights movement was at its height. A strike was almost

inevitable. . . . The union had been forced into a corner. It was promised a contract, but the agency had no intention of negotiating it, and the membership wanted a strike. . . .

Union leaders began to argue that members must "break the cycle of fear," and assert their independence from management. On April 26, 1967, the membership approved a motion to strike for the following nine demands:

1. union pay plan retroactive to January 1, 1967;
2. grievance procedure for all agency employees;
3. union fringe benefit proposal;
4. union security;
5. no reprisals;
6. emergency checks for aid recipients at the agency district offices;
7. agencywide distribution of the union's handbook for aid recipients;
8. civil service coverage for all agency employees;
9. submission of remaining contract proposals to advisory arbitration.

The union now confronted an institutional environment that was distinctly less favorable than the one it had faced during its first blitzkrieg victory. Seymour Simon's replacement by the more conservative Ogilvie was only the most obvious change. The union now faced a Director with strong ties to some of the community and recipient groups that had supported its first strike. The West Side Organization, with William Robinson as its head, had endorsed the first strike. Now that Robinson was the agency's director, he was invited to W.S.O. meetings to "Tell His Story to the Poor." The W.S.O.'s perspective changed sharply. "Lazy caseworkers with no feelings for aid recipients should stand behind their boss who is firmly behind doing more for the poor." (leaflet.) Robinson himself continued to lobby for some of the demands of welfare rights organizations, and allowed them to distribute literature to clients in public aid offices.

Support for the second strike was no easier to obtain directly from recipients or even other employees. Union leaders found that "clients stayed away" from the union. The union asked clients to flood public aid offices with special requests, with little effect. A visit to the Delegates' Assembly by recipients supporting Director Robinson almost turned into a fist fight. Robinson also maintained relations with nonstriking employees through talks in the district offices and frequent bulletins. Only 29 percent of 4,200 bargaining-unit employees stayed out.

For a time, some picketers enjoyed the camaraderie of the picket line. High levels of involvement kept up an active sense of progress among some strikers:

> During the first four weeks of the strike, there was so much going on. We negotiated for four weeks while we were on strike, and we'd go to the picket lines, go to negotiations, come back, and of course we had a Rep Council [Delegates' Assembly] meeting every night.

Strikers at some offices distributed leaflets urging nonstrikers to "GIVE ANY FORM OF SACRIFICE YOU CAN. . . . MAKE OURS AN OFFICE TO BE PROUD OF." Clerical members, largely absent from the first strike, made an important contribution to the second. Many strike meetings and rallies were held in black communities, and for some supporters a connection was drawn between the strike and the civil rights movement. However, as weeks passed and the strike dragged on, support began to wane. An increasing sense of a shared fate among picketers maintained the commitment of some of them. "We were all in it together and we knew we would sink or swim together." Others, however, began to defect from the strikers' ranks.

> It was a good thing for the clericals because during that time the shouting militant caseworkers, either they left and took other jobs, or went other places, or went on their trips to Europe and whatever.

Attitudes toward the many nonstriking employees became increasingly harsh. Leaflets directed to these former coworkers expressed the sentiments of vocal strikers in many offices:

> WE'RE GOING TO STAY OUT HERE AND LOOK YOU IN THE EYE AND CALL YOU A SCAB. WE'VE SEEN YOU SNEAKING IN THE BACK DOOR. SCAB (SCARED COWARDLY APATHETIC BETRAYERS). ANGRY AT SCABS LIKE YOU WHO DON'T HAVE ENOUGH BACKBONE. OTHER OFFICES LAUGH WHEN WE TELL THEM ABOUT THE OLD LADIES AND RESIDUE OF MANHOOD . . . THAT WE HAVE TO CONTEND WITH.

A tentative settlement was finally reached by the fourth week of the strike. Although it contained none of the changes in welfare policy the union had sought, at least partial concessions to many of the original demands were included. After gaining this limited victory, however, the union found it could go no further. The Cook County Board of Commissioners failed to ratify the contract, and the strike continued. Neither union appeals to other unions and to clients, leaflets at City Hall, nor militant demonstrations at the offices of the Board's Commissioner were able to wring the contract from the Board.

After six weeks, the union could only obtain a "face-saving" agreement with the Commissioners and was "forced to crawl back." To many activists, it seemed that the strike "didn't accomplish anything," and had just "gutted the union." Less than one-third of the membership turned out to approve the settlement, although they did so by a three-to-one margin. The resolution accepted by the Commissioners had offered the hope of some improvements for the union. The Commissioners agreed to request salary increases, to review levels of paperwork, and to equalize county and state employee benefits. The agreement also anticipated that the Commissioners would establish a grievance procedure, negotiate a contract, and take no punitive action against strikers. However, efforts to implement these agreements stalled for months. Unionists complained of punitive actions against them, and no grievance procedure was initiated.

Finally, the bill to authorize public employee collective bargaining was defeated in the Illinois State Senate.

> In the closing hours of the Legislature, the Chicago Democratic Machine succeeded in defeating Senate Bill 452 which would have authorized collective bargaining for public employees. The machine's spokesman then informed the IUPAE that, despite their previous commitment to collective bargaining for the Department of Public Aid, the County Board could not enter into a signed agreement with the union; they would, however, urge the *State* to implement everything in the contract which their representatives had negotiated. . . . Thus, the machine, which had previously been persuaded (at politically propitious moments) to grant the union's demands, now (in a different political climate) feels free to back down on its commitment. (*IUPAE News*, August 9, 1967:1.)

The lasting impression of some activists was simply that "you can't fight City Hall."

Relations between former strikers and nonstrikers were bitter in the district offices. One unionist recalled that there were many employees "you could not speak to." Many members concluded that the idea of changing the welfare system with union-recipient action was not feasible, and left the agency. Overwhelmed by the experience of the strike's defeat, members' involvement in the union dramatically declined.

CONCLUSIONS

Throughout its first year, the primary goal of the Illinois Union of Public Aid Employees had been to achieve official recognition, to be followed by a contract. Both victorious presidential candidates in the first year had accepted the primacy of this goal, and a more hierarchical structure was adopted in part to facilitate its achievement. The institutional acceptance connoted by recognition was expected to lead to greater consultation with agency officials, and to a greater flow of resources to the union from its institutional environment (Gamson, 1975:31–34). Like many unions lacking adequate ties to the network of organizations in their primary institutional environment, the I.U.P.A.E. was willing to expend substantial resources in order to gain acceptance (Snyder, 1975).

Twice within one year, the union called its members out on strike to achieve recognition. The response to this effort differed markedly between the two strikes. In the first strike, community groups, other unions, and some politicians all supported the public aid employees. The strike brought the union to the attention of all employees, and ensured its continuing ability to organize. Even though some of the early radical activists were bitter over the leadership's failure to demand and achieve improvements in working conditions or service policy, most viewed the strike as beneficial. Membership increased rapidly after the strike, and union activists felt they had become a powerful force in the agency.

The agency was more determined to prevail in the second strike, and the political bodies controlling public aid policy were less favorable to the union. Community groups that had aided in the first strike remained aloof in the second. The union was also unable to secure adequate levels of involvement from employees. In spite of the prodigious efforts of many strikers, on and off the picket lines, the union was unable to overcome an overall deficiency in resources. A victory that had been "too easy," was now joined by a defeat that was "pure hell."

Both strikes had united supporters of the union's factions. On the picket lines, differences in goals appeared less significant. The gravity of the strikers' situation, and their common interest in securing a contract created a temporary solidarity, and thus saved the resources that might otherwise have been expended in factional conflict. However, solidarity in itself was insufficient to secure union victory.

By the end of the second strike, the union was further from achieving its goal of recognition than when it had begun the strike. Committed to a goal it could not achieve, failing with tactics to which it had been committed, the union now found its membership disillusioned in spirit and declining in numbers. Unable to obtain adequate resources from its social or institutional environments, as an organization the union itself was severely impaired.

CHAPTER SIX

Bread, Butter, and
Social Consciousness

After two years of rapid growth and frenetic activity, union expansion slowed to a crawl (Figure 1). The failure of the second strike in 1967 raised fears that "the union was in the throes of death," as one member remembered it. Membership ceased to grow, conflict frequently erupted between factions, and membership criticism of union leaders was often sharp. In two elections, candidates for president were recruited after the filing deadline had passed. Prior to the 1969 election, the union's newspaper carried the desultory headline: "SLIM PICKINGS IN THE IUPAE ELECTION APRIL 30." (*IUPAE News*, May 1969.) Doug Cater, the minister who had led the union during the second strike, was replaced by a militant black caseworker, Carter Williams, in May 1968. Williams was in turn defeated for reelection by the minister in May 1969. As a result of a change in the union's elections from May to September, Cater's second term only lasted four and one-half months. Before it was over, Cater found himself "voted back to the office" by the Delegates' Assembly, and spent the last month of his term working without compensation. The next president, David Fuller, found his proposals for action in local politics consistently voted down by the Delegates' Assembly.

Union efforts to influence the agency after the second strike were often unsuccessful. By the summer of 1968, the union's president called for a new grievance procedure and an investigation of the Department. The goal of securing ratification of the contract negotiated after the first strike seemed increasingly less achievable. It was finally abandoned at a poorly attended meeting of the union's membership in 1971. In an editorial entitled "A Union That Failed," an activist lamented,

In our analysis we found that we have not obtained
implementation of our contract, due to insufficient power. . . .

> At a membership meeting the less than 150 persons, some
> nonmembers, voted to desert the strategy that grew out of
> four years of struggles; to desert the demand for a contract
> already agreed upon. (*IUSSE News*, March-April 1971:2)

Yet the union did not expire, in spite of its many problems. While
it had difficulty influencing the agency, the factors that had led
employees to start the union continued to draw new employees into
it. Many of the grievances revealed in the emergence of the union
were still unresolved. Rising case loads continued to generate charges
that the agency emphasized "paperwork and not people," in "a huge
factory in an office." A March 1968 union statement to the Illinois'
Legislative Advisory Commission on Public Aid (leaflet) attempted
to speak for the caseworkers experiencing these problems:

> Caseworkers' frustration is not a statistic or hypothesis or
> some other abstraction to us. It is we who, simply because we
> are human and there, must suffer with them.

Unable to resolve their frustrations on the job, some caseworkers
turned to the union.

Outside the agency, the political environment had become more
turbulent. For some new caseworkers, contact with the inner city
itself seemed to demand more than routine casework. "The West
Side was burning, and I felt I had to do something." The riots after
the assassination of Martin Luther King, Jr., contributed to a feeling
that traditional approaches to the problems of the poor were no
longer appropriate.

> I was due to report to work on Monday, following that
> weekend, and out of our fifty-member orientation group, five
> people showed up. . . . [The office] had been burned down.
> . . . My district . . . had been devastated by the riots. There
> were no grocery stores in walking distance; . . . they had just
> been burned down. There were police everywhere——
> everywhere in the district. You couldn't walk half a block
> without seeing a canine patrol car. . . . They were using
> helicopters still to patrol.

The student movement's continued growth and radicalization also
influenced the public aid work force. Radical student activists found
that a combination of public welfare work and union activity was
"a natural progression from college." The factors in the social environment that explained the emergence of the union also accounted
for its ability to persist in the face of daunting external difficulties
and internal discord.

SOURCES OF UNION MEMBERSHIP

The bases of the union's appeal can be specified in terms of the grievances, resources, and constraints associated with membership in the union. Statements of former union activists, information from union publications, and statistical analyses of employee responses in the 1973 survey will be used to identify these sources of union membership.

The 1973 survey of C.C.D.P.A. employees occurred at the end of the post-strike period, after the union had changed its name to the Illinois Union of Social Service Employees (I.U.S.S.E.). At that time, most employees in the agency were in one of five general occupations: clerical, case aide, caseworker, supervisory caseworker, and specialized professional jobs (professional specialists). The job duties of employees in at least four of these occupations differed substantially, as did their levels of pay and education.

Clerks maintained files on clients or worked as typists, stenographers, and switchboard operators. College training was not required for these positions, and their average (mean) salary was just $5,978. Mean salaries for particular clerical jobs ranged from a low of $4,741 for Clerk I to $10,009 for Clerk V and $10,671 for Secretary II. Beginning in 1969, the C.C.D.P.A. had begun to hire case aides and case aide trainees to assist caseworkers and perform some casework tasks. Although the actual distinction between the duties of the "professional" caseworkers and the "paraprofessional" case aides was a subject of continuing debate, differences between the requirements and rewards for the two positions were pronounced. Case aides were required to have only two years of college, and earned an average salary of $7,158. Caseworkers, who were responsible for visiting clients and evaluating their financial and service needs, were required to have college degrees. They earned an average salary of $9,618 in 1973. Accounting for thirty-five percent of the agency work force, their numbers were exceeded only by the clerical group. (See Appendix Table A-3.)

The work of caseworkers was overseen by supervisory caseworkers. Supervisory caseworkers evaluated the work of units of up to five caseworkers, and met with their unit to discuss policy issues. They were promoted to the supervisory position from the ranks of caseworkers, and received an average annual salary of $12,675. Agency employees in several other occupations were responsible for specialized professional tasks. This category included Property and Insurance Consultants, Medical Social Workers, Deputies, and Public Aid Representatives. Their average salary ranged from a low of $8,906 for

Deputy I to $12,689 for Medical Social Workers, for a combined average of $10,826.

Indicators of grievances, individual resources, and acceptance of traditional constraints against collective action were each measured. The five potential grievances were: job dissatisfaction (JOB), importance attached to ability to serve clients (SERVICE), importance attached to increasing general employee economic benefits (ECON), importance attached to increasing economic benefits for paraprofessional employees (PARA), and importance attached to decreasing employee work loads (WORK) (see Appendix). Several indicators of resources available to employees—amount of socializing with fellow employees (SCLZE), nondependence on income from the job in public aid (JOB NEED), nonmarried status (SINGLE), and amount of education (EDUC)—were also measured. Rejection of a view of clients as victims (CLIENTS), trust in government and business (PLTCS), and seniority (SNRTY) indicated the extent to which employees were subject to constraints against union action.

A regression analysis of union membership was conducted in order to identify the independent impact of grievances, resources, and constraints, as well as of occupation, gender, and race. An equation of the form $Y = a + b_1X_1 + b_2X_2 + \ldots b_iX_i + e_i$ expresses the regression model of the linear effects of the independent variables (X_i) on the dependent variable (Y). The effects themselves are captured by the slope coefficients (b_i), while "a" is the value of Y when all the independent variables have a value of zero (the Y-intercept) and e_i is the error made in predicting Y from the X_i (the residual variation). When the slope coefficients (b_i) are calculated for standardized units of Y and all X_i, they are termed β_i (beta) and provide an indication of the relative strength of the effect of each independent variable regardless of the units used in measuring the variables.

The regression results are reported in two stages. First, the results of regressing membership on the five grievances are reported. These results indicate the extent to which union members tended to have different goals than nonmembers, regardless of their other attitudes or characteristics. Second, membership is regressed on the entire set of variables, in order to identify the independent impact of each. In the analysis of the bases of union membership, findings from these regression analyses are presented simultaneously with the related findings from interviews and union publications.

Concern neither with strictly economic gains (ECON) nor with ability to serve clients (SERVICE) was higher among members than nonmembers. As indicated in Table 2, the beta coefficients for these two variables were zero in the first stage of the regression analysis, and did not achieve statistical significance at any stage. The union's appeal was not primarily on the basis of the economic grievances commonly associated with blue-collar unionism nor the concern with client service sometimes associated with traditional professional associations. Of the five grievances included in the regression analysis, it was the two that focused on the nature of public aid work itself that were related to membership.

Job dissatisfaction (JOB) was significantly higher among union members than among nonmembers, as indicated by the coefficients of .13 and .11 for JOB in the first two stages of the regression analysis (see Table 2). The impact of job dissatisfaction was also reflected in the comments of union activists.

Table 2. Regression Analysis of Factors in Union Membership, Cook County, 1973 (Beta Coefficients)

Independent Variables	Specification 1	Specification 2	Specification 3
Grievances			
Job dissatisfaction (JOB)	.13***	.11***	.05
Service to clients (SERVICE)	.00	.00	−.03
Work load (WORK)	.08**	.05	.07*
General economic benefits (ECON)	.00	.03	.02
Paraprofessional benefits (PARA)	.05	.08*	.03
Occupation[a]			
Clerical (CLERK)[b]		.04	−.08
Case aide (AIDE)		.05	−.01
Caseworker (CW)		.13*	.06
Supervisory caseworker (SUP)		.11**	.09*
Resources			
Socializing (SCLZE)			−.06
Need for job (JOB NEED)			−.08*
Marital status (SINGLE)			.03
Education (EDUC)			−.16***
Constraints			
Belief in clients (CLIENTS)			.09**
Institutional alienation (PLTCS)			.09**
Seniority (SNRTY)			−.05
Demographic background			
Age (AGE)			−.13***
Gender (MALE)			.05
Race (BLACK)			.08*
R^2	.04	.05	.12
$\bar{R}^2$[c]	.03	.04	.10
N	1195	1133	1064

[a] Professional specialists omitted.
[b] Includes Homemakers and Janitors.
[c] Adjusted R^2.
 * $P \leq .05$
 ** $P \leq .01$
 *** $P \leq .001$

It was like an assembly line in Intake. It was not pleasant, but it was good pay—a very frustrating job. The college grads felt they had been trained for a better job.

Many activists had also had an adverse reaction to high case loads.

As the War on Poverty ended, funds diminished. I didn't enjoy the job. . . . There was little time for individual clients. I had to see about twenty clients per day. The job was mostly paper pushing.

The impact of desire to reduce case loads (WORK) was not significantly altered statistically by the inclusion of other attitudes and characteristics in the regression analysis. Frustration with high case loads in itself seemed to be enough to motivate union membership. However, the effect of job dissatisfaction (JOB) diminished in stage III when the correlated effects of age, race (BLACK), and attitudes toward clients (CLIENTS) were controlled.

Propensity to reject a negative perspective on client problems (CLIENTS) differed markedly between union members and non-members (beta = .09). Employees who viewed clients as victims of the welfare system, rather than as abusers of it, were more likely to join the union. The regression analysis also revealed that employees who had low levels of trust in government and business (PLTCS) were more likely to be in the union (beta = .09). Such an orientation appeared frequently in the comments of activists.

I decided to join the union right away [in 1969] because I had been politically active in college in the McCarthy campaign, and I wanted to continue my involvement in those issues. The union was ideal for this, with its work actions and marches. . . . The office . . . had just been involved in a march. . . . So, when I was given a choice of three offices to begin work at, I chose [it]. . . . I didn't like employees being pushed around and the running of the agency as a dictatorship.

Often associated with low levels of institutional trust were leftist politics.

If it wasn't respectable and the administration hated it, then I knew that's where I wanted to be.

And opposition to the Vietnam War had brought some to work in public aid.

> I applied because I was a Conscientious Objector, and public aid work was my alternative service. I had been in the Peace Corps.

Membership was more common among younger than older employees (AGE). But seniority in the job itself (SNRTY) had no effect.

The resource variables did not have the predicted effects on union membership. While frequency of socializing (SCLZE) was higher among members, its effect was not significant. Single employees, expected to have more time for union activity, were no more likely to be in the union than those who were married. Employees with more education, who were expected to have more of the skills useful in union activity, were nonetheless significantly less likely to be members than those with less education when their political attitudes and other characteristics were taken into account. Rates of membership were similar among men and women, but black employees were more likely to be union members than whites. Those less dependent on their public aid job, in terms of either present economic need or future job prospects, seemed less interested in commiting themselves to it further through joining a union. In other words, the union seems to have had some appeal to those employees with a greater potential interest in job security, either due to greater current economic needs or fewer opportunities in the larger job market.

These findings are largely consistent with the historical analysis of bases for the union's emergence. The union seemed to appeal more to those employees who were generally dissatisfied and disappointed with their jobs, and to those who were particularly concerned with reducing case loads. It was these grievances that were exacerbated in the 1960s, not concerns with wages and service policies per se.

Grievances of any kind played only a limited role in distinguishing members and nonmembers. The union's appeal was primarily rooted in other attitudes and characteristics. Employees who rejected the psychological perspective on client problems that had traditionally been associated with adjustment to work in social service agencies were more likely to join the union (Blau, 1960). Such a tendency to "blame the system" rather than "blaming the victim" was encouraged by the social movements of the 1960s, and was apparent in the orientations of many of the early union activists.

The "climate of the times" was also consistent with the higher levels of distrust of government and business found among union members. The same values voiced in the student movement had reappeared in the public aid work force, and were associated with the same predisposition toward collective action. A greater tendency toward union membership among younger employees suggests a demographic pattern consistent with this larger explanation of the union's appeal. However, concerns with job security seemed to motivate membership for a minority of members. This basis for union membership, initially apparent in factional conflict before the first strike, was to grow in importance.

Union Goals and Action

Member grievances were translated into union goals. However, the process of translation was not direct. From the array of grievances felt among the membership, some were the focus of unionwide efforts. Other goals were pursued briefly and then neglected, while actions to secure some goals were taken only by limited sectors of the membership.

After the interlude of unity created by the stress of the second strike, factional conflict reemerged within the union. The two factions that dominated intraunion politics during this period differed in the goals they sought to emphasize, and thus appealed to members with different grievances. One faction focused on "bread and butter" issues, the economic concerns of the membership, while the "socially conscious" faction sought to elicit substantial union efforts on behalf of, and in concert with, welfare clients. Although the "bread and butter" faction succeeded in electing each union president, the supporters of the "socially conscious" faction often dominated the Delegates' Assembly, and played pivotal roles in several public aid offices.

Underlying the development of a new opposition faction in the union were the efforts of new radical recruits to the public aid work force.

> Of course some of the people had been in SDS [Students for a Democratic Society] chapters, and some of the people had been in civil rights, and some people had been active in the anti-war movement. So when we came into public aid as caseworkers, we were already radicalized to an extent by coming out of colleges at the time that we did.

Others had started as caseworkers "pretty much for political reasons," and found that it proved to be a "real rich job" for organizing.

> In 1969, "those like-minded people" formed a study group. It was sort of a debating society and a drinking society and a revolutionary society: . . . We wanted to make bigger than bread and butter changes.

For a year, the study group included union members with ties to various radical groups. After that, a new study group focusing on trade union organizing and dominated by the Progressive Labor Party emerged. "That was the beginning of the idea of having a caucus and meeting clandestinely." This group formed what was called the "Rank and File Caucus," and began to emphasize a "socially conscious" client-centered position.

PL, as it came to be known, was a radical 1960s offshoot of the U.S. Communist Party. For several years, PL focused its organizing efforts on welfare clients as well as welfare employees. Their general policy was to encourage militancy wherever possible, and an interpretation of immediate work place problems in terms of class struggle. As a leaflet on "Welfare and the War" explained, "we must expose the federal government not only as an imperialist government but as a boss that keepts [sic] its own workers down." Within public aid employee unions, PL organizers sought to foster an alliance between workers and welfare clients.

Opposed to the efforts of the radical caucus were members who believed that union should emphasize economic and other employee concerns. There was "no point in organizing with clients," and client groups shouldn't expect the union "to fight their battles for them." Other opponents of the radical opposition disliked their emphasis on militancy.

> The Caucus was bent on destruction. It wanted to strike—strike—strike. This would have been disastrous. I saw them as a young bunch of hotheads—college kids going out for kicks, who didn't really have employees' interests at heart. The rest of us had worked to build up the union.

Union activity during the post-strike period can only be understood in the context of this factional conflict. The goals that were the focus of union activity, and the tactics employed to achieve particular goals, were shaped by the relative ability of both factions to mobilize resources, as well as by member grievances.

Case Loads

Pressures due to high case loads continued after the union's emergence. Caseworkers recalled that "emergency cases . . . in piles six feet tall on clerks' desks . . . had to be taken care of immediately, and wouldn't get taken care of for weeks. . . . Everybody [the clients] needed everything." The union charged that caseworkers handled an average of 171 cases, while the H.E.W. case load standard was sixty (*IUSSE News*, November 1970:2).

The problems experienced by caseworkers with excessive case loads demanded attention from the union, and supporters of both factions recognized the issue's importance. Union work actions over case loads sometimes developed in district offices, and involved the union's central leadership only after a call to union headquarters, post hoc. In the summer of 1968, members in one office voted to refuse to do redeterminations of eligibility on cases assigned in excess of normal case loads.

> The . . . members recently took a stand against doing the meaningless work [redetermination visits] on uncovered loads. . . . In a letter addressed to the DO [District Office] Supervisor, the . . . unionists in an educative tone made it clear that they would do everything possible, short of insubordination, to avoid doing the meaningless work on the uncovered loads. (*Information and Action*, July 9, 1968:2.)

Some new workers were subsequently hired. Another office won a twelve-point grievance that demanded improvements in their intake system.

The practice of transferring employees from their regular case loads to uncovered case loads became common as the agency attempted to cope with an insufficient staffing level. Some case workers felt they were being forced to neglect their own clients and make up for agency shortcomings.

> The ADC Review is a useless piece of paper, a waste of our time, a camouflage. Processing the reviews prevents us from providing essential services. (*IUPAE News*, May 1969:4.)

Sometimes this agency transfer of workers to uncovered loads led to union action. At one office, members voted a sit-down to protest an attempted transfer of several caseworkers and clerks to uncovered case loads. After warning notices were issued to those refusing the transfer, however, the action ended. (*IUSSE News*, March-April 1971:3.)

The most concerted union effort to reduce case loads occurred in October 1970, with an agencywide work slowdown. Participating employees refused to service cases when they exceeded the numerical limit formally established for caseworkers. However, the only response by agency administrators was to point out that they could not assume responsibility for a problem caused by a statewide hiring freeze (*IUSSE News*, November 1970:1). Employees then voted to hold a strike referendum if union demands were not met (*IUSSE News*, February 1971:1), but in the union's weakened state the threat could not be carried out. By the fall, the idea of striking had been abandoned.

Discipline

Union tactics also frequently focused on the problem of disciplinary suspensions and terminations of probationary employees. As the temporary suspensions of employees after the union's first walkout had galvanized united union action, so calls for action over suspensions in later years elicited support from both factions. For union activists, disciplinary procedures were a matter of vital concern. Such agency action was viewed by the union as a threat to its ability to function, as well as an injustice to those disciplined.

> Now that the Agency has responded [to union actions] with a rash of suspensions, it becomes more important than ever that the Union meet this response by demanding full justice for all employees. This of coarse, [sic] means a rescinding of all suspensions and a halt to any more such action. It also means that the issue must be presented to the public in order to force a change in personnel policies of CCDPA.

Throughout 1968, 1969, and 1970, the union tried a variety of tactics to stop the suspensions and terminations. While union leaders emphasized grievances and attempts to negotiate with the agency, supporters of the opposition faction often encouraged collective actions by employees.

At times, the grievance procedure established by the agency after the first strike provided a means for responding to disciplinary actions. In June 1968, a union grievance stopped a member's suspension. At about the same time, a discrimination charge filed by the union with the state Fair Employment Practices Commission helped to secure the rehiring of Puerto Rican caseworkers who had not passed an English language test (*IUPAE News*, January 1969:1). In many such cases, the union was not successful. "Justice is not the concern of the bureaucrats who run this department," the union charged after nine employees were suspended in an "anti-union" action (*Information and Action*, August 19, 20, 1968).

The agency agreed to negotiate with union leaders over the suspensions problem, but some members felt that negotiations alone would not suffice. These activists organized a demonstration to end suspensions and harassments, reduce workloads, and increase salaries for clerks, maintenance workers, and homemakers as an accompaniment to union–agency negotiations. As described in a leaflet distributed the following day, the action drew over five hundred people from twenty-three offices. It was remembered fondly by union militants for years to come.

A bunch of us were down there, the Bread and Butters [supporters of economic goals] and the other ones, all trying to decide what to do. . . . The picket line had been going clear around the whole Loop block. . . . Suddenly, . . . people were going inside CAO [the agency's Central Administrative Offices]. . . . [A] bunch of people . . . crawled out on the fire escape [after walking up eighteen flights of stairs to get to the negotiating room]; . . . we were just sort of milling around, didn't know what to do.

In spite of the drama of the event, however, the action had little impact. Negotiations were subsequently adjourned, to the dismay of union activitists. Ultimately, the problem of disciplinary suspensions was partially resolved in court. A federal judge agreed with the union's contention that lack of a hearing prior to suspension violated the due process clause of the fourteenth Amendment and granted a temporary restraining order. The agency soon adopted a new suspension procedure that included hearings before the suspensions were to occur (*IUSSE News*, November 1970:1).

Economic Gains

Economic gains were of concern to many activists, even if they were not associated with union membership itself. A 1970 union newspaper article voiced the complaint that,

in a year of soaring cost of living and unprecedented wage gains won by other Chicago workers, CCDPA employees are not only not getting any real increase in purchasing power, but will probably even fall behind the rise in cost of living (*IUPAE News*, August 1970:1)

Little effort was expended to achieve economic gains for caseworkers, however. Most union efforts focused on economic gains for clerks and other low-paid employees. The mean annual salary for clerks was just $6,000 as late as 1973. Case aides received just over $7,000, compared to a caseworker mean of just under $10,000 (Illinois Department of Public Aid, March 15, 1973). Action to increase clerical and paraprofessional salaries thus seemed to speak to an important grievance among a group of employees whose resources were sorely needed in the union. Both factions tried to champion their cause.

Union leaders had recognized the importance of clerical involvement during the second strike. While caseworkers quit in frustration over agency policies or union failures, clerks tended to treat their public aid job as permanent. Yet the union had had little success in increasing clerical involvement. A leaflet entitled "WAKE UP CLER-

ICAL," for example, pleaded with clerks, "won't you sacrifice four dollars a month [union dues] for the betterment of *yourself* and co-workers." The union's Organization Vice-President reported that clerical members had not been participating in union committees, and clerical activists struggled to convince their coworkers that "OUR SALVATION IS SIMPLY—'COME TOGETHER'" (*IUPAE News*, March 1970:4).

The union began to emphasize the importance of raising the salaries and benefits of clerks, maintenance workers, and homemakers ("CMHS" workers) in 1969 (*IUPAE News*, July 16, 1969:1). When health aides paid from U.S. Office of Economic Opportunity funds were laid off, the union called demonstrations, distributed publicity, and held meetings with government officials over the problem. After these actions, the aides were rehired (*IUPAE News*, May 1969:11). Pay increases for clerks in 1968 were attributed by the union president to his contacting agency, county, and state officials. The union also focused on problems of agency Homemakers. "Homemakers are in bondage; they are slave laboroers [sic]." The union reported winning grievances concerning public aid homemakers' problems with their promotions, examinations, and firings (*IUPAE News*, July 16, 1969:2; *Information and Action*, July 9, 1968).

The highpoint of the CMHS campaign came in the summer of 1969. Unionists staged an emotionally charged confrontation at the offices of the Illinois Department of Public Aid in Springfield.

> A clerk IV complained angrily of the inadequacy of her salary in relation to the responsibilities of her work. This brought a confirming chorus from other clerks, who demanded that their real responsibility—training caseworkers who were given inadequate training in the first place—be rewarded with a salary that matched their work (*IUPAE News*, June 1969:1).

However, the Director of the I.D.P.A. refused to recommend CMHS pay increases to the state's Department of Personnel (*IUPAE News*, June 1969:1).

The union then organized three hundred employees to march around the Director's office. A demand for his resignation now accompanied the demand for a pay increase. Failing to secure the Director's prompt acquiescence, the union called a one-day work stoppage and then a work slowdown (*IUPAE News*, July 16, 1969:1). "Following agency policy to the letter as it is written is the most effective way of grinding the complex agency machinery to a halt," the union's newspaper claimed (*IUPAE News*, September 1969:1). Rhetoric notwithstanding, the slowdown had little impact (*IUPAE News*, September 1969:1).

While some of its actions at the office level met with success (*IUPAE News,* March 1970:1), the most substantial union contribution to the welfare of CMHS employees proved to be its sponsorship of a credit union, discount buying plans, and low-cost charter trips to Bermuda and Las Vegas. An article written by a clerical activist in 1971 summarized the impact of union action on clerical involvement: "We have become easily pacified, and we quickly drop back into our ruts—nice, safe, comfortably warm, secure ruts" (*IUSSE News,* March-April, 1971:6).

Service Policy

Contact with clients on the job, public protests by welfare rights groups, and actions by other organizations of the poor continued to draw the attention of some union activists toward client issues and related community concerns. This concern no longer focused on attempts to persuade the agency to change policy. Union President Doug Cater, as the author of the "Manifesto for a Humane Welfare System," "tried to get the [union's] Agency Improvement Committee going again, but there was not enough interest, and there was no possibility of implementing changes through a contract." Instead, protest activity with community groups became the primary outlet for union activists concerned with agency service policy.

At times, such community-centered activity dominated union activity. The March 1968 issue of the union newspaper, for example, contained five articles on community groups. Union activists furnished food for a seventy-two-hour vigil of recipient activitists against new restrictive welfare policies, and argued that "IUPAE needs the support of labor *and* welfare unions" (*IUPAE News,* March 12, 1968). The IUPAE issued statements of support for Jesse Jackson's Operation Breadbasket and for a boycott of the A&P food chain. Union members helped United Farm Workers supporters picket stores selling California grapes (*Information and Action,* August 6, 1968; July 9, 1968).

In some offices, it seemed that most union activity was directed to "the community." As a new caseworker recalled,

> The union was very client-oriented at that time. I don't remember the union fighting for employees much. . . . But the union was fighting for clients, around grants, assistance, and insane agency policies.

Union actions on behalf of clients, and in conjunction with client groups, became the focus of factional conflict. A Community Relations Committee had been formed within the union to focus on client issues. It was dominated by unionists who rejected the traditional professional social work approach to client problems. They adopted social reform as their goal and direct action as the means to achieve it. Many of these committee activists also participated in the caucus of the radical opposition.

One of the basic tenets of the professional social work approach was to maintain objectivity toward clients.

> One of the cardinal rules of social work is to try to remain as objective as possible so as to be able to make rational decisions with regard to the client (Berk, 1968:143.)

A survey of public welfare caseworkers in fifteen cities had found that thirty percent endorsed a "largely objective" approach to social work, while another sixty percent supported an equal amount of objectivity and subjectivity in relations with clients (Berk, 1968:143).

The Community Relations Committee activists rejected the validity of this approach. The agency, they argued, was simply trying to inculcate "the myth of being professionals" by encouraging caseworkers to complete MSWs and to evaluate clients "objectively" (*IUPAE News*, November–December 1968:7).

> The old-line social work philosophy sort of was that the clients were crafty, yet ignorant, and that we had to protect the clients from themselves, and we had to dress in a professional manner, act in a professional manner, and always be objective about the clients. And "objectivity" was a real word that they used to flaunt around. . . . The CRC people . . . saw welfare rights unions as being unions like us. . . . Our oppressor was a common oppressor—you can't be standoffish and you can't be "objective" because you see yourself in the same struggle.

The Committee distributed a welfare rights handbook to clients, and passed out at least one leaflet to the public protesting restrictive welfare policies. It also participated in demonstrations with welfare rights groups to publicize the plight of the poor, and to protest restrictive amendments to the Public Assistance Code (*IUPAE News*, November 1967).

The success of welfare rights groups in the late 1960s and early 1970s was a major source of support for the Community Relations position, and helped the union to overcome its problems in relations with community groups manifested in the second strike. The successes of the National Welfare Rights Organization (N.W.R.O.) proved to some union activists the ability of client groups to influence public aid policies (*IUPAE News*, March 12, 1968:3). Although formed only in 1966, after a series of demonstrations for welfare rights, the

N.W.R.O. had developed into a prominent national organization by its peak at the end of the decade. At this point, it represented over 173 groups in twenty-three states, with a national membership of 22,500. It sought to achieve its goals by disrupting the welfare system to secure increasing concessions for the needs of the poor. N.W.R.O. often organized demonstrations in welfare offices to support demands for school clothing grants and other special benefits, and distributed simplified handbooks of welfare regulations (Piven and Cloward, 1971:323–24; Steiner, 1971:297–98).

Activists in the union's Community Relations Committee sought to channel this client militancy into joint action against the agency. As a Community Relations Committee report explained, "a group of angry united clients in the Intake office [is] the most crucial and visible lever" for demanding changes in agency policies. In the recollections of a committee member, "twenty or more clients would come into the office and scream at the supervisor." In 1968, the I.U.P.A.E. and the Latin American Defense Organization jointly demanded an emergency clothing allowance and more agency staff (*IUPAE News*, November-December 1968:2). Mothers from the Kenwood-Oakland Community Organization were arrested at another district office during a sit-in for more clothing allowances. However, many union members viewed such activity as inappropriate for an employee union.

SOURCES OF FACTIONAL CONFLICT

A series of regression analyses using the 1973 survey data help to identify the sources of support for the two factions. Measures of the union goals and tactics that members favored, the resources they could make available to the union, the constraints on member action, and their satisfaction with the union are all included. This analysis parallels the previous analysis of the bases of union membership. Resources and constraints are measured with the same variables. Three of the measures of grievances, support for paraprofessional benefits (PARA), concern with work loads (WORK), and job dissatisfaction (JOB) are also used in the analysis of factional conflict. However, two additional grievances, concerns with general employee benefits and with client benefits were also measured in the 1973 survey in terms of desirable goals for the union. It is the measures of desired union goals (EMP and SERVE) rather than of individual grievances that are used in the analysis of factional conflict.

The correspondence between the variables used in the analysis of union membership and the analysis of factional conflict reflects the assumption that the factors giving rise to a new organization continue to influence the organization after its emergence. As with analysis of the effect of grievances, resources, and constraints on union membership, this analysis of goals, resources, and constraints is able to clarify the bases of factional conflict and its outcome. However, the differences between the processes of organizational emergence and factional conflict require some differences in the analysis of their sources. The measures of support for particular union goals (EMP, PARA, WORK, and SERVE) are treated initially as dependent variables, in order to identify the extent to which different groups in the union backed different goals. An additional index, employee support for militant tactics (MILTNT), is included to identify the role of tactics preferences in factional support. Job dissatisfaction (JOB) is again used as a predictor in this analysis. Measures of the extent of participation in union activities (PART) and of plans to soon leave the agency (EXIT) to help determine the differences in individual resources available to the two factions. A regression analysis is also done on a measure of satisfaction with the union (USAT) in relation to the other variables. (See Appendix.)

Due to the number of dependent variables, only the final stage of the regression analyses are presented. This final stage includes the measures of support for the four union goals as independent variables in the regression analyses of militancy, participation, plans to leave, and union satisfaction. This indicates the extent to which members with different goals have different orientations to union tactics, involvement, and the union in general. Comparison of the coefficients obtained in this final stage with those produced in earlier stages indicates that little information about the structure of the effects is lost by not presenting the earlier stages.

Prior to controlling for other variables, occupation had a significant impact on support for three of the four goals (Table 3). Clerks, the lowest paid, were most supportive of union efforts to improve wages and benefits for all employees (EMP), while both clerks and case-aides evinced significantly higher levels of support for improving the wages and benefits of paraprofessionals in particular (PARA). Caseworkers and supervisors, on the other hand, were most concerned with efforts to reduce work loads (WORK). None of the occupational groups was significantly more or less supportive of union efforts to improve benefits for clients (SERVE).[1]

Most of the occupational effects were explained by the influence of other correlated variables, however. After controlling for social background, for example, the distinctive clerical concern with general economic goals (EMP) was largely eliminated (see Table 4). Support for general economic goals decreased with seniority and was higher among black than white members (BLACK). The greater level of

Table 3. Effect of Occupation on Member Support for Union Goals, Cook County, 1973

Occupation[a]	Union Goals (Beta Coefficients)			
	General Employee Benefits (EMP)	Paraprofessional Benefits (PARA)	Work Load (WORK)	Client Benefits (SERVE)
Clerical (CLERK)[b]	.15*	.39***	.04	−.02
Case aide (AIDE)	.07	.32***	.10	.05
Caseworker (CW)	−.05	.04	.17*	.10
Supervisory caseworker (SUP)	.00	.05	.14*	.03
R^2	.04	.17	.02	.01
$\bar{R}^{2}$[c]	.03	.17	.01	.00
N	587	589	589	583

[a] Professional specialists omitted.
[b] Includes Homemakers and Janitors.
[c] Adjusted R^2.
  * $P \leq .05$
 ** $P \leq .01$
*** $P \leq .001$

clerical support (CLERK) for general economic goals was explained by higher clerical seniority levels and the high percentage of clerks who were black. Support for general economic goals (EMP) also decreased with job satisfaction (JOB), and was higher among members who socialized more with each other (SCLZE).

Predictors of support for the economic needs of paraprofessionals (PARA) differed from those for general economic goals. Clerks and case aides were significantly more supportive of union efforts to achieve economic gains for their own job classification (PARA). Support for paraprofessional economic goals also increased with support for clients (CLIENTS) and with alienation from business and government (PLTCS). As in the regression analysis of general union economic goals (EMP), blacks (BLACK) had higher levels of support for paraprofessionals' economic goals (PARA).

Support for work load reduction efforts (WORK) increased with seniority (SNRTY) and with frequency of socializing with other employees (SCLZE). Members dissatisfied with their jobs (JOB) and those alienated from business and government (PLTCS) also attached more importance to work load reduction. None of the occupational position or social background variables significantly influenced support for improving client benefits (SERVE). Support for service goals increased with support for clients (CLIENTS) and with alienation from institutions (PLTCS), both considered indicators of lower levels of attitudinal constraints on employees.

Table 4. Regression Analysis of Member Support for Union Goals, Cook County, 1973

| Independent Variables | Union Goals (Beta Coefficients) | | | |
	General Employee Benefits (EMP)	Paraprofessional Benefits (PARA)	Work Load (WORK)	Client Benefits (SERVE)
Occupation[a]				
Clerical (CLERK)[b]	.07	.30***	.02	−.04
Case aide (AIDE)	.02	.28***	.05	.03
Caseworker (CW)	−.06	.07	.07	.09
Supervisory caseworker (SUP)	−.00	.07	.10	.03
Resources				
Education (EDUC)	−.06	−.06	.01	−.05
Socializing (SCLZE)	−.12**	−.07	.11**	−.03
Need for job (JOB NEED)	.02	.00	.09	.02
Marital status (SINGLE)	−.01	.02	.05	.04
Demographic background				
Age (AGE)	−.01	.00	.02	.07
Gender (MALE)	−.00	.03	−.02	.03
Race (BLACK)	.16**	.18***	.07	−.04
Constraints				
Belief in clients (CLIENTS)	−.08	.16***	−.05	.38***
Institutional alienation (PLTCS)	.06	.13***	.22***	.14***
Seniority (SNRTY)	−.11**	.00	−.08*	.07
Grievances				
Job dissatisfaction (JOB)	.09*	−.01	.19***	−.03
R^2	.10	.26	.14	.21
$\bar{R}^2$[c]	.07	.24	.12	.19
N	587	589	589	583

[a] Professional specialists omitted.
[b] Includes Homemakers and Janitors.
[c] Adjusted R^2.
* $P \leq .05$
** $P \leq .01$
*** $P \leq .001$

Support for union militancy (MILTNT) varied substantially across particular agency occupational categories (Table 5). Case aides and caseworkers were significantly more supportive of militant tactics than members in clerical and supervisory positions. Militancy increased with job dissatisfaction (JOB) and alienation from institutions (PLTCS) (Table 6). It was also higher among younger workers, those with less education, and those who socialized more with fellow workers (SCLZE).[2] The higher levels of militancy of case aides and caseworkers were largely explained by their greater propensity to socialize and their younger average age.

Both social background and occupational position thus influenced orientation toward union goals and tactics, but the role of occupation

Table 5. Effect of Occupation on Members' Union Orientation, Cook County, 1973

	Union Orientation (Beta Coefficients)			
Occupation[a]	*Work Action Support (MILTNT)*	*Participation (PART)*	*Job Attachment (EXIT)*	*Union Satisfaction (USAT)*
Clerical (CLERK)[b]	.11	.08	−.03	.19**
Case aide (AIDE)	.15**	.06	−.11*	.00
Caseworker (CW)	.30***	.28***	−.44***	−.17*
Supervisory caseworker (SUP)	.08	.08	−.08	−.15*
R^2	.04	.04	.15	.12
$\bar{R}^2$[c]	.03	.03	.14	.11
N	575	581	550	579

[a] Professional specialists omitted.
[b] Includes Homemakers and Janitors.
[c] Adjusted R^2.
  * $P \leq .05$
 ** $P \leq .01$
*** $P \leq .001$

was more limited. Clerks and case aides were more supportive of economic goals when such goals were expressed in terms of their own economic needs (PARA). Not taking the effect of other variables into account, employees involved in service—case aides, caseworkers, and supervisory caseworkers—were more supportive of a union goal of reducing work loads (WORK) than were those at the clerical level (although the effect was not statistically significant for case aides). Service workers did not, however, attach particular importance to union efforts to improve service to clients. (See Table 3.)

Factors other than occupation seemed important in influencing support for union goals. Black employees were more supportive of general and paraprofessional economic goals (EMP and PARA), regardless of their own occupation. Members who rejected a negative perspective on clients (CLIENTS) and were politically alienated (PLTCS) were also more supportive of union goals on behalf of paraprofessionals (PARA). Job dissatisfaction (JOB) increased support for general wage improvement (EMP) and case load reduction (WORK). (See Table 4.) However, these underlying "ideological" constraint factors were associated with occupation, and thus contributed to a factional cleavage between those at the clerical level and the caseworkers with more radical orientations. (See Table 4 and 6.) As one caseworker supporter of the Community Relations Committee observed,

> The clerks were not happy—conditions were very bad for
> them. They were low paid. . . . Clerks saw caseworkers as

Table 6. Regression Analysis of Factors in Members' Union Orientation, Cook County, 1973

| Independent Variables | Union Orientation (Beta Coefficients) | | | |
	Work Action Support (MILTNT)	Participation (PART)	Job Attachment (EXIT)	Union Satisfaction (USAT)
Occupation[a]				
Clerical (CLERK)[b]	.04	.01	−.03	.16
Case aide (AIDE)	.04	.01	−.06	.01
Caseworker (CW)	.07	.22**	−.16*	.02
Supervisory caseworker (SUP)	.00	.04	−.02	−.07
Resources				
Education (EDUC)	−.13*	−.09	.06	−.06
Socializing (SCLZE)	−.22***	−.19***	.00	−.01
Need for job (JOB NEED)	.01	−.03	−.08*	−.06
Marital status (SINGLE)	−.02	.04	.01	.03
Demographic background				
Age (AGE)	−.17***	.06	.39***	.08*
Gender (MALE)	.06	.04	.00	.05
Race (BLACK)	−.07	−.03	.08	.17***
Constraints				
Belief in clients (CLIENTS)	.00	.02	−.01	.03
Institutional alienation (PLTCS)	.15***	.04	−.02	−.03
Seniority (SNRTY)	−.01	−.16***	−.01	.00
Grievances and Goals				
Job dissatisfaction (JOB)	.19***	.08	−.22***	−.26***
General employee benefits goal (EMP)	.04	.06	.06	.05
Paraprofessional benefits (PARA)	.05	.16***	.03	.05
Client benefit goal (SERVE)	.01	−.02	−.03	.06
Work load (WORK)	.05	.00	.05	−.05
R^2	.28	.16	.39	.26
$\bar{R}^2$[c]	.25	.13	.37	.23
N	575	581	550	579

[a] Professional specialists omitted.
[b] Includes Homemakers and Janitors.
[c] Adjusted R^2.
* $P \leq .05$
** $P \leq .01$
*** $P \leq .001$

just being radical. It was difficult to get oriented to the needs of the clerks, the needs of caseworkers [understaffing], and the needs of clients.

On the issue of union militancy the bases for cleavage were pronounced. Union militants (MLTNT) tended to be young, white, more politically alienated (POLTCS), and dissatisfied with their jobs (JOB). Caseworkers, case aides, and the more educated, because they also were more likely to share such characteristics, were the more militant unionists. Nonmilitants, on the other hand, were likely to be black, older, less politically alienated, and more satisfied with their jobs. There were thus mutually reinforcing cleavages in terms of militancy on the bases of occupation, age, race, politics, and job satisfaction. (See Table 6.)

A regression analysis on the bases of satisfaction with the union (USAT) yields a similar picture of the sources of factional conflict. Satisfaction with the union was substantially higher among black than among white members, and increased with members' age. Satisfaction with the union increased with job satisfaction (JOB), but was not independently related to the ideological attitudes toward clients (CLIENT) nor institutional alienation (PLTCS). (See Table 6.) The effect of race largely explained the higher level of union satisfaction among clerical-level workers at the zero-order level (Table 5).

THE ROLE OF RESOURCES

The distribution of resources across groups with varying goals and tactical preferences helped to determine the impact of this pattern of support for particular union goals and tactics. While low levels of membership involvement were of general concern to union activists throughout the post-strike period, participation among black union members seemed to be particularly low. Black union activists sometimes complained about the problem.

> You, through your lack of involvement in our union, support your present status of low-paid and over-worked employees. . . . It is not enough just to be infuriated; we must channel our energies into meaningful activities aimed at removing the sources of our anger. (*IUPAE News*, September 1970:2.)

> There is not a handful of blacks active in any of the union's functions. You whisper about the shites [sic] that surround our president, and it bothers him too, but you are too "busy" to assist him. (*IUPAE News*, May 1969:2.)

Regression analyses of the 1973 survey data, however, on the bases of participation in union activities, reveal that these perceptions may have confounded the effects of race with those of occupation, and discounted the impact of caseworkers' higher rates of leaving the agency. Participation in union affairs (PART) and plans for leaving the agency soon (EXIT) both varied with the occupation of union members (Table 5). Caseworkers were more likely to participate in union activities than members in other occupations, but they were also much more likely to be planning to leave the agency. Participation in fact decreased with seniority, and was highest among caseworkers even after other factors were controlled. Employees who were more supportive of paraprofessional work benefits (PARA) also tended to participate more in union affairs (PART).

However, neither youth nor alienation nor job disatisfaction, all predictors of militancy, were related to participation. Plans to leave the agency soon (EXIT) increased with age and job dissatisfaction (JOB). Employees with higher levels of job need, as well as those who were not caseworkers, were less likely to be planning to leave soon.

The pattern of effects of occupation and several other variables on these dependent variables reveal the consequences of involvement for factional conflict. Members expecting to leave the agency sooner (EXIT) tended to be young caseworkers who were dissatisfied with their jobs. These factors were also associated with dissatisfaction about the union and with militancy. The members who were likely to be a source of militancy and opposition in the union, and who were most likely to be able to create pressure in the union for their positions through participation, were less likely to be planning to remain in the agency. The value of their participation as a potential resource for the union—and their ability to support an opposition faction—was substantially lessened.[3]

DECLINE OF THE "SOCIALLY CONSCIOUS" FACTION

The survey results help to explain the difficulties the opposition faction encountered during the post-strike period. Factional conflict had rested in part on differences in grievances among union members. Those members who had been most concerned with client issues had not been able to find enough members with similar interests. Moreover, these concerns had been rooted more in political orientation and social background than in workplace situation. As the proportion of paraprofessionals in casework in the agency expanded, these bases of concern with client issues declined. In addition, the declining activity of the student movement signalled a decrease in the radical political orientation that had motivated the client concerns of many opposition supporters. Among union members, the resources available to the opposition faction were insufficient. Clerical members continued to prefer the union's leadership, and provided a reliable base of support for it. The union leadership's support for militant actions in response to the widely felt problems with excessive case loads helped to reduce the appeal of the opposition faction.

The reaction of the union's institutional environment to the tactics of supporters of the Community Relations position also contributed to its demise. Actions sponsored by the union's Community Relations Committee met with occasional success (*IUPAE News*, November-December 1968), but only in the face of stiff agency resistance. Agency officials tried to avoid joint meetings with clients and unionists, and viewed joint employee-client demands as a threat to the agency's authority and central mission.

Decreasing activity of community organizations concerned with welfare rights also contributed to the Community Relations Committee's demise. Nationally, the National Welfare Rights Organization declined rapidly after 1969 (Piven and Cloward, 1977:316–31). Special grants, which had been the object of much N.W.R.O. organizing, were increasingly eliminated, and the federal government ended its support for welfare rights groups with the close of the War on Poverty. N.R.W.O. leaders devoted a growing portion of their organization's resources to lobbying in Washington in an attempt to reverse these changes, but by 1975 the N.W.R.O. was bankrupt (Piven and Cloward, 1977:349–61; Steiner, 1971:297–98). At about the same time, the Progressive Labor Party decided to shift its organizing efforts from welfare to factories. Organizers remaining within welfare worker unions were to shift their focus from client to "union" issues. Although they continued to talk about client issues and call for a worker–client alliance, "we weren't nearly as serious . . . about the worker–client kind of thing."

Within the union, the Community Relations Committee strategy regularly failed to win majority support. Neither Committee leaflets asserting that the goals of "putting real butter on your table" were compatible with "making the social climate a little more bearable" nor union meetings with clerks "to develop a dialogue . . . between the forces for the improvement of working conditions and for the community" were able to quell "bread and butter" opposition.

By 1972, the "socially conscious" position had largely disappeared from union politics. The "socially conscious people" regularly lost to the "bread and butter people" in proposals to the Delegates' Assembly to replace the union's Grievance Vice-President with a Community Relations Vice-President. When a Community Relations Committee leader proposed to amend a soon-to-be-forgotten motion for a strike referendum in February 1971, to stipulate that contract demands "be primarily concerned with working conditions, salary, and *equally important* . . . *client demands*," "all hell broke loose. . . . The meeting clearly split into two factions over the exclusion of client demands." The amendment was defeated resoundingly, 71 to 36. (*IUSSE News*, February 1971:1, 3, emphasis added.)

STRUCTURAL CHANGE

Throughout the post-strike period, supporters of both factions, as well as the union as a whole, struggled to increase levels of membership involvement. Although low levels of clerical involvement were often singled out for criticism, participation in regular union meetings was generally low, and no growth occurred in membership. In March 1968, the union's Publicity Vice-President noted that "a very sad thing appears to be happening—the union is losing its voluntary participation character: . . . Members—especially stewards and delegates—seem to feel that they can leave everything to the people who are being paid by the Union" (*IUPAE News*, March 1968:8). Three years later, the President's report complained that "some of you are dissatisfied with others, so you take the easy way out: You quit the union. . . . You quiet ones and fence sitters had better move, become active, show some strength" (*IUSSE News*, February 1971:3). A union newsletter warned that "WITHOUT ACTIVE REPRESENTATION IN EACH OFFICE IT BECOMES VERY DIFFICULT TO KEEP PEOPLE INFORMED, AND AN UNINFORMED MEMBERSHIP LEAVES A UNION VERY WEAK, IF NOT DEAD."

In 1969, some activists decided that a new constitution could solve the union's malaise and lessen internal conflict (*IUPAE News*, March 1970:6). It would be "a sign of the coming-of-age of IUPAE." A new constitution, they argued, should provide for more effective traditional political action, encourage greater involvement of the agency's "permanent" workers (clerks, etc.), and give more power to the union President. "Is participatory democracy as practiced by certain elements in our society a SUCKER CONCEPT," asked the union's President.

> The most active participant or practitioner is the transient sent to the agency whose real affiliation and loyalty is not to this organization. His technique is to force the union to over-participate in negative and, in many cases, irrelevant issues, thereby excluding the rank-and-file members. (*IUPAE News*, March 1970:2.)

The proponents of constitutional revision also sought to limit the number of official union goals. The existing structure was "too loose. . . . People used it for too many things." "Did we bite off more than we can chew?" queried an author of an article in the union's newspaper who supported constitutional change (*IUPAE News*, March 1970:6). The old constitution's goal of establishing "professional equality with highest standards of private and public social work" seemed unreasonable, given the *"outright failure* of many long-cherished social work dogmas" and their irrelevance to the real needs of the poor.

The radical caucus quickly expressed its opposition. The union's membership "must take upon itself increasing responsibility in union affairs," they maintained (*IUPAE News*, November–December 1968:3), as they challenged the need for greater Executive Board power:

> The proposed constitution strips all power from the delegates' assembly, turning it into a simple "information passer" from the executive committee to the rank and file membership. . . . As members, we do not want to give up our representation in the union and replace it with reliance on a small elected leadership, over which we have no control.

Radical caucus supporters on the staff of the union's newspaper editorialized that the "Delegates' Assembly is often chaotic, and other times a bore, but it is the sounding board for the varied ideas within IUPAE" and "should retain power" (*IUPAE News*, May 1969:2).

In debate during the union's second Constitutional Convention, the proponents of change were largely successful. Both union goals and structure were altered (*I.U.S.S.E.*, 1970). The union's main goal was declared to be "the strong labor organization goal of collective bargaining for the protection and gain of maximum benefits of its members, using any economic means necessary." The value of promoting "understanding between our membership and the public we serve" and of trying to influence legislation "which directly or indirectly affect[s] social services workers' standard of living and the common good" were acknowledged, but the old constitutional language concerning welfare policy and professionalism were gone.

Several changes in the union's formal structure increased the power of union leaders. Executive Board members were to be elected every two years, rather than annually, and the President was to be paid a full-time salary without periodic approval by the Delegates. The four vice-presidents, for organization, publicity, casework, and clerical-level concerns were replaced by one Vice-president, and the Delegates' Assembly was replaced by a Representative Council. The Rep Council, as it came to be called, was to include both Representatives elected by each agency office in proportion to office size, and para-professional and professional Representatives-at-Large to be elected by a plurality vote of their constituents throughout the union. The Rep Council was given the function of establishing policy.

Its authority was to be second only to that of an official membership meeting on all issues other than strikes and membership referenda. The new constitution also changed the union's name to the Illinois Union of Social Service Employees (I.U.S.S.E.), signalling the intention to organize throughout the state.

CONCLUSIONS

The union's GIST configuration had now changed markedly from that of its earlier years. The new structure was distinctly more representative than participatory, and extrinsic concerns were now emphasized in its goals. After repeated experiments with militancy, the union's emphasis on achieving collective bargaining rights indicated its continued desire to rely on institutionalized tactics. Membership involvement had declined from a peak in the period after the union's emergence to a persistently low level.

The union had survived after the failure of its second strike due to the continued high level of grievances among public aid employees, the availability of resources for the union from some employees and other organizations, and the absence of effective constraints against organizing. However, involvement of the membership as a whole in union affairs remained low, and the activities of supportive organizations in its secondary institutional environment diminished. In its primary institutional environment, the union was able to secure only limited gains. In general, then, the union experienced a severe resource deficit in spite of occasional high levels of activity in some agency offices.

Factional conflict within the union reflected the environmental pressures on it. Variations in grievances among the union's membership were reflected in the different goal priorities of its two factions. Paralleling the perceptions of union activists, radical politics tended to underlie support for a union emphasis on service issues, while clerical or paraprofessional status and minority group membership were associated with support for economic goals. Although members with radical political orientations were also more supportive of paraprofessional economic goals than those without such perspectives, they were unable to translate this shared concern into support from economically oriented union members.

The goals of reducing case loads and lessening the threat of suspensions and dismissals had the broadest appeal. They were both demands whose outcome would affect conditions throughout the agency and the welfare of all groups within the union. Increasing the pay of the lowest paid employees was a goal that directly benefited only a more limited number of members. However, members who were particularly sympathetic to clients and were more institutionally alienated, as well as black members, were more supportive of efforts to improve pay for those at the bottom of the agency's pay scale. Efforts to achieve this economic goal did not generate factional conflict at this stage of the union's development. But union efforts to improve service to clients were not supported by a large number of members, and they generated intense factional conflict.

The availability of substantial resources for both union factions helped maintain conflict at a high level for several years. Supporters of the radical opposition faction participated more readily in union affairs, and were able to form some supportive alliances with community organizations. Supporters of the "bread and butter" faction were less likely to leave the agency, and somewhat more numerous in the union. As support for radical politics and the activity of welfare rights groups and other organizations diminished, the base of resources for the radical faction declined.

Lacking ties to the union's primary institutional environment, the union's radical faction supported the expansive goals and participatory structure associated with a high level of dependence on the social environment for resources. Seeking firmer ties to the primary institutional environment, supporters of the union's leadership sought to change the union toward the limited goals and more bureaucratic structure associated with institutionalization. By the end of the poststrike period, the shift in resources available to the two factions enabled supporters of the union's leadership to implement the changes they desired. Little benefit for the union was apparent from them, however. The I.U.P.A.E. was still only a marginal actor in its primary institutional environment.

CHAPTER SEVEN

Reorganization of Public Aid

In the mid-1960s, rapidly rising case loads, inadequate fiscal resources, and a highly mobile casework staff had exacerbated the level of grievances among employees and contributed to the emergence of the union. By the end of the decade, these bases for employee grievances had not abated. The welfare rolls continued to rise into the 1970s. Food stamp participation rose from four million to twelve million cases between January 1970 and July 1972. Atlanta experienced a 104 percent increase in public assistance cases, including a 492 percent increase in cases of Aid to Families with Dependent Children from 1965 to 1971 (Joint Economic Committee, 1972:26). During 1971 alone, the number of recipients in Illinois increased by 630 per month (*Illinois Welfare News*, January 18, 1973).

Rules governing assistance to recipients also proliferated. The federal Health, Education and Welfare (HEW) Public Assistance Handbook weighed in at six pounds (Aaron, 1973), and rules for local welfare agencies could fill a four-foot-wide bookshelf (Joint Economic Committee, 1972:5). Simply processing a new welfare applicant often required completion of more than twenty-five different forms. The number of public aid employees failed to keep pace, as casework staffs less than doubled in size from 1966 to 1971 (Joint Economic Committee, 1972:27). A HEW limit of sixty cases per service worker was abandoned in 1969. From Atlanta to Detroit, case loads rose to over two hundred cases per service worker (Joint Economic Committee, 1972:28). Around the country, the crisis in public welfare was intensifying, rather than letting up.

This continuing crisis incurred substantial costs for welfare agencies. Caseworker error rates increased (Joint Economic Committee, 1972:35–36; Steiner, 1966:64; *From the State Capitals*, July 1, 1971), and dissatisfaction remained high. The disillusionment, loss of idealism, and decline in commitment to social services among new agency employees was associated with high rates of turnover (Katzell, Korman, and Levine, 1971:28–29, 56–60). A 1969 HEW study of public welfare in eleven cities found five with caseworker turnover rates above 40 percent, and none with turnover rates below 21 percent (Joint Economic Committee, 1972:33). Thirty-eight percent of the employees surveyed in a 1972 study of twelve public aid agencies reported they would not choose their agency as a place to work if they could start over. Employees in public aid agencies reported lower levels of satisfaction with their work situation, less approval of agency policies, and fewer feelings of accomplishment than employees in other social and rehabilitation agencies (Olmstead and Christensen, 1973:261–98; see also Steiner, 1971:39; Street, Martin, and Gordon, 1979:24–28, 56–59). "Dysfunction—both in the sense of failure to operate and in the sense of waywardness in operation— pervades the welfare system," concluded a Congressional Subcommittee on Fiscal Policy (Joint Economic Committee, 1972:2).

PRESSURES FOR CHANGE

The public aid environment simply could not provide the experience that caseworkers with professional aspirations sought. Such aspirations were more likely to be associated with exit from the agency or attempts to reform it than with dedication to the job. The possibility of professionalizing casework and thus lessening such problems was no longer viable, however. The eclipse of the effort to professionalize casework in the early 1960s seemed permanent.

Welfare costs had been driven upward by liberalization of benefit policies, as well as by the rising case load itself. A 1967 revision of the Social Security Act tripled Illinois payments to medical vendors (*From the State Capitals*, September 1, 1967; October 14, 1968). Court invalidation of a one-year residence requirement for welfare necessitated a deficiency appropriation in Illinois (*From the State Capitals*, February 1, 1969). By the end of the decade, the cost of welfare exceeded $1.12 billion and absorbed 85 percent of the growth of state revenues. Control of the "fiscal monster" of public aid was high on the political agenda (*From the State Capitals*, July 1, 1971:2), and it seemed that "almost everyone [in politics] is against welfare" (Salamon, 1978:4; Street, Martin, and Gordon, 1979:34–40).

The effort to reduce welfare costs focused in part on welfare benefits themselves. At the national level, restrictive proposals by Senator Wilbur Mills were adopted in 1967. As a result, the U.S. Senate placed a cap on social service expenditures for fiscal year 1973 (Joint Economic Committee, 1972:114–16). These pressures were also felt in both the Illinois Department of Public Aid and, within Illinois, in the Cook County Department of Public Aid. Illinois legislators proposed to tighten eligibility standards and institute forced work requirements; one even sought to require sterilization of welfare mothers

(*From the State Capitals*, April 1, 1971; July 1, 1971; November 1, 1971; December 1, 1971). Illinois Governor Ogilvie proposed a comprehensive eleven-point plan to reform public aid and reduce "welfare abuse" (*From the State Capitals*, July 1, 1971:3; see also *Sun-Times*, September 7, 1973:4).

Efforts to control costs also extended to the nature of casework in public aid. The complexity of rules for determining family budgets and allowances for special needs had impaired cost-control efforts (Joint Economic Committee, 1972:11–12). Two-thirds of the instances of "welfare abuse," the Illinois Governor asserted, were later found to be mistakes by caseworkers themselves (*From the State Capitals*, July 1, 1971:3; see also *Sun-Times*, September 7, 1973:4). The solution seemed to be to reduce the number of decisions that caseworkers had to make on their own, thus increasing adherence to agency guidelines.

The basic structure of public aid casework still reflected its occupational origins. Like their counterparts in private social work, public aid caseworkers were responsible for consulting with clients and trying to meet most of their needs. As a result, public aid caseworkers had substantial discretionary decision-making powers (Lipsky, 1980:3; Prottas, 1979:86–88). Diffuse relationships with clients ensured that caseworkers would encounter many complex, unpredictable situations (Toren, 1969), and many that required a response to "the human dimensions" (Jacobs, 1969). These features of casework, also found in the traditional professions, precluded the high degree of routinization found in more bureaucratized positions (Scott, 1969).

Caseworker discretion had never been more than a mixed blessing for public aid agencies. Caseworkers' discretionary power enhanced their self-esteem, as well as the high esteem in which they were held by clients, but it could also easily be used to subvert agency rules. A Chicago caseworker recalled that, in the early 1970s,

> You could find loopholes in policy so that you could deliver something to clients . . . . You never had to say "No."

The consequences of these practices for agency policy were suggested when New York City welfare officials modified a plan to reduce intake hours. They concluded that if the formal rules were changed, caseworkers would simply accept welfare applications outside of the agency (Lipsky, 1980:22).

Maintenance of caseworker discretion became less tenable as pressures to reduce costs mounted. Chronic shortages of resources and rising demands for services increased the need to monitor caseworker decisions, but such monitoring was impaired by caseworkers' discretionary powers. At the same time, the vague, conflicting, and frequently changing goals of welfare policy failed to provide consistent guidance for caseworkers in the exercise of their discretion (Lipsky, 1980:27–28). The job of casework had become "impossible to do in ideal terms" (Lipsky, 1980:82).

Casework practice changed to some extent before there was any change in the "ideal terms." A special Citizens Committee on Cook County Government found that in 1968,

> Field caseworkers are charged with administering public
> assistance to needy citizens and providing rehabilitative
> services to help families and individuals develop alternatives
> to public assistance. This is "social" casework in its proper
> perspective. . . . It was very disheartening to discover, during
> our visits to field offices, that the emphasis is not on "social"
> casework at all, but is, instead, financially oriented. (*IUPAE
> News*, January 1969:4.)

The discretionary power of caseworkers thus seemed anachronistic in light of caseworkers' actual responsibilities.

CHANGE IN CASEWORK

Reduction of Caseworker Discretion

The potential benefits of reducing caseworker discretion seemed clear. If they had to make fewer decisions independently, caseworkers could work faster, this work could be monitored more effectively, and the frustrating gap between real and ideal work practices would be reduced (Haug, 1973; Jacobs, 1969; Olmstead and Christensen, 1973:157–160; Oppenheimer, 1973). "Many of the problems . . . would theoretically disappear" (Lipsky, 1980:15). However, since it was the structure of casework that required discretionary decision making, casework itself had to be reorganized.

Two major changes in casework occurred in the early 1970s. First, the Social Security Act of 1969 mandated separation of the income maintenance and the service functions formerly combined within the caseworker job. An Illinois Department of Public Aid pamphlet (1972:5,6) summarized the rationale for separation:

> The traditional approach places responsibility for all actions on
> the shoulders of a caseworker. . . . Under the separation
> mandate, social workers will no longer handle the tasks
> involved in determining eligibility and authorizing payment of
> cash assistance and issuance of food stamps and medical
> cards. They will concentrate, instead, on helping families and

individuals obtain services which increase independence and improve the quality of life. . . . Income maintenance specialists and clerical staff will be primarily responsible for the administration of payments.

Income maintenance caseworkers, referred to as "case managers," were to initiate income maintenance after a case was approved by intake staff. Case management was, implicitly, no longer considered a professional job. "We no longer assume that the person who needs food, shelter, clothing, and medical care also needs the assistance of a *professional* caseworker" (Illinois Department of Public Aid, 1972:10, emphasis added). Caseworkers in special service units were to respond to the special service needs of clients referred from intake or income maintenance (Illinois Department of Public Aid, 1972:12).

While ending caseworkers' dual responsibilities for financial support and social services lessened the rationale for caseworker discretion, administration of the myriad possible welfare grants still provided a means for exercise of discretion. Clients could seldom be expected to know all the grants for which they were eligible, nor could welfare agencies reliably assess all the caseworker decisions made in the course of providing financial assistance.

Adoption of the "flat grant" system of welfare payments simplified the tasks involved in income maintenance. It represented the second stage of the effort to routinize income maintenance activities. Officially termed the "Consolidated Standard Plan," the flat grant system began in Illinois on October 1, 1973. Before it was instituted, the size of welfare grants had been determined by the number and ages of children, family living arrangements, and other family income. Ninety special allowances were available, and could be awarded in 135 different ways.

> This state now has the most complex system in the country. . . . Dozens of factors must be considered in determining the amount a family will receive for food, clothing, and shelter. . . . Under the current error-prone system, payments are based on the "subjectivity" of the caseworkers. (Joel Edelman, Director of the Illinois Department of Public Aid, quoted in *Sun-Times*, August 7, 1973:4.)

Under the new flat grant system, welfare grants were based on family size and area housing costs, with just fifteen special allowances (*Chicago Tribune*, August 30, 1973; Zashin and Summers, 1980:6,7). Thus was "the tension between the workers' desires to help clients and their need to control disbursements" eliminated (Lipsky, 1980:149).

Introduction of Paraprofessionals

Although few public aid caseworkers had professional social work training, a bachelor's degree had traditionally been required for employment as a caseworker. Of course, the aspirations for professional work associated with college education had long been frustrated by conditions in public aid (Alutto and Belasco, 1974:217; Olmstead and Christensen, 1973:309–11). This "mismatch" between employee desires and job characteristics had produced dissatisfaction even before the rationalization of casework (Etzioni, 1969:96–97; Hall, 1968:102; Teare, 1981:91–94). After this change, the even larger gap between the aspirations of college graduates and the reality of casework could be expected to produce even more discontent (Oppenheimer, 1973:214–16).

A response to this problem had been envisioned by those promoting the reorganization of casework.

> Social casework is a skill requiring a good deal of specialized training. In universities this skill is taught at the graduate level. The financial aspects of public assistance, on the other hand, can be adequately handled by persons who do not have the skills of the social caseworker. . . . A careful determination of any need for casework or rehabilitation services which may accompany financial need can be made by the intake division. . . . By referring only those in need of rehabilitation services to the casework division, caseworkers' time could be devoted to those tasks requiring their special skills. We would get the most [in exchange] for the higher cost of training and higher salary of these workers. At the same time, we would reduce the high cost occasioned by the excessive turnover rate. (Citizens Committee on Cook County Government, as quoted in *IUPAE News*, January 1969:4).

In other words, the flat grant and this division of labor between service casework and income maintenance management made it no longer necessary to rely on employees with advanced training in income maintenance (U.S. Dept. of Health, Education and Welfare, 1974:20–22).

By the time the flat grant and separation of casework from financial case management were implemented, the basis for a distinction between income maintenance and social service work requirements had already appeared. But contrary to the recommendation of the Citizens' Committee, it was college graduates who were distinguished from nongraduates, rather than those with *graduate* social work training from those without.

The 1967 Harris Amendments to the Social Security Act had required states to begin to train and use subprofessional staff (U.S. Dept. of Health, Education and Welfare, 1974:19). Motivated in part by demands for greater employment of the poor (U.S. Dept. of Health, Education and Welfare, 1974:20–22), the use of what came to be known as "paraprofessionals" complemented rationalization of the work process (Haug, 1973:198–200). By 1971, about fifteen thousand paraprofessionals, most having only a high school education, were employed across the nation in state and local public welfare departments (U.S. Dept. of Health, Education and Welfare, 1974:125–33). In the Cook County Department of Public Aid, the number of paraprofessionals was to increase by 248 percent (from 249 to 866) just between November 1972 and June 1973, resulting in an increase in the percentage of paraprofessionals among "caseworkers" from 16 percent to 52 percent (Illinois Department of Public Aid, March 15, 1973). During the same time, the number of professional (nonparaprofessional) caseworkers was to decrease by forty-one percent (from 1,336 to 786).

Paraprofessionals were termed "Case Aides" and "Case Aide Trainees" when they were first introduced into the C.C.D.P.A. in 1969. Receiving $200 less per month in salary than Caseworkers, the Aides and Trainees were to perform routine duties under the guidance of Caseworkers. After the implementation of the separation between casework and case income management in January, 1975, the Case Aide Trainee and the Case Aide were reclassified as Caseworker I and II, respectively. Caseworkers at levels I and II were reclassified to the new levels of Caseworker III and IV. The job title for Supervisory Caseworkers was changed to that of Caseworker V. Caseworkers I were assigned to Intake units, Caseworkers II and III (paraprofessionals and professionals) to Income Maintenance, and Caseworkers IV either to Service units or to supervising Intake workers. Supervision in Income Maintenance and Service was performed by Caseworker V (Illinois Department of Personnel, n.d.; Zashin and Summers, 1980:5–6).

Educational requirements varied between caseworker classifications. Appointment as a Caseworker I required only a high school degree, a Caseworker II was expected to have two years of college, a Caseworker III or IV, a college degree. In part due to union pressure, the agency also waived the educational requirements (except for Caseworker IV) for employees with a certain number of years of seniority in lower level classifications (including clerical).

Distinctions between the job duties of different caseworker levels were somewhat more difficult to maintain than the education and experience distinctions. While separation of service and financial award casework ensured a clear distinction between the duties of Caseworkers III and IV, and made the intake role of the Caseworker I unique, the distinction between Caseworker II and Caseworker III duties, like that between Case Aides and Caseworkers before 1975, was not always clear. According to state job descriptions, the Caseworker II was to handle *"progressively* responsible" entry-level casework duties under *"general supervision,"* while *"in training"* for case load management. A Caseworker III was to perform *"responsible professional* duties" *"under direction,"* while managing a case load and performing *"responsible"* services (Illinois Department of Personnel, n.d., emphasis added). In practice, however, the work performed by these two adjacent classifications was difficult to distinguish (Illinois Union of Social Service Employees, *Brief,* 1976).

Several other service occupations accounted for less than ten percent of agency staff. Educational Rehabilitation Workers were engaged in occupational counseling, job placement, and related functions. Investigators conducted field investigations of eligibility. Public Aid Representatives evaluated caseworker decisions concerning levels of support, and conducted other skilled investigative work. Employees in these three occupations will be referred to as "professional specialists." Employees working as "Homemakers" were sent to the homes of incapacitated recipients to perform housework chores. No formal education was required for this job.

Extension of the Agency

Two other changes in the organization of the Illinois public welfare system changed the union's social environment. Most important was the centralization of control of public aid under the Illinois Department of Public Aid. The years of "buck passing" and conflict between the county and state departments were over on January 1, 1974. The Cook County Department continued to function with much the same administrative staff, but its authority was now both more limited and more clearly defined. Included within the Illinois Department now were the employees working in all public aid offices in the state, of which there was at least one in each county. Unlike the many large offices in Cook County, many offices in the "downstate" area were staffed by just a handful of employees.

The union's social environment was also extended with the inclusion of the state's Division of Vocational Rehabilitation within the welfare department. Vocational Rehabilitation Counselors were employed throughout the state in offices much smaller than most public aid offices, with from one to forty counselors. Rehabilitation Counselor job descriptions stressed professional duties. Four years of college, with courses in guidance, counseling, psychology, or closely related areas were required. Rehabilitation Counselors had more autonomy in their work than public aid caseworkers, and tended to view themselves as professionals (Olmstead and Christensen, 1973:107–8).

RESPONSES TO REORGANIZATION

Reorganization was a painful process at first. As new procedures were tried on an experimental basis in some offices, and then as work was redistributed and workers reassigned according to the new division of labor, strains were exacerbated in many offices.

> Nobody on top ever talked to us. Random, emergency measures were announced to us in unit meetings, in a curt, starting-tomorrow-or-maybe-it-was-yesterday fashion. . . . For two weeks we worked with no [district] maps, with our cases in other people's stat boxes. (*IUSSE News,* June 1971:1,5.)

In the first months after the separation was implemented countywide, the union newspaper was filled with members' complaints.

> First "they" (the nebulous heads) told us to update our 299s, send the 552s to Financial, and destroy the stat cards. So we started to update our 299s, when they told us to stop. Then they told us to send our stat cards and 552s to Financial. Before we started, "they" told us to stop. Next they told us to check our 552s against our stat cards and rewrite missing stat cards. (*Common Sense,* November 20, 1972:1–2.)

These strains led to a rapid rise in the level of grievances among employees in many offices, and many union activists felt a collective response was required. A Separation Committee tried to formulate a plan.

> The State wants to ignoe [sic] us as they reorganize our jobs; *we are not going to let them get away with it so easily.* (*Common Sense,* November 20, 1972:5, 7.)

The union newspaper, its editorial staff still dominated by supporters of the opposition caucus, editorialized that,

> The end result of "Separation" will be replacing white college-educated caseworkers with white college-educated case aides!!!!!!! (*Common Sense,* January 17, 1973:2.)

Employees mobilized in several offices in response to the separation of tasks, and received temporary reprieves or additional staff. At the Southern District Office (DO), the "sick-in" emphasized the employee needs for more staff in all areas, a fuller explanation from CAO on the meaning of Separation and separating Southern DO into two district offices to relieve overcrowding. (*Common Sense*, February 14, 1973:2.)

Employees at the Englewood District Office followed suit.

It was decided that . . . caseworker/managers would no longer do any work on uncovered loads except for the most pressing emergencies, and that financial workers would work on one group only. (*Common Sense*, June 13, 1973:3.)

In spite of these outbursts of militancy in particular offices, however, separation continued with only temporary modifications due to union action. Office protests resulted in new district maps, a brief postponement of separation, hiring of new clerks and case aides, and "the satisfaction of Watching Them Squirm" as members felt they had gotten "out from under the thumb of the bureaucratic fist" (*IUSSE News*, June 1971:1, 5; *Common Sense*, December 20, 1972:1; March 14, 1973:1; April 11, 1973:1; August 21, 1973:1; *Southern Newsletter*, n.d.). The union's leadership during the process of separation inveighed against the lack of adequate staff (*Common Sense*, January 17, 1973:3), estimated by the agency's director to be 1,350 caseworkers (*Chicago Tribune*, February 14, 1973). However, no attempt was made to organize against implementation of the plan as a whole (*Common Sense*, December 20, 1972:1). A motion to resist separation proposed by opposition members failed in the union's Representative Council by a two-thirds margin (*Common Sense*, December 20, 1972).

Implementation of the flat grant did not have the disruptive effect on employees that separation did. Rhetoric against the flat grant was still sharp, but no spontaneous protests occurred. Again, the opposition caucus was most opposed to the change, and explained its position in a leaflet:

We can build a fighting alliance with recipients who understand that [Governor] Walker and [Director] Edelman are launching an attack on both workers and recipients. . . . The flat grant hurts all of us.

Even the union's president announced that,

I'll be damned and burn in Hell before I agree that the paperwork of union workers be reduced by going along with a flat grant that hurts recipients. (*Common Sense*, September 19, 1973:1.)

Nonetheless, a motion by union radicals for "stronger action, including a strike" was defeated, 23½ to 2½ (with 1 abstention).

The union made one concerted effort to demonstrate opposition to the flat grant and support for welfare rights groups organizing against it. On October 1, the union newspaper announced, "HUNDREDS WALK OUT/JOIN RECIPIENTS" (*Common Sense*, November 6, 1973:1). A union leaflet argued,

> If you feel flat grants will not help either the poor or the jobs we perform, do not go to work on Monday. Instead, join WRO on the Picket line. . . . *ABOVE ALL, DO NOT CROSS PICKET LINES.* Remember if we cross WRO's picket lines on Oct. 1, WRO can easily state in the future, "What difference do your picket lines make?" or they may cross your line to take your job for their grant.

After the one-day action, however, the flat grant was no longer a focus of union activity.

In comparison to the union's brief but militant responses to separation and the flat grant, union efforts to respond to the other aspects of reorganization were more extended, but less dramatic. By 1973, the union filed a suit concerning the duties of case aides, and in order to deal more effectively with its new employer affiliated with a national union. These responses would eventually result in major changes in the union itself.

CONCLUSIONS

Reorganization of public aid substantially changed the distribution of both grievances and resources in the union's social environment, and altered its relation to its institutional environment. At first, the difficulties involved in implementing separation had caused complaints. Overall, though, reactions to reorganization were not negative.

> People . . . felt that some parts of the "separation" plan were good (like the functional units), but also felt that the office was understaffed overall (*Common Sense*, November 20, 1972:1–3).

With respect to the flat grant, a union activist recalled, "members were divided."

Many welcomed the opening of casework positions to those without college degrees. A black caseworker felt that "when case aides were able to move to caseworkers, this was a beautiful professional job for the union." However, some case aides were dissatisfied with demands placed on them, while some caseworkers were unhappy when case aides were given the opportunity to become caseworkers.

> They [the agency] said we would aid caseworkers, but we were given case loads. After a while, the expectations for case aides were no different than for caseworkers. . . . I felt abused.

The union's president

> used to get hate letters from white caseworkers for [his] role in this change [enabling clerks to move to caseworker positions]. White caseworkers attacked [him] for eroding professionalism and the value of the college degree.

In general, however, removal of the college degree requirement for work in income maintenance also lessened one of the major sources of grievances concerning the nature of casework: the gap between the expectations of new employees and the requirements of their jobs. In addition, reduction of caseworker discretion in income maintenance units simplified work, while social service units provided greater opportunities for those with professional aspirations. Inclusion of Vocational Rehabilitation Counselors brought another group with generally higher levels of job satisfaction into the union (Olmstead and Christensen, 1973:107-8).

Reorganization of casework also reduced ties between caseworkers and welfare recipients. Caseworkers could no longer receive satisfaction from manipulating rules to help some clients, while clients could not as easily view some caseworkers as confederates in attempting to meet their needs. The appeal of welfare rights groups was diminished as a result. Welfare rights groups had recruited new members in part because of the aid the groups' members provided other recipients in seeking the maximum benefits to which they were entitled. By sharply reducing special categories of benefits, the flat grant largely ended the efficacy of this strategy. The new paraprofessionals in casework generally had higher levels of economic need themselves, and less interest in service issues, than the caseworkers with college degrees (U.S. Dept. of Health, Education and Welfare, 1974:130-33).

The potential for grievances over service issues appeared to have been diminished by reorganization, while the potential for economic grievances seemed to increase. The level of resources available in the union's social environment had declined. Lower levels of education and fewer alternative job opportunities among the paraprofessional staff suggested a decline in the resources available for union activity. Reduced involvement with clients deprived the union of a resource that had previously been used effectively by the union's opposition faction.

While the union's social environment had changed, its primary institutional environment was also redefined. Centralization of control of public aid at the state level allowed the union to focus more of its tactics at one level of government, and removed ambiguity about those responsible for responding to those tactics. At the same time, the expanded scope of the union's institutional environment brought it into competition with other unions with aspirations for influence at the state level. It proved to be these changes at the institutional level that directly precipitated a new stage in the Illinois Union of Social Service Employees' own development.

CHAPTER EIGHT

Affiliation, Bargaining, and a Contract

Four years of relative organizational stagnation were followed by an equivalent period of rapid growth. The Illinois Union of Social Service Employees (I.U.S.S.E.) established new chapters throughout the state, and its membership more than doubled, from 1,700 to 4,600 between 1973 and 1976 (Figure 1). Union lobbying efforts secured a substantial raise for employees, even over a gubernatorial veto. I.U.S.S.E. members consistently reelected the same president for the first time in the union's history, in spite of the radical faction's determined opposition. By the end of this period, the radical faction was no longer a force in union politics.

Underlying these changes in the union were changes in its environment. Expansion brought new employees with different perspectives into the union. In anticipation of state takeover of the Cook County Department of Public Aid and a new opportunity to secure collective bargaining rights, the I.U.S.S.E. affiliated with the American Federation of State, County, and Municipal Employees (A.F.S.C.M.E.). As a local of A.F.S.C.M.E., the I.U.S.S.E. fulfilled the dream of its founders in negotiating a collective bargaining contract.

REAFFIRMATION OF THE CONTRACT GOAL

The 1972 union election affirmed the continued appeal of the strategy of institutionalization for the union's membership. In that election, Barbara Merrill, the union's president and a former Clerical Vice-President, was opposed by Max Liberles, the union's vice-president and a former Casework Vice-President, as well as by a leading activist loosely associated with the radical opposition. Although receiving strong support from clerical members, the union's president was seen by many activists as having been ineffective. Max Liberles campaigned on the basis of years of processing grievances for members. His slate emphasized the need for a business-like approach to unionism, as one of his supporters recalled:

> The union as a business was our platform. Max had a lot more specific good ideas, such as a contract, and a career ladder, and he knew how to do it. The political climate was starting to change. Rather than continuing to butt heads with the agency, the union was getting politically involved and more into legal action.

Statements of the second opposition slate, led by a militant activist in the union's Representative Council, Jim Kelly, reflected disagreement with the institutionalization strategy. An opposition member recollected its position:

> The union . . . was too legalistic; . . . the union should concentrate on monetary issues to pick up power. The ball game is power—talk is inadequate, for we need power . . . . Max had an investment in legal questions. The delays were too long, and there was not always [a] victory.

While none of the three candidates stressed client issues, the Kelly slate selected a vice-presidential candidate who had distinguished himself as oriented to client needs.

Supporters of the radical opposition were not able to agree to support either of the opposition presidential candidates. "PL couldn't be sure that either Kelly or Max would better represent PL's interests. It was only a question of the lesser of two evils."

The Liberles slate won all four Executive Board positions in a close three-way race. Although the Kelly slate secured many seats in the Representative Council, and remained as a potential force in union politics, the union's top leadership now firmly supported a strategy of institutionalization. Max Liberles, the union's new president argued that,

> WE CAN AND MUST CONTINUE TO PUT ASIDE OUR PETTY DIFFERENCES. WE CAN AND MUST CONTINUE TO WORK TOGETHER TOWARD OUR COMMON GOAL OF DETERMINING OUR OWN DESTINY AND BRINGING DIGNITY TO OUR JOBS THROUGH COLLECTIVE BARGAINING. (*Common Sense*, December 1974:4.)

Within the first year of the new union leadership, it became possible to implement this strategy.

THE BEGINNING OF BARGAINING

Desire for a contract had remained high among union presidents since the union's first strike. In 1970, Carter Williams, a former president and still a leading activist, called for an overall campaign to build "up to the point where we can say 'we want a contract now. We will fight for it by any means necessary.'" (*IUPAE News*, March 1970:3.) In 1971, union President Barbara Merrill asked members, "Do you see where we are going? One day maybe next week, next month, next year, but one day we are going for that CONTRACT." (*IUSSE News*, February 1971:3.)

After the election of Max Liberles, the need for a contract continued to be debated, and to receive majority support. A "Strategy Workshop" held in 1973 heard arguments for organizing to promote collective bargaining legislation and to win a contract, which were counterposed to opposition support for organizing to prevent layoffs (the layoffs did not occur in any case). The pro-contract position was given priority in the final resolution of the workshop.

> The Objectives of IUSSE is [sic] a Contract. The main, but not exclusive, focus in obtaining a contract is the issue of layoffs. (*Common Sense*, March 14, 1973:3.)

Obtaining a contract finally became possible later in 1973. In June, the union was able to secure recognition of its right to represent employees throughout the Illinois Department of Public Aid. Intensive lobbying efforts in Springfield were successful, as the I.U.S.S.E. became the first state employees' union recognized by the State of Illinois (*Common Sense*, July 18, 1973:1). In September, political efforts by the American Federation of State, County, and Municipal Employees also bore fruit. Illinois' new Democratic Governor, Dan Walker, issued an executive order on September 5, 1973, allowing collective bargaining by state employees.

AFFILIATION

Union leaders recognized that "the framework in which the union operates has had a decisive and abrupt change. *It is a whole new ballgame.*" (*Common Sense*, Special Edition, n.d.:4.) The prospect of collective bargaining elections for state employees seemed to make affiliation with a larger union imperative, while fear of layoffs and downgrading of caseworkers due to reorganization and the state takeover of public aid contributed to the perceived need for such affiliation (*Common Sense*, August 21, 1973:4; September 19, 1973:3).

To rest on our recognition rights for Cook County would be a disastrous mistake—*we must organize statewide in Public Aid in order to have the power to affect changes in Springfield.* . . . The IUSSE needs affiliation in order to obtain financial assistance, help in Steward's training, help in political action work, etc. Most of all, we need the clout (political) within the State to win our fight for the contract. (*Common Sense*, September 19, 1973:3.)

The union's president concluded that affiliation "WITH A STRONG INTERNATIONAL AFL–CIO UNION *ON OUR TERMS* BECOMES THE MOST CRUCIAL AND IMPORTANT ISSUE FACING THE UNION" (*Common Sense*, September 19, 1973:3).

Support for affiliation was not unequivocal. Some members retained the distrust of "big labor" evident in the union's formative period. After narrowing the affiliation choices to the Service Employees International Union (S.E.I.U.), the successor to the B.S.E.I.U. whose Local 73 had opposed the I.U.S.S.E.'s formation, and the American Federation of State, County, and Municipal Employees (A.F.S.C.M.E.), this distrust surfaced (*Common Sense*, Special Edition, n.d.:1). One union staff member noted that A.F.S.C.M.E. was "more left-leaning, and so [was] more politically close to caseworkers."

The union's radical opposition faction publicly but only hesitantly supported affiliation.

Affiliation will be good for IUSSE *only* if we understand that we will have to fight every step of the way to keep our independence and autonomy" (*Common Sense*, Special Edition, n.d.:3).

The attitude of the Progressive Labor Party was even more ambivalent. As a member recalled,

What we wanted all the time . . . is to have the rank and file active, and we were pretty sure that the rank and file would get squeezed out of the action if we got into the International, unless the party itself could really stir up a hell of a lot of shit in the International. . . . We never did give a very clear answer.

An affiliation agreement with A.F.S.C.M.E. that ensured I.U.S.S.E. would not have to join a "service council," would be guaranteed autonomy in internal operations, and would receive a full rebate of dues paid to A.F.S.C.M.E., as well as extra money for one year after affiliation, reduced the concerns of some union members (*Common Sense*, November 6, 1973:2). For opposition activists, the desire to "stir" in A.F.S.C.M.E. was apparently greater than fear of the "squeeze." Union Representatives voted unanimously in favor of affiliation with A.F.S.C.M.E. (*Common Sense*, November 6, 1973:1).

On November 28, 1973, a record seventy-five percent of the I.U.S.S.E. membership turned out for the final vote on affiliation. Ninety-three percent (1,696 members) voted in favor (*Common Sense*, December 18, 1973:1). I.U.S.S.E. President Max Liberles congratulated the membership for having "finally matured as a union—that we can act together—unified as one" (*Common Sense*, December 18, 1973:1). The I.U.S.S.E. became Local 2000 in A.F.S.C.M.E.

BARGAINING UNITS

In spite of Local 2000's ability to achieve unity over one issue, the union's leadership and other activists were deeply concerned about its ability to maintain a unified structure throughout the state. The Governor's executive order allowing collective bargaining had given an Illinois Office of Collective Bargaining (O.C.B.) the responsibility for determining the composition of bargaining units. Other states that had adopted collective bargaining laws had established bargaining units on the basis of occupational classification, rather than by state agency or department. In an early leaflet to his members, the union president warned,

> If we are forced to compete with unions representing
> highwaymen and revenue employees, the ILLINOIS UNION
> OF SOCIAL SERVICE EMPLOYEES *will be busted.*

The Local's initial jurisdiction was "vertical," involving employees throughout the Department of Public Aid. Union activists soon decided that the state preferred "horizontal" bargaining units.

> It is the Union's position that all classifications throughout the
> Department, with the exception of management, should be in
> the same bargaining unit. The State, on the other hand, will
> prabably [sic] argue for classification units and maintain that
> the clerks, for example, should be in a clerical unit in all
> agencies throughout the state. (*Common Sense*, July 25, 1974:1.)

The State did in fact take this position. After lengthy deliberations, the Office of Collective Bargaining rejected the I.U.S.S.E.'s request for continued representation of the entire Department of Public Aid, and ruled in favor of the state's position. Separate bargaining units were established for clerks, paraprofessionals, and professionals.

Anticipating a negative O.C.B. decision, the I.U.S.S.E.'s leadership had persuaded the union's Representative Council to back a plan to organize for the collective bargaining elections even if horizontal (also termed "functional") units were adopted. Supporters of the militant opposition caucus argued against the elections in their handbills.

> The Rank and File Caucus opposes separate elections based on job titles; . . . *any* election other than one for *departmental* bargaining units which would unite all agency employees regardless of job title . . . would mean that clerks, who are generally the most oppressed and the best fighters, would be prevented from leading all agency workers.

A militant caucus motion to oppose the elections failed by 49½ to 17 votes (with 3 abstentions) in the Representative Council.

After the O.C.B.'s decision, the Local leadership and the Illinois A.F.S.C.M.E. continued in its leaflets to encourage employees to accept the ruling and organize for the election.

> AFSCME in no way agrees with the artificial criteria used by the OCB to delineate these two units [professional and paraprofessional]. . . . The units are set, however, and AFSCME's program to deal with this situation is to jointly petition for the two units and insist that there be a joint election.

However, opposition to the election by the most radical portion of the opposition caucus grew more vehement:

> progressive labor party says:
> BOYCOTT THE RACIST "ELECTION" FRAUD!
> STOP THE SPLIT! SAVE OUR UNION!
> We can save our union by dumping the sell-out misleaders and running the union directly as the organized rank and file.

In spite of this opposition, A.F.S.C.M.E. achieved victory in all three bargaining units. In the clerical unit an employees' association that had only been organized in downstate Illinois also campaigned in the election, but A.F.S.C.M.E. won with 54 percent of 8,141 votes (*Common Sense*, November 1975:1). Unopposed in the paraprofessional and professional units, A.F.S.C.M.E. won with 91 percent and 84 percent of, respectively, 1,762 and 4,998 votes cast.

GOALS AND TACTICS

The Campaigns for Economic Benefits

The union's expanded ability to act together was demonstrated in a campaign for a pay raise by Illinois A.F.S.C.M.E. Prior to affiliation, the I.U.S.S.E. had attempted to improve employee economic benefits, but it had met with only limited success. A state freeze on wages was lifted late in 1971, and the I.U.S.S.E. had argued for retroactive payment of all raises due during the freeze period. When the payments were granted, the union was quick to take credit (*IUSSE Bulletin*, November 22, 1971; February 29, 1972). On the verge of state takeover in 1973, the union expressed concern over the ability of the Cook County Pension Fund to make refunds to all employees. The refunds were distributed in 1974, although it was not clear what effect, if any, the union's efforts had.

Union impact was clearer, although less successful, in an effort to obtain cost-of-living raises in 1973. First, I.U.S.S.E. members signed petitions to their state representatives requesting a $35-per-month raise. When this action was rewarded with a favorable vote in the Illinois House of Representatives, union members then sent telegrams of support to their state Senators. However, after the Senate passed the pay raise bill, the Illinois Governor vetoed it. The Governor did agree to a lower raise, but union impact overall was weak (*Common Sense*, May 16, 1973:1).

After affiliation, union effectiveness in Springfield dramatically increased. This was apparent in the success of a new effort to secure $100 per month pay raises for state employees. The campaign was first proposed by an opposition activist in an I.U.S.S.E. Representative Council meeting. At the time, the rest of Illinois A.F.S.C.M.E. had decided to seek a 10 percent pay raise. However, arguments that "something green in their wallets . . . should be IUSSE's main image" and that a flat amount of increase would upgrade the relatively low salaries of the lower-paid employees won a majority of Representatives to the $100 campaign. Shortly afterwards, Illinois A.F.S.C.M.E. changed its position to correspond to that of its largest Illinois local. (*Common Sense*, May 16, 1974:1.)

The public aid local and the rest of Illinois A.F.S.C.M.E. began a campaign to build support for the $100 raise in the state legislature. Petitions, telephone calls, telegrams, and visits were used as pressure tactics. These tactics led to success in the legislature, but the Governor once again frustrated the union's efforts with an amendatory veto cutting the size of the raise in half. At this point, Illinois A.F.S.C.M.E. began a mass mobilization. A former I.U.S.S.E. activist later remembered that,

> [The IUSSE] took about fifteen buses down the first time we
> went. One night just about 8:00 in the evening we got a
> telephone call that said the legislature is going to open in the
> morning and the first thing that is going to hit the floor is the

> public aid pay raise. So we got on the phone, we didn't go home, and stayed until 1:00 at night calling employees to get 'em to go down to Springfield with us. . . . When people came to work that day we just loaded 'em on the buses . . . to rally for the $100 pay raise.

Two thousand state employees then "marched to the State Capital [sic] where a rally was held; we then went inside the Capital [sic] chanting" (*Common Sense*, January 2, 1974:1).

Success in the House was followed by a 44 to 11 vote in the Senate to override the Governor's veto.

> [The] $100 a month pay raise finally became a reality when the Senate overrode Walker's veto on Dec. 4. Hundreds of state employees . . . packed the Senate galleries. . . . As the YES vote hit the required 36 votes, the galleries erupted with cheering and applauding by very happy state employees. (*Common Sense*, December 11, 1974:1.)

A leader of the I.U.S.S.E.'s opposition faction announced that "we can be very proud of ourselves and our Union in this campaign" (*Common Sense*, December 1974:1), and the ability of economic demands to mobilize the membership was clearly perceived.

> IUSSE has a record of spending a lot of time on things that are not universally felt or desired by the rank-and-file (= you). No wonder it is a very difficult task to get momentum behind a union drive. . . . Pay raises . . . is [sic] an undeniably popular objective. Never in my four years plus of union activism have I seen such unanimous support. (*GA Blues*, July 23, 1973.)

A Career Ladder

The union was also able to resolve the problem of job opportunities for case aides and clerks. Since case aides and case aide trainees had been introduced into the department in the late 1960s, the union had attempted to formulate a position on their job opportunities that did not conflict with the interests of established members.

> We should have incisive, constructive ideas on how case aides can be productive and can serve human beings. . . . If we demand these [advancement] rights for case aides, can we demand less for ourselves? What specific kind of training should our clerical staff receive both on the job and during released paid educational time? (*IUPAE News*, May 1969:3.)

When the agency allowed caseworker job applicants preference points for two years of college on their civil service tests, the union protested (*IUPAE News*, September 1970:1). When the agency instituted a new exam for caseworker applicants, the union charged that "CW Exam is Farce."

> The exam was slanted toward those who were used to taking various types of examinations, namely: college students. . . .
> The agency has no intentions of creating open-end employment for case aides or trainees. *They are both dead-end jobs.* (*Common Sense*, December 20, 1972:1.)

"Too few" of the 2,800 people taking the exam were agency employees, and only 12 percent of the blacks taking the test passed, compared to 63 percent of the whites (*Common Sense*, January 17, 1973).

Concentrating on the pay disparities between Case aide and Caseworker positions, the union filed a suit charging discrimination in December 1973. The suit demanded that Case Aides and Trainees be promoted or upgraded to the Caseworker position with retroactive pay, and that all clerks who had ever expressed an interest in becoming a caseworker or attempted to take the Caseworker test be upgraded (*Common Sense*, December 18, 1973:1).

Even before the suit was resolved, the agency proposed a career ladder for employees. The union's impact on the proposal was recognized when the Civil Service Commission backed the union's request for union–management meetings prior to the plan's final approval. In these meetings, the union won recognition of the "important principle of seniority." The final plan affected 3,653 staff. Of these, 70 percent experienced a salary increase, 16 percent kept the same salary, and just 14 percent were downgraded to a lower pay level (*Common Sense*, January 1975:1, 4).

Union efforts to "fix the ladder" continued. Feeling that the distinction between Caseworker II and Caseworker III could not be justified, the union encouraged Caseworkers II to request desk audits of their duties. Hundreds of upgradings were the result. In spite of agency reluctance, the union was able to negotiate an agreement with the agency that opened the career ladder for clerks, by which "specific time requirements in clerical functions would be sufficient to be eligible for promotion to Caseworker." In 1979, a federal district court judge agreed with the union that case aides had been "qualified to perform tasks designated for Caseworkers, did in fact perform those tasks, but were not paid in accordance with their assumed responsibilities" (*Max Liberles, et al., v. David L. Daniel, et al.*, September 10, 1979).

Case Aide Layoffs

While the campaign for the $100 pay raise and negotiation of the career ladder both involved new tactical approaches by the union, the old more direct style of militant confrontation was still practiced in response to more immediate work-based problems. Militancy appealed to many members when the department notified seventy-two case aides on February 1, 1974, that they were to be laid off in two weeks. The "Wacker 72," as they were soon dubbed, initially had been assigned to a temporary general assistance review unit on Wacker Drive, but believed their jobs as case aides to be permanent. Given the number of uncovered case loads in Cook County, the union met the department's claim that the case aides were no longer needed with disbelief.

Union leaders quickly notified media sources, eliciting a favorable TV news editorial and at least one newspaper editorial that criticized the "false economy in welfare" (*Sun-Times*, February 25, 1974). Union leaders contacted local politicians, while exploring possibilities of a legal suit. Members of the union's Representative Council sought more direct action, however. A motion proposed by the opposition caucus to hold a strike referendum within two weeks was passed at a highly charged meeting of the Council. A union leadership plan to bus representatives to Springfield for lobbying, and then to build gradually for a statewide strike was rejected (*Common Sense*, March 5, 1974).

The strike never occurred. Within one week, the union's Executive Board had negotiated an agreement with state officials. All case aides were to be placed in new jobs, although up to 15 percent could be laid off for one month. In spite of vehement radical opposition to this last provision, the agreement carried in the Representative Council by 46½ to 7½, with 4 abstentions. In fact no case aides were laid off for any extended length of time.

Redetermination

Another crisis developed in the summer of 1975, as "caseworkers throughout the State are feeling the pinch of the 2158B redetermination program." Initiated because of high rates of overpayment and ineligibility, and a new federal requirement of minimal error rates, the redetermination program led to a sharp increase in work loads (*Common Sense*, June 1975:1).

> There was a tremendous increase in the amount of forms that came out of nowhere . . .—Management by Objectives. . . .
> He [Director Trainor] went from a system where you weren't

that accountable to one where performance requirements were explicitly spelled out, with the discipline that could result from insufficient work. This happened overnight.

In several offices where supporters of the opposition faction dominated union politics, a work slowdown over the redetermination program was begun. Those involved in the slowdown only processed redetermination forms. "Since the immediate disciplinary action was being taken on the forms, we said, 'O.K., we'll comply with your forms.'"

The union's Representative Council then adopted a plan for a statewide sick-out (*Common Sense*, August 1975:1–2). Ten hours before it was to begin, union leaders reached an agreement in negotiations with the agency. A union–management committee to develop recommendations was established, and agreed on a quota of thirty redeterminations per worker per month, rescission of all disciplinary action related to the wildcat actions, and hiring of more staff, with clerical-to-caseworker promotions where possible (*Common Sense*, September 1975:1, 4).

Working Hours

Militant action had less appeal when working hours in Cook County were extended to 5 P.M., in accordance with downstate agency hours. The extension of working hours without extra pay was unanimously opposed in the Representative Council, but the opposition caucus arguments that "we can stop these attacks only by organizing and fighting!!" were rejected. An opposition motion to take direct action failed by 44 to 28 (with 1 abstention) in the Representative Council, and by 101 to 37 (with 3 abstentions) in a meeting open to the entire membership. Arguing that "the State was and is trying to divide us and cause a strike in Cook County," President Liberles secured Council approval for binding arbitration of the issue. (*Common Sense*, July 25, 1974:5.) The arbitrator eventually approved the lengthened workday, but refused to allow an agency attempt to abolish presuspension and predisciplinary hearings.

RESURGENCE AND DEMISE OF THE RADICAL OPPOSITION

After its neutral stance in the 1972 election, the radical opposition began to organize again. While "the leadership of [our] group was always Progressive Labor Party," some new caseworkers joined the new "Concerned Caucus" to express their opposition to the union's direction. Differences in goals between the opposition and the union leadership were now minimal. Instead, tactical militancy became the key issue in debate between the opposition and the union's leadership.

Calling for a strike was the "Concerned Caucus" response to each major problem faced by employees.

> How do we make our bosses stick to certain laws or enforce a contract—STRIKE! (*Common Sense*, June 13, 1973:4.)

This was the answer to the flat grant, too. "Our union must begin to prepare to use the ultimate weapon of all union [sic]—the STRIKE." (*Common Sense*, September 19, 1973:2.)

The union's president, on the other hand, cautioned members that,

> THE CONTRACT IS OUR PRIMARY OBJECTIVE; . . . do not get sidetracked by the diversionary and divisive tactics of a certain faction that continues to call strike over any issue they can lay their hands on. (*Common Sense*, November 6, 1973.)

By the 1974 election of executive officers, the militant opposition was ready to field a complete alternative slate. It was headed by the losing opposition candidate in the 1972 election, Jim Kelly, who was now closely allied with the radical faction. At this point, collective bargaining was yet to be achieved, and provided a focal point for the debate over union tactics.

> The Campaign for a Strong Local 2000 believes that the real difference between ourselves and the current leadership is strategy. We believe that a union's strength and its ability to win real gains for its members comes first from the membership's action and only second from legal action and cultivating "important friends." We all want and need a good contract. . . . To get what we need requires mobilizing union power, . . . aggressive legislative lobbying campaigns, willingness to take work actions, . . . developing a credible strike threat and having the ability to strike if necessary. (*Common Sense*, September 11, 1974:3.)

The union's leadership mobilized for the election as the "Contract Action Slate," and emphasized the value of focusing on a contract.

> Fighting for and the winning of a decent contract will bring long overdue dignity and first class citizenship to employees of Public Aid and DVR [Division of Vocational Rehabilitation]; . . . the ultimate goal of all unions is to obtain a Decent Contract. Then to make sure management lives up to their end. (*Common Sense*, September 11, 1974:2.)

Again, the union's leadership warned members,

Do not believe that resorting to the Union's ultimate weapon
for every issue that faces us is the way to positive change;
. . . there is no room at the top for hysteria!

Although the opposition caucus lost the 1974 election with less
than 40 percent of the votes cast, they announced in a leaflet that,
"WE ARE HERE TO STAY." For the next two years, the opposition
continued to argue for militancy in response to major union problems.
Some activist supporters of the union leadership felt the militant
opposition made a worthwhile contribution to union politics, but
most were more critical in their reminiscences.

The internecine warfare—it was debilitating, and took time
and emotional commitment. We always referred to them as
"the crazies." They took absurd positions. PL was always for
striking no matter what. They were planning according to an
ideological framework.

Militancy was a continuing theme in opposition motions in the
Representative Council from the summer of 1973 to the summer of
1976. Thirty-three motions were made concerning major changes in
the agency and the union. Factional conflict accompanied twenty-
seven of these motions, and differences in tactics were involved in
twenty. In each case when there was both conflict and a focus on
tactics (fifteen motions), the opposition caucus took the more militant
stance. However, it was these motions for militant action that were
most consistently defeated. Only two of the eleven votes on union
activity won by the opposition caucus during this period involved
militant action. One of these successful motions called for a one-day
walkout against the flat grant. However, an earlier opposition proposal
to strike against the flat grant had already been defeated. The other
successful militant motion simply required the union to establish a
strike preparedness committee prior to negotiation of the union's first
contract.

Support for the militant caucus varied little throughout these years.
It was unable to expand significantly its base of support beyond the
agency offices on Chicago's north and west sides, with a predomi-
nantly white casework staff. Due to the union's expansion outside
of Cook County, and the efforts of the union's full-time organizers,
however, many more Representatives joined the Council. The result
was a substantial eclipse of the opposition's strength in that policy-
making body. Militant caucus candidates for Representative Council
Chair were defeated by increasingly wide margins (Figure 5). Votes
on motions in the Council became heavily skewed against the opposition caucus after 1973. During twenty-three meetings, in which

votes were taken on fifty-two motions, the mean number of votes cast for the union leadership's position rose from 31.1 in 1973 to 44.6 in 1974–75 and 61.4 in 1976. For the same three periods, the mean vote for the militant caucus position was 20.2, 16.3, and 30.7.

As the 1974 election aproached, factional conflict intensified. A spring meeting to elect negotiators for the Human Services bargaining units (professionals and paraprofessionals) was open to the entire union membership. Opposition caucus supporters therefore felt that their losing pattern in the Council could be reversed, and proclaimed that "our union needs negotiators who aren't afraid of THE MAN." Nonetheless, their slate lost by 95 to 19; the highest militant caucus vote-getter received only 47 out of 160 votes cast.

The Progressive Labor Party began to publicize its positions directly, and called on members to

FIGHT FOR A $200 RAISE

The best way is to strike. . . . The other way to win more is to put mass pressure on the legislature. . . . Because our goal

Fig. 5. Votes for Rep Council Chair by Faction and Year, 1973–1975.

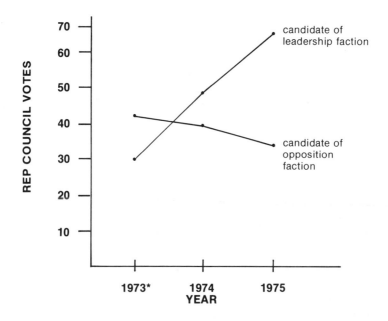

* In 1973 a more militant caucus member ran as a third candidate initially, and received only 9 votes. He then supported the other opposition candidate in the runoff election.

is a workers' revolution for socialism, we have no stake in the present boss-run system. We are not bound by the bosses' laws or their budgetary problems. (*PLP News*, April 5, 1976.)

Response from supporters of the union's leadership was direct:

There is a group of people within our Local which includes the PLP and its friends. This group, made up of white middle-class college kids, seems determined to undermine the union. . . . [The] PLP mis-leader . . . encouraged . . . clericals [to] vote "NO UNION," advertising it on the union bulletin board. Now he says he wants a good contract for clerks. (*Black Facts*, n.d.)

In its campaigning for the fall 1976 election, the opposition changed its approach. The radical caucus adopted a "sophisticated look," complete with "slick," professionally designed articles and leaflets.

The only way we will ever win a strong contract and a decent pay raise is to end the lack of leadership and disorganization that has paralyzed Local 2000 (*Common Sense*, September 9, 1976:2).

In a fancy brochure headed: "THE CAUCUS: ACCOUNTABLE UNION LEADERS WORKING FOR A UNION YOU CAN BELONG TO," they listed their goals as

FINANCIAL AND JOB SECURITY . . .
DELIVERY OF NEW UNION BENEFITS . . .
PROFESSIONALLY TRAINED [LEADERSHIP] . . .
ACCOUNTABILITY . . .

The regular leadership Contract Action Slate continued to emphasize the value of a contract:

He [Max] believes that these contracts will bring long overdue dignity and first-class citizenship to the employees of DPA and DVR. . . . Tish [the Slate's vice-presidential candidate] believes that our strategy must change, because the contracts will serve as our big gun. (*Common Sense*, September 1976:3.)

In spite of the "slick" strategy, the opposition again lost, getting only one-third of the vote. Results of the election of Representatives-at-Large for the Representative Council revealed a particularly weak militant caucus appeal among clerks. While the number of votes cast for the least popular Contract Action candidate for Professional Representative-at-Large was only 1.06 times the number of votes cast for the most popular militant caucus candidate, the least popular

Contract Action Clerical Representative-at-Large candidate received 2.64 times more votes than the most popular opposition caucus Clerical At-Large candidate.

Dismayed by their failures, leading opposition activists left the agency, and the radical faction "kind of kaputzed." Some later recognized critical weaknesses in their strategy.

> We [the Progressive Labor Party] intended to make it very clear to people what we stood for; on the other hand, to the extent that people understood what we stood for, a lot of people weren't going to go for that.

Some ultimately rejected altogether the feasibility of a radical role in union elections.

> Our internal weaknesses were an idealistic campaign. "We would do this and that if elected." In reality, we probably wouldn't have been able to accomplish these things. . . . We were opportunist. . . . Max *could* handle grievances better. . . . There shouldn't be a Rep Council—just membership meetings.

Most opposition supporters simply lost heart and left the agency.

CONCLUSIONS

The four years immediately preceding negotiation of the first contracts were a period of substantial change in the union. Economic goals became the union's primary concern. The dominance of "bread and butter" issues was reflected in the electoral success of candidates emphasizing these traditional trade union issues and in the widespread appeal of the union's campaign for a $100 pay raise. Even more striking evidence of the dominance of economic goals was the shift of the opposition faction from raising "socially conscious" issues to stressing bread and butter gains. Although the shift was reinforced by the opportunity to ally behind a presidential candidate in 1974 who had an unswerving devotion to economic goals, the shift was more directly a result of a conscious decision to change strategy.

Union members were still concerned with changes in working conditions. Perceived threats to their economic security and substantial increases in work loads even led to localized work actions. However, little attention was given to client issues. The major change in this period in client benefits—the institution of the flat grant—occasioned only a brief, symbolic union response.

Institutionalization of labor relations brought a decisive shift in union tactics. Contract negotiations were emphasized, and union leaders encouraged members to look to the contract to resolve many work place problems. The marches and demonstrations for a $100 pay raise certainly were more militant, but unlike most earlier actions, they were centrally coordinated and aimed at government bodies having control over public aid. Work actions still disrupted offices on some occasions. However, except for the changes negotiated by union leaders in the redetermination and layoff crises, these actions had only a temporary impact.

No longer differing with union leaders in terms of desired goals, the opposition faction distinguished itself by its repeated calls for work actions and strikes. While members in offices with substantial levels of support for the opposition heeded these calls at times, the opposition's militant stance failed to secure unionwide support. The appeal of the newly institutionalized mechanisms for achieving union goals finally led even the opposition to try to change its image to that of simply more effective negotiators.

Affiliation substantially increased the resources available to union leaders, and resulted in changes in the local's structure. The new Local 2000, which had increased its dues at the time of affiliation, also received money from A.F.S.C.M.E. with which to hire full-time organizers. The number of paid union staff grew, they were distributed throughout the state, and the union leadership was given authority to hire and fire its own staff directly. The editor of the union's newspaper, previously a supporter of the opposition caucus, was replaced. For a time, union organizers brought multiple proxies for those not in attendance to the union's Representative Council meetings. While this policy was partially rescinded after a sharp Representative Council debate, votes of many downstate Representatives continued to be cast by proxy. This bureaucratization of the union's structure placed the opposition at a substantial disadvantage. The relative advantage accruing to the opposition caucus from the high levels of commitment of opposition activists was greatly reduced, and for the first time in union history the incumbent president was reelected twice in succession.

Involvement in the union rose rapidly during this period. After four years of unchanging membership figures, the union grew again. Most members of the union's Representative Council attended its meetings consistently, and many participated vigorously. While much of the union's growth could be attributed to extension of its jurisdiction, involvement of members from the union's traditional base of support in Cook County public aid also rose.

The importance of the union's external environment in stimulating this change in the union's GIST configuration was clear. While the union began this period with a new set of leaders, their basic orientations to a more traditional union strategy were consistent with that of previous successful presidential candidates. On the other hand, substantial change occurred at both levels of the union's environment. Its primary social environment changed markedly as clerical staff, who were identified in the 1973 survey as being more concerned with economic goals, were able to move to caseworker positions. The flat grant and separation of service casework and case financial management reduced the opportunities for those caseworkers still oriented to client issues to develop joint activities with clients. The union's increasing institutionalization also provided greater opportunities for influence from its institutional environment. Union leaders maintained frequent contacts with agency officials throughout most of this period, and the militant direct action typically favored by opposition activists less often appeared to be a necessary tactic for goal attainment. Negotiations successfully prevented layoffs, and legal action opened new occupational mobility opportunities for hundreds of employees.

The I.U.S.S.E. was not a passive recipient of environmental influence. Union members consciously sought to change the union in anticipation of, or in response to environmental changes. Affiliation and the focus on collective bargaining were both policies proposed by union leaders and ratified by membership votes. However, union options for change were severely constrained by the environment. Attempts by opposition activists to oppose the major changes in the union were markedly unsuccessful.

Other changes in the union also reflected the dependence of union development on its larger environment. While the shift to a more traditional structure began prior to institutionalization, with the hope of encouraging it, this change had little effect until the process of institutionalization began. The greater resources available to union leaders after affiliation and expansion statewide enhanced the hierarchical structure's effectiveness, and facilitated negotiations with state and A.F.S.C.M.E. officials.

Institutionalization appeared to create new opportunities for union influence, and levels of membership involvement rose in anticipation. The low levels of involvement during the previous period were more likely to have been due to a perceived lack of success of the union in its institutional environment, rather than to an inevitable process of decreasing member interest with organizational age. Change in the union's relations with other organizations thus seemed to be more consequential for its development than its relations with its membership. A more complete evaluation of the impact of changes in the union's primary social environment requires analysis of data obtained from members in the 1976 statewide survey.

CHAPTER NINE

New Members in a
Changed Environment

Two major changes had occurred in the union's environment during the four years prior to negotiation of the first state A.F.S.C.M.E. contract in 1974. The union's social environment had changed as a result of reorganization of public aid and expansion of the union. New types of members entered the union, and the proportion of some social categories among the membership declined. The union's institutional environment changed due to affiliation with a national union and establishment of a collective bargaining relationship with the state. Relations with other organizations were transformed as a result. In addition, the consistent alignment of particular offices in Cook County with the leadership or opposition factions influenced member orientations quite apart from these other changes.

These changes were manifested in the union's membership. Changes in the social environment necessarily affected the distribution of grievances and resources among union members. Membership involvement and pressure for particular union goals changed as a result. The domination of particular Cook County offices by supporters of the opposition or the leadership factions exerted a strong influence on the orientations of members within those offices. Since most members had little direct contact with union headquarters, the orientations of activists within members' own offices shaped their view of and involvement in the union. Changes in the union's relation to its institutional environment altered the meaning of particular tactics and the likelihood of their success. Events had begun to overtake memories of the union's defeat in the second strike.

Analysis of the union's history suggested that these changes influenced members' orientations and were translated into factional conflict within the union. However, the interview and archival information on which the historical analysis was based do not provide a reliable picture of the entire membership. For this purpose, survey data collected in 1976 will be used. The survey was administered to a stratified random sample of paraprofessional and professional members just prior to the start of negotiations for their contracts with the state agency. Including indicators of employee grievances, support for militancy, union participation, and likelihood of leaving the agency, the survey data allows a quantitative analysis of the bases of factional conflict and involvement among the membership. (See Appendix for methodological details.)

CHANGES IN UNION AND AGENCY

The Social Environment

Introduction of former paraprofessionals and clerks into the caseworker ranks was the most significant change in the union's social environment. At the time of the first survey, paraprofessionals were still a relatively new addition to the agency staff. By 1976, many paraprofessionals and clerks had moved upward into the "professional" casework position. As a result, caseworkers employed in the same job (Caseworker III) differed in their educational backgrounds and employment histories much more than they had earlier.

Expansion of the union outside of the Cook County Department of Public Aid brought many new employees into the union. Some had previously been organized by A.F.S.C.M.E., but many had no prior exposure to welfare employee unionism. Most downstate employees worked in small offices with more general responsibilities, and with somewhat lower work loads than in Cook County. Incorporation of the State Division of Vocational Rehabilitation also brought another group with different work experiences and social backgrounds into the union. Working in smaller offices throughout the state, in jobs requiring more advanced training and involving more responsibilities for clients. Rehabilitation Counselors approximated traditional professionals more closely than did the Public Aid Caseworkers.

Although they were not new to the union, the low-paid Homemaker staff in Cook County had been a special concern of the union's president. Several improvements in the job security and pay of the Homemakers that resulted from Max Liberles' efforts had led some of them to become particularly active in union politics. The Illinois Office of Collective Bargaining placed Homemakers in the paraprofessional bargaining unit, so they were included in the 1976 survey.

In 1976, differences in education, seniority, pay, and social background between the occupations within the union were substantial (Table 7). Education, seniority, and salary each increased with Caseworker rank. Caseworkers I and II in Cook County had median levels of 14.3 years of education, 1.7 years of seniority, and $748 per month salary. The corresponding figures for Caseworkers V were 16.8, 12.8, and $1,321. Differences between the professional Income Maintenance Caseworkers III and their counterparts in Service units, Caseworkers IV, were less marked. The median education of Caseworkers III was one-half year less than that of Caseworkers IV. Caseworker III members also tended to have less seniority than Caseworker IV members, and earned a median salary that was $205 less per month.

Rehabilitation Counselors had the highest median years of education of the occupations in the sample, and the second highest median salary. Homemakers, on the other hand, had the least education (a median of 9.8 years), the lowest salaries in Cook County, but a level of seniority second only to that of Caseworkers V. Occupations within the professional specialty group in Cook County were closest on the average to Caseworkers IV in terms of salary, to Caseworkers V in terms of education, and to Homemakers in terms of seniority.

Table 7. Characteristics of Union Members by Occupation, Illinois, 1976

Occupation (Number[b])	Median Salary (per month)	Median Education (years)	Median Seniority (years)	Percent Female	Percent Black[a]
Cook County					
Homemaker (29)	$ 723	9.8	10.6	97%	100%
Caseworker I, II[c] (76)	748	14.3	1.7	76	75
Caseworker III (91)	946	15.8	4.3	67	54
Caseworker IV (76)	1,151	16.3	6.8	50	34
Caseworker V (28)	1,321	16.8	12.8	57	46
Professional Specialist (41)	1,130	16.6	9.6	37	32
Rehabilitation Counselor (29)	1,247	17.0	6.2	41	31
Downstate					
Homemaker (1)	—	—	—	—	—
Caseworker I, II[c] (16)	$ 718	13.5	3.2	87%	27%
Caseworker III (55)	888	14.4	3.8	86	27
Caseworker IV (54)	1,151	16.1	6.5	72	13
Caseworker V (4)	1,327	16.5	8.5	100	0
Professional Specialist (13)	938	16.8	3.1	33	8
Rehabilitation Counselor (31)	1,271	17.1	7.0	19	13

SOURCE: All figures from 1976 survey.

NOTE: Figures reported are also similar to those for the entire sample, including nonrespondents.

[a] The 23 nonwhites who are not black are included in the category designated Black.

[b] The sample is a disproportionate stratified random sample. These Ns are unweighted and thus do not exactly correspond to the occupational distribution of the entire union membership.

[c] Because there are only ten Caseworker I staff in the sample, a number too small to yield reliable estimates of effects, the categories of Caseworker I and II are combined. Both positions are classified as paraprofessional.

Interoccupational differences in social background indicators were pronounced. The percentage of whites increased steadily with caseworker rank in Cook County, while the percentage of males increased only slightly less regularly. There were no white Homemakers in the sample, and only 31 percent of the Caseworkers I and II in the entire sample were white. In contrast, 72 percent of the Caseworkers IV and 80 percent of the Rehabilitation Counselors in the entire sample were white. There was thus a fairly close correspondence between the ranking of occupations by education and salary and their ranking in terms of percentage white and male. The only exception to this pattern in the Caseworker series was among Caseworkers V. Women, and in Cook County, nonwhite women, were more likely to be Caseworkers V than expected on the basis of this otherwise regular pattern. Perhaps due to fewer outside job opportunities they tended to accumulate longer seniority in the agency, and thus move upward to supervisory positions more often than men.

The Organization

Union politics in several agency offices in Cook County[1] were dominated by the radical opposition faction throughout this period. Most of the opposition-oriented offices were on Chicago's north side, serving primarily white, Hispanic, or racially mixed neighborhoods. Most offices on the city's largely black south side were consistently aligned with the union's leadership. In a few offices there was a fairly even split in support for the two factions; such splits often represented markedly different orientations of the union's casework and clerical membership. Throughout the downstate counties, support for the leadership faction was high and relatively constant.

Two variables are used to indicate office political context: the percent of members voting in the office who voted for the incumbent president, Max Liberles, in the unionwide election three months after the survey (PCTMAX), and the average responses of members to six questions concerning the union's performance "in the last two years" (UPERF) (see Appendix). Higher scores on the union performance index indicate higher levels of satisfaction with the union. Scores on this index are averaged for members in each agency office to derive an office-level measure.

This office-level data confirm the substantial variation in support for the incumbent president among Cook County public aid offices (Table 8). In 29 percent of these offices, less than 40 percent voted for the incumbent president, while in 42 percent at least 70 percent voted for him. Evaluation of union performance (UPERF) also varied widely between offices. Both downstate and in Division of Vocational Rehabilitation offices, support for the incumbent president was uniformly high. Lacking exposure to the internal conflicts in the Cook County offices, members downstate and in vocational rehabilitation had had little exposure to, and apparently little interest in, the opposition faction.

The Institutional Environment

Governor Walker's executive order establishing the right of state employees to bargain collectively changed fundamentally the role of state employee unions. The advent of collective bargaining made it possible for union leaders to press union demands during contract negotiations, and made a constructive state response to those demands, rather than inaction, the appropriate, normative action.

In response to these new opportunities for institutionalized influence, I.U.S.S.E. leaders increasingly eschewed direct action by employees in favor of resolving problems through contract negotiations. Previously, such militant actions as petitioning, work slowdowns, picketing, and striking represented a single continuum of increasingly militant actions. Institutionalization created a qualitative distinction between strikes and the other forms of militancy. Strikes to back up contractual demands when negotiations failed to settle them are considered legitimate within the context of institutionalized labor relations. Other militant actions, such as the walkouts and work slowdowns that had often been instigated at the office level in the I.U.S.S.E., explicitly violated the conditions of the collective bargaining relationship. They now could be considered actions against the union leadership, as well as against the agency (Schutt, 1982).

Table 8. Union Support Among Cook County Public Aid Agency Offices, 1976

Percentage of Support for Incumbent President (PCTMAX)	Percentage of Offices	Mean Satisfaction with Union Performance (UPERF)	Percentage of Offices
20%–29%	22.7%	< 2.5	4.2%
30 –39	9.0	2.6–2.7	12.6
40 –49	9.0	2.8–2.9	29.4
50 –59	4.5	3.0–3.1	21.0
60 –69	9.0	3.2–3.3	25.2
70 –79	22.7	3.4–3.5	8.4
80 –89	9.0		100.8%*
90 –99	13.6		(24)
	99.5%*		
	(22)		

* Percents do not add to 100 due to rounding error.

Reflecting this new distinction between forms of militancy, union leaders often argued for the importance of preserving the right to strike over a contract, but usually discouraged militant action outside of this context. The radical opposition, on the other hand, frequently resorted to calls for walkouts, work slowdowns, or strikes outside of the collective bargaining context, in response to work place problems.

IMPLICATIONS FOR ORGANIZATIONAL CHANGE

These changes in the union and its environment had the potential for altering the distribution of grievances and resources among the union's membership. The mobility opportunities established for former paraprofessionals and clerks brought many employees without college degrees into the professional caseworker position. Lacking initial expectations for professional work at the time of their employment, the mobile caseworkers had less basis for experiencing the gap between expectations and achievement underlying the professional–bureaucratic conflict model of semiprofessional discontent. The bases for militancy and job dissatisfaction identified in earlier years (chapter 6) may have been lessened as a result.

Differences in the orientations of white caseworkers and black clerks had been apparent to union activists in many offices.

> The majority of the people that were involved in
> worker–client activities, as far as caseworkers were concerned,
> were white. That was always a problem that we never were
> able to [overcome].

Some attributed these differences to race, and others to occupation.

> There was always some friction between the so-called
> professional staff and the clerical staff, . . . the clerks feeling
> that when we have a problem the professional staff doesn't
> really want to get involved.

In another office, a supporter of the opposition faction noted,

> There was a real racial tension between financial and field
> staff. . . . It was like walking into a war zone at times. . . .
> The racial tensions at the office were really bad; . . . we had
> meetings after meetings of everybody getting together and
> listing what they couldn't stand about one another.

While differences in grievances were a major basis for factional conflict, low levels of participation of minority members in the union had continued to be of concern to union activists.

[The union's vice-president] pleaded for greater participation from Blacks and other minorities in IUSSE's union activities. To date there has been very little positive responses [sic] and flimsy excuses. . . . JUDGING FROM THE ATTENDANCE OF THE UNION MEETING IT WOULD BE VERY DIFFICULT TO CONVINCE ANYONE THAT AN APPRECIABLE NUMBER OF BLACKS WORKED FOR THE AGENCY. (*Common Sense*, March 14, 1973:4.)

Headlines in the union's newspaper continued to query, CLERICAL AND PARA-PROFESSIONAL: WHERE ARE YOU? (*Common Sense*, September 19, 1973:4.) The increasing prevalence of employees from clerical/paraprofessional and minority backgrounds thus seemed to presage problems of involving members in the union.

Variation in work place politics often influences member orientations. The political climate in printing shops influenced member voting in the International Typographical Union (Lipset, Trow, and Coleman, 1962:ch. 16); the presence of militant colleagues increased the likelihood that teachers would participate in a strike (Cole, 1969). Political context also influences the bases of member involvement. In non-militant contexts, social status and social integration predispose members toward participation, while in militant contexts, antagonism toward the company may motivate union member participation (Dean, 1954a, b; Tannenbaum and Kahn, 1958).[2]

The importance of the office political context was apparent in the comments of union activists.

We walked out a lot, and it was, you know, "it's too hot in there, it's too cold in there, we have an uncovered case load, we want a worker," you know. So it was like, at the drop of a hat, people would say, "We don't like this shit anymore," and off we'd go. . . . So, you kind of got into the whole milieu that you didn't put up with a lot of shit. Somebody got out of line or they did something you didn't like, you said, "O.K., we're not working anymore, we're walking out!" Paychecks were late, you just didn't work anymore. You walked down to CAO [the agency's Central Administrative Offices] or wherever, and said, "First of all, we're getting paid for this. Second of all we want this rectified," that kind of thing.

In such office contexts, the likelihood of member support for militant action was likely to be greater than in the offices in which such actions did not regularly occur.

Establishment of collective bargaining rights fundamentally changed the role of militancy in the union, however. Contract strikes tend to be planned, legal actions organized by formal union leadership and involving members throughout the union's jurisdiction (Schutt, 1982). Other work actions, such as sick-outs, are normally not sanctioned by union leaders, are relatively spontaneous, typically illegal, and often based on immediate work place concerns (Gouldner, 1965). Explicit differentiation of the attitudes of union leaders and opposition activists toward the role of militant tactics accompanied the institutionalization of labor relations in public aid. While supporters of the leadership asserted that "we will build a strike if necessary to get our needs, but we won't discuss it every day," opposition activists believed "that the real power of our union lies in member participation and action." The ability of the alternative union factions to mobilize members would be affected to the extent that different groups of members varied in their support for the institutionalized and non-institutionalized forms of militancy.

QUANTITATIVE FINDINGS

Both frequency of members' participation in union affairs and their likelihood of leaving the agency were related to various aspects of their work place position and social backgrounds.[3] Upper-level Paraprofessionals (Caseworkers I and II), were less likely to participate in the union, while professionals, paraprofessionals from clerical backgrounds (CLERK), and professionals from paraprofessional backgrounds (PARA) (see Appendix, Table A-3) were more likely to participate than others (Table 9). Members in paraprofessional and professional positions from clerical backgrounds (CLERK) were less likely to leave the agency (Table 10). This greater commitment to the agency was shared with Homemakers (HMK), another occupational group composed largely of black women (see Table 7). Caseworkers III who were not from clerical or paraprofessional backgrounds (CW III), on the other hand, were more likely to leave the agency. As indicated by the significant interaction effect in table 9, Rehabilitation Counselors (VOC) had the highest levels of participation among the occupational groups in Cook County, but had particularly low levels of participation downstate.[4]

Independent of these occupational effects, background factors influenced participation and exit. Members with higher levels of education and those who were younger were more likely to be planning to leave the agency soon, although no more likely to participate in union affairs. Black members in the professional and paraprofessional positions surveyed participated in the union more frequently and

Table 9. Regression Analysis of Union Participation (PART), Illinois, 1976 (Beta Coefficients)

Independent Variables	Specification 1	Specification 2
Organizational Position		
Downstate (DWN)	.09	.30***
Education (EDUC)		−.06
Seniority (SNRTY)		.02
Occupation[a]		
Homemaker (HMK)	−.03	.00
Caseworker I, II (CWII)	−.12*	−.11
Caseworker III (CWIII)	.01	.04
Caseworker V (CWV)	−.03	−.03
Professional Specialist (PFL)	−.03	.00
Rehabilitation Counselor (VOC)	.01	.30***
Ex-clerk (CLERK)	.10*	
Ex-aide (PARA)	.12*	
Demographic Background		
Race (BLACK)		.13**
Gender (MALE)		.12**
Age (AGE)		−.06
Office Political Context		
Incumbent Support (PCTMAX)		−.14*
Office Size (SMALL)		−.08
Interaction Effects		
Rehabilitation Counselor downstate		
(VOC * DWN)		−.38***
R^2	.05	.10
$\bar{R}^2$	.03	.08
N	511	511

[a] Caseworkers IV omitted.
* $p \leq .05$
** $p \leq .01$
*** $p \leq .001$

were less likely to be planning to soon leave the agency than whites. This greater commitment to the agency did not extend to black members outside of Cook County, however, as indicated by the significant interaction effect of race and county in table 10.

Office politics also influenced members' likelihood of participating in the union and planning to leave the agency soon. Participation was lower, but planning to soon leave the agency was less, the higher the degree of support for the incumbent union president, Max Liberles. Members in downstate offices were also more likely to participate in the union and less likely to leave the agency than those in Cook County.

Overall job satisfaction (SAT) was high among Homemakers (who worked only in Cook County), and Rehabilitation Counselors downstate (Table 11). Male and older members were also more satisfied with their jobs, while members with higher levels of education reported less job satisfaction. Members who worked in small offices

Table 10. Regression Analysis of Union Member Job Departure Plans (EXIT), Illinois, 1976 (Beta Coefficients)

Independent Variables	Specification 1	Specification 2
Organizational Position		
Downstate (DWN)	−.10*	−.19**
Education (EDUC)		.20**
Seniority (SNRTY)		−.10
Occupation[a]		
Homemaker (HMK)	−.11*	.09
Caseworker I, II (CWII)	.04	.01
Caseworker III (CWIII)	.13*	.09
Caseworker V (CWV)	−.05	−.03
Professional Specialist (PFL)	.03	.05
Rehabilitation Counselor (VOC)	−.01	−.02
Ex-clerk (CLERK)	−.25***	
Ex-aide (PARA)	−.01	
Demographic Background		
Race (BLACK)		−.28***
Gender (MALE)		−.06
Age (AGE)		−.13*
Office Political Context		
Incumbent Support (PCTMAX)		−.11*
Office Size (SMALL)		−.02
Interaction Effects		
Blacks downstate (BLACK * DWN)		.11*
R^2	.08	.20
$\bar{R}^2$	.06	.17
N	488	488

[a] Caseworkers IV omitted.
  * p ≤ .05
 ** p ≤ .01
*** p ≤ .001

downstate and those who worked in offices with high percentages of support for the incumbent president also were more satisfied with their jobs.

Satisfaction with union performance (UPERF) was affected by some of the same factors that influenced job satisfaction (Table 12). Thus, Homemakers were more satisfied with union performance, as were older members and those with less education (EDUC) (although the latter effect was not statistically significant). Members in small agency offices (SMALL) were also more satisfied with the union than those in other offices, as were members in offices with higher percentages voting for the incumbent president (PCTMAX) (although also not a statistically significant difference). In addition to these effects, union satisfaction was higher among black members (BLACK) than among whites, and among those who had been promoted to caseworker positions from the clerical staff (CLERK).

Support for work actions (MILTNT) and support for a contract strike (STRIKE) had only one predictor in common: Support for both

Table 11. Regression Analysis of Union Member Job Dissatisfaction (SAT), Illinois, 1976 (Beta Coefficients)

Independent Variables	Specification 1	Specification 2
Organizational Position		
Downstate (DWN)	–.16***	–.04
Education (EDUC)		.12*
Seniority (SNRTY)		.07
Occupation[a]		
Homemaker (HMK)	–.12*	.00
Caseworker I, II (CWII)	–.08	–.09
Caseworker III (CWIII)	–.03	–.03
Caseworker V (CWV)	–.09	–.10*
Professional Specialist (PFL)	.01	.11*
Rehabilitation Counselor (VOC)	–.24***	–.04
Ex-clerk (CLERK)	.01	
Ex-aide (PARA)	.10	
Demographic background		
Race (BLACK)		.09
Gender (MALE)		–.13**
Age (AGE)		–.24***
Office Political Context		
Incumbent Support (PCTMAX)		–.16**
Office Size (SMALL)		–.15*
Interaction Effects		
Rehabilitation Counselor downstate		
(VOC * DWN)		–.16*
R^2	.08	.17
$\bar{R}^2$	.07	.14
N	479	479

[a] Caseworkers IV omitted.
* $p \leq .05$
** $p \leq .01$
*** $p \leq .001$

forms of militancy decreased with age (Tables 13 and 14). Otherwise, their predictors differed. Support for work actions was particularly low among Homemakers (due to their higher average age), and relatively high among men (Table 13). Strike support, on the other hand, was higher among members of the lower status occupations: Homemakers, Caseworkers II, and Caseworkers III (Table 14). Members downstate were particularly low in strike support, while black members had particularly high levels of strike support. Salary per se was not related to either form of militancy.

The correlates of both forms of militancy differed somewhat in downstate offices. Rehabilitation Counselors downstate were less supportive of striking, although in Cook County their level of strike support did not differ significantly from that of the other relatively high status occupations, the Professional Specialist and Caseworker V. Members from clerical backgrounds (CLERK), who were not more supportive of work actions generally, were so if employed downstate.

Table 12. Regression Analysis of Member Satisfaction with Union Performance (UPERF), Illinois, 1976 (Beta Coefficients)

Independent Variables	Specification 1	Specification 2
Organizational Position		
Downstate (DWN)	.07	.12*
Education (EDUC)		−.09
Seniority (SNRTY)		−.04
Occupation[a]		
Homemaker (HMK)	.29***	.21***
Caseworker I, II (CWII)	.02	.01
Caseworker III (CWIII)	−.01	.03
Caseworker V (CWV)	−.01	−.01
Professional Specialist (PFL)	−.06	−.10*
Rehabilitation Counselor (VOC)	−.06	−.09
Ex-clerk (CLERK)	.10*	
Ex-aide (PARA)	.10	
Demographic Background		
Race (BLACK)		.13**
Gender (MALE)		.04
Age (AGE)		.12*
Office Political Context		
Incumbent Support (PCTMAX)		.10
Office Size (SMALL)		.12*
R^2	.13	.17
$\bar{R}^2$	.11	.14
N	499	499

[a] Caseworkers IV omitted.
* p ≤ .05
** p ≤ .01
*** p ≤ .001

Mobility and Race

The variables of race, education, mobility history, and current occupation were highly correlated in the agency work force. The effects of these variables on union member orientations were generally similar, but with some important differences. Caseworkers who had formerly been clerks, and black members generally were more likely to participate in the union, less likely to be planning to leave the agency, and more satisfied with union performance than white members and those who had started in professional positions. Homemakers, all black, were also more likely to be staying and satisfied. In addition, black members, including Homemakers, were more supportive of striking over negotiation issues than were white members. Caseworkers I and II (paraprofessionals) were also more supportive of striking, although they were less likely to participate in union affairs. Levels of job satisfaction tended to decrease, and plans for leaving the agency tended to increase with education independently of these other effects.

Table 13. Regression Analysis of Member Support for Work Actions (MILTNT), Illinois, 1976 (Beta Coefficients)

Independent Variables	Specification 1	Specification 2
Organizational Position		
Downstate (DWN)	.00	−.02
Education (EDUC)		.05
Seniority (SNRTY)		−.07
Occupation[a]		
Homemaker (HMK)	−.13**	−.04
Caseworker I, II (CWII)	−.07	−.10
Caseworker III (CWIII)	.04	.02
Caseworker V (CWV)	.00	.02
Professional Specialist (PFL)	−.06	−.04
Rehabilitation Counselor (VOC)	−.10	−.10
Ex-clerk (CLERK)	.01	
Ex-aide (PARA)	.05	
Demographic Background		
Race (BLACK)		.01
Gender (MALE)		.08*
Age (AGE)		−.15**
Office Political Context		
Incumbent Support (PCTMAX)		−.04
Office Size (SMALL)		−.02
Interaction Effects		
Ex-clerks downstate (CLERK * DWN)		.15**
R²	.08	.08
R̄²	.02	.06
N	510	510

[a] Caseworkers IV omitted.
* $p \leq .05$
** $p \leq .01$
*** $p \leq .001$

In general, then, the upward mobility of clerks, the positive ties of the union to Homemakers, and the decreasing levels of education in the overall work force brought employees into the union with greater commitment to the agency and less critical attitudes toward the union. However, while race was related to these other factors, black members were even more supportive of striking for a contract than other employees. While their unexceptional levels of support for work actions indicated that they would not be particularly likely to back the radical opposition because of its stance in favor of direct confrontation with the agency, the high support of black members for strikes distinguished them from other groups of relatively conservative members in the union.

Members Downstate

Union members downstate were less supportive of strikes, more likely to participate in the union, and less likely to be planning to leave the agency than their counterparts in Cook County. As a group,

Table 14. Regression Analysis of Member Support for Contract Strike (STRIKE), Illinois, 1976 (Beta Coefficients)

Independent Variables	Specification 1	Specification 2
Organizational Position		
Downstate (DWN)	–.10*	.07
Education (EDUC)		–.02
Seniority (SNRTY)		.05
Occupation[a]		
Homemaker (HMK)	.10*	.11
Caseworker I, II (CWII)	.16**	.08
Caseworker III (CWIII)	.13*	.09
Caseworker V (CWV)	–.06	–.06
Professional Specialist (PFL)	.01	.05
Rehabilitation Counselor (VOC)	.01	.16
Ex-clerk (CLERK)	.01	
Ex-aide (PARA)	.07	
Demographic Background		
Race (BLACK)		.30***
Gender (MALE)		.08
Age (AGE)		–.23***
Office Political Context		
Incumbent Support (PCTMAX)		–.08
Office Size (SMALL)		–.04
Interaction Effects		
Rehabilitation Counselor downstate		
(VOC * DWN)		–.20**
R^2	.06	.17
$\bar{R}^2$	.05	.14
N	497	497

[a] Caseworkers IV omitted.
* $p \leq .05$
** $p \leq .01$
*** $p \leq .001$

downstate members were also more satisfied with the union's performance. For some particular downstate groups, however, location had a different effect. Rehabilitation Counselors downstate were noticeably less supportive of strikes, more satisfied with their jobs, and much less likely to participate in the union than their Cook County colleagues. Upwardly mobile clerks, on the other hand, were more supportive of work actions downstate, while black members downstate were more likely to plan to leave the agency than those in Cook County.

Expansion of the union downstate thus brought employees into the union who were generally more conservative, less militant, and more satisfied with the union. Given downstate members' high levels of participation in union affairs and attachment to the agency, this new set of members represented a powerful new force in union politics. Their dispersion and distance from union headquarters in

Cook County, however, could have lessened the impact of these resources.

Rehabilitation Counselors

Rehabilitation Counselors tended to be less supportive of militant action and much more satisfied with their jobs than union members in other occupations. Downstate, Rehabilitation Counselors were less supportive of striking over contract demands, more satisfied with their jobs, and less likely to participate in the union. Thus, Rehabilitation Counselors, like other members downstate, represented a new membership component that was more satisfied with its conditions. While the high average level of participation of Cook County Rehabilitation Counselors suggested a greater potential for influence on the union's direction, their orientations on union and job-related issues did not differ from those of other union members in public aid.

Office Context

Union members in agency offices with more supporters of the incumbent president were less likely to participate in union affairs, but also less likely to plan to leave the agency than those in opposition-dominated offices. Satisfaction both with union performance and with the job was higher among members in the more proleadership offices.

These findings on the effect of office context on individuals are complemented by findings from office-level analysis of the correlates of satisfaction with the union leadership. Both the percentage of members in Cook County offices voting for Max Liberles for union president and the average level of satisfaction with union performance in these offices were correlated with averaged aggregate values of the other variables used in the individual-level analyses (Table 15).

Offices with lower levels of support for the incumbent president tended to have significantly lower average union member job seniority and age levels. Opposition offices in Cook County tended to have more union members in the professional and paraprofessional categories who were Caseworkers III. Support for work actions and plans for soon leaving the agency were also higher in these offices. These variables were also related to the average level of satisfaction with the union's performance. Union satisfaction was greater in offices with higher levels of seniority and age, with lower levels of work action support and higher levels of job attachment. Higher average levels of union satisfaction were also apparent in offices with more

Table 15. Office Correlates of Political Alignment and Union Satisfaction, Cook County, 1976

| | Pearson Correlation Coefficients | |
| | Percent Vote for Incumbent President (PCTMAX) | Satisfaction with Union Performance (UPERF) |
Independent Variables		
Ex-clerk (% CLERK)	.04	.04
Ex-aide (% PARA)	−.10	−.20
Homemaker (% HMKR)	.08	.69***
Caseworker I, II (% CWII)	−.18	−.06
Caseworker III (% CWIII)	−.34*	−.46**
Caseworker IV (% CWIV)	.08	−.18
Caseworker V (% CWV)	−.06	−.09
Professional specialist (% PFL)	.39*	−.11
Rehabilitation counselor (% VOC)	.20	−.19
Seniority ($\bar{X}$ SNRTY)	.60***	.44**
Education ($\bar{X}$ EDUC)	−.25	−.76***
Race (% BLACK)	.27	.55***
Age ($\bar{X}$ AGE)	.49**	.50**
Job attachment ($\bar{X}$ EXIT)	.54**	.45**
Support for work actions ($\bar{X}$ MILTNT)	−.51**	−.43**
N	25	27

black members, and among Homemakers (who worked out of a single office), and in offices with a lower educational level.

Institutionalized Militancy

One result of the union's institutionalization was to distinguish work actions from strikes over contract issues. These different tactics tended to have different sources among the paraprofessional and professional union members. Strike support, the institutionalized form of militancy, was higher among members in lower status occupations, and among black and younger members. Work actions, the non-institutionalized form of militancy, received more support from male and younger union members, and less from Homemakers.

CONCLUSIONS

Some of the same factors that had generated differences in member orientations in 1973 were still reflected in the 1976 survey results. Members who were older, more educated, and white were more likely to oppose the incumbent union leadership. As in 1973, characteristics of those most likely to oppose the union's leadership were also associated with plans to leave. However, several important changes had occurred. A new, more resourceful group had emerged in support of the union leadership. Upwardly mobile clerks, like their non-mobile colleagues studied in 1973, were less likely to be dissatisfied with the union's performance. Unlike clerks in 1973, those clerks who had moved into Caseworker II or III positions by 1976 were also more likely to participate in union affairs than others. Coupled with their lesser likelihood of leaving the agency, these high rates of participation suggested that upwardly mobile clerks were a powerful group in union politics. By decreasing the proportion of caseworkers with college educations in the union's membership, the career ladder reduced the ability of such employees to serve as a source of opposition in union politics.

Inclusion of downstate offices within the union had an effect in some ways similar to that of the new career ladder for clerks. Downstate members were less supportive of striking, more satisfied with their jobs and the union, and more likely to participate in the union and less likely to plan leaving the agency than Cook County members. These members thus represented another more conservative force in union politics. Incorporation of downstate Rehabilitation Counselors into the union had a similar effect.

While upwardly mobile clerks in Cook County were largely black, race also had effects independent of mobility history and current occupation. Like upwardly mobile clerks, black members generally tended to be more satisfied with the union's performance, more attached to the agency, and more likely to participate in the union. Their higher levels of strike support, however, distinguished their orientations from those of other members. Increasing numbers of black members in Caseworker positions, and thus in public aid generally, thus suggested the possibility of conflict with members downstate and with Rehabilitation Counselors.

Changes in the union's social environment thus had the potential for fundamentally changing its direction. New members downstate, in the Division of Vocational Rehabilitation, and those upwardly mobile from clerical positions were generally more conservative and more satisfied with the union than others. Their inclusion in the union appears to have accounted in part for the diminishing appeal of the union's radical opposition faction, historically based among the college-educated white caseworker staff. The impact of these changes was heightened by the substantial resources of these new groups of members. However, the differences of orientation in members downstate and those in Cook County, and between white and black members, suggested continued bases of conflict. In the next stage of the union's development, these bases of conflict were translated into the emergence of new factions within the union.

Chapter Ten

Union Business

Union attention focused on new actors in the primary institutional environment as negotiations for the first contract began in 1976. Local 2000 now had to place its demands before the state's Department of Personnel, rather than before the familiar administration of Cook County Public Aid. As part of Illinois American Federation of State, County, and Municipal Employees (A.F.S.C.M.E.), the Independent Union of Social Service Employees (I.U.S.S.E.) Local 2000 had to work for these demands together with representatives from other Illinois locals, and under the aegis of A.F.S.C.M.E.'s professional staff. These expanded institutional connections created new possibilities and problems for the union.

Contract Negotiations

Union leaders were eager to reap the benefits of establishing a collective bargaining relationship with the state, and assured the members of its value in a leaflet.

> For too many years, we in DPA and DVR have watched workers across the country enjoy the benefits and protections of a contract while we had none. THIS IS ABOUT TO CHANGE!

As negotiations commenced, first for clerks and then for paraprofessionals and professionals, members were told that they involved *"you* and *your* co-workers working together, united, for one pertinent cause—*your* contract."

Union leaders responded firmly to an effort of the opposition caucus to pressure the legislature for a raise before the start of the 1976 negotiations.

> No more begging in the Legislature. Through collective bargaining, we sit down as equals with management and negotiate with the power we possess as a Union, not only

154

[for] pay increases, but fringe benefits and your everyday working conditions: Promotions, work loads, holidays, leave, grievance procedure, etc. . . . *Let's start being realistic and prepare for the contract fight.* . . . *A decent pay raise can be negotiated, but if you are not protected on the job and if the other important conditions of work are not dealt with in the contract, you will have been sold out in the worst way.* (*Common Sense*, March 1976:4.)

Union representatives rejected an opposition caucus motion to take immediate action for a raise, in favor of an effort to secure improvements in employee pension provisions, a nonbargainable benefit.

Union negotiators plunged enthusiastically into debates over contract language and personnel procedures. Readers of the union newspaper were informed that the grievance procedure agreed on "required lengthy negotiating, and is the most important article in the contract" (*Common Sense*, November 1976:1). Negotiated personnel procedures were billed as the foundation for "the construction of the house . . . the wage package on top of the strong foundation" (*Common Sense*, November 1976:4). When the state balked at referring to clerks as "vital and necessary" in their contract, union clerical activists retorted that "you know and most important of all THEY know that they *CANNOT*" function without clerks. Throughout the union, supporters of the union leadership declared that "strong contract language will be our protection against anyone who tries to subvert the benefits which we will legitimately achieve in our contract" (*Common Sense*, November 1976:1).

For participants, contract negotiations were an exciting experience:

I loved participating in negotiations. It was one of the greatest experiences in my life. I was totally involved: seeing the contract being formed, with union input; learning how management thinks.

The experience also served to moderate the expectations of some activists.

We were in a group with employees from all over Illinois. We had different backgrounds, which made you realize why you don't get things. . . . AFSCME was new in many areas. . . . There was more realism in negotiations due to the presence of others.

PAY RAISE ACTIONS

Interest in achieving a pay raise could not easily be moderated among the union's membership. The union's president had to justify the postponement of negotiations over a raise until after other contract provisions had been worked out.

> Our first order of business is to get some of that power the State has had over us for years and to get back our dignity [through contract provisions protecting employee rights] and then deal and fight on the pay raise and cost-of-living issues (Common Sense, May 1976:4).

By the time negotiations for a raise were the order of business, however, Governor Walker, who had promulgated the Executive Order allowing collective bargaining for state employees, had been defeated by a Republican, James Thompson. Much to its chagrin, A.F.S.C.M.E. found that Walker had decided to leave a decision on the pay raise up to his successor. While the lame-duck Governor was willing to sign the contract without a raise, he refused to begin bargaining for a raise.

After emergency meetings of statewide negotiating committees, Illinois A.F.S.C.M.E. rejected "Governor Walker's ultimatum." On January 3, 1976, the I.U.S.S.E. Local 2000 announced to its membership in a contentious leaflet:

UNION REJECTS CONTRACT
tells Walker to shove his ultimatum

The I.U.S.S.E. Local 2000 decided to hold meetings with its membership to plan subsequent action.

> After we hold enough of these meetings, a referendum of the membership will be taken, in which you will be asked to authorize your Executive Board to call for an action, which may include work actions up to and including a strike—if absolutely necessary. (Common Sense, February 1977:1.)

Having decided to "go down fighting rather than to submit" (Common Sense, February 1977:1, 3), union leaders held the referendum in March 1977. The referendum included a provision authorizing a dues increase once the raise was obtained. Upon passage of the referendum, union leaders asserted they would be returning to negotiations "with a loaded gun."

The gun was first displayed as negotiations were being conducted at a Chicago hotel. Chanting "No Pay, No Work," picketers outside of the hotel demonstrated they had reached "a fever pitch to demand a raise." Illinois A.F.S.C.M.E. then brought thousands of union members from locals around the state to a march on the Capitol in Springfield. Temporarily revitalized by the activity, some former members of the radical opposition caucus even led a group of marchers into the Governor's office to demand the wage increase.

Although no raise was forthcoming as a result of the demonstrations, the state agreed to have the issue arbitrated. On June 22, 1977, union and state negotiators approved the fact finder's recommendation. It granted a one-time $100 increase (to have no effect on base pay), liberalized rules for promotion to higher pay grades, and a $50 per month pay hike in the next year. The only provision for a raise before that time involved what came to be called the "if-come money." *If* the state had excess revenues at the end of the current fiscal year, it stipulated that a raise proportionate to the size of that surplus (up to a maximum of $50 per month) would *come* to employees.

The minimal pay raise agreement turned out to be a major setback for the union. Union members had expected to receive a much higher pay raise as a result of contract negotiations. "When the $67.50 checks came out [the $100 bonus, after taxes], members lined up for revocation cards [to terminate their union membership] at some offices"; in one large office in Cook County, fifty members withdrew their union affiliation. Local 2000 had found at least temporary defeat in the jaws of victory.

RENEWED CONFLICT WITHIN AND WITHOUT

The affiliation of the Independent Union of Social Service Employees with the American Federation of State, County, and Municipal Employees initially worked to the advantage of both. The I.U.S.S.E.'s backing helped A.F.S.C.M.E. to win each of the bargaining unit elections, and the prestige of A.F.S.C.M.E.'s name, as well as the funds A.F.S.C.M.E. provided for organizing, contributed to the I.U.S.S.E.'s renewed growth. As stipulated by the affiliation agreement, however, the extra funds for organizing, including the rebate of A.F.S.C.M.E.'s per capita membership tax, were ended after one year. At this point, relations between the local and its adopted parent began a period of deterioration.

Conflict Without

The first overt indication of serious differences between the local and A.F.S.C.M.E. appeared in contract negotiations. Feeling that A.F.S.C.M.E. staff were not allowing Local 2000's negotiators enough autonomy, Local 2000's leaders led a temporary walkout from the negotiations.

Another major controversy occurred when Illinois A.F.S.C.M.E. tried to persuade Local 2000 to participate in its regional council structure for grievance handling and contract administration.

> With the signing of these [first] contracts, the emphasis of the state [A.F.S.C.M.E.] organization will shift from organizing to the administration and enforcement of the negotiated contracts. This shift in emphasis will necessitate the formation of some type of Statewide council structure. (*Common Sense*, February 1977:1.)

In its normal operational arrangement, A.F.S.C.M.E. divided large states into regions, within which staff worked to process grievances and attend to other routine matters in all the State departments within each region. In Illinois, A.F.S.C.M.E. planned to create four regional "district councils" to provide these day-to-day services, with a "Technical Council" to coordinate administration of statewide functions. By the end of the year, I.U.S.S.E.'s leadership had concluded that the council structure would dilute their local's power and fragment member services (*Common Sense*, November 1977:1). The disparate structures of the I.U.S.S.E. Local 2000 and A.F.S.C.M.E. could not easily be brought together.

Conflict Within

Some I.U.S.S.E. Local 2000 activists did not support the Local's position toward A.F.S.C.M.E. One interviewee argued:

> AFSCME and Local 2000 are one, and disagreements should not lead to such fights. . . . We can accomplish change through working together.

When other members of Local 2000 walked out of contract negotiations to protest A.F.S.C.M.E.'s position, these activists remained. In the months after the negotiations, they formed a new faction within the Local.

Most of the initiators of the new faction had been backers of the "Contract Action Slate" headed by Max Liberles in the 1976 election. Now, they adopted the name "Contract Action" for themselves, and began actively to organize against the current union leadership. When write-in votes for a Representative Council candidate were not counted, a Contract Action supporter filed charges with the Local's Mediation Council. When the union's leadership tried to reduce travel costs to an A.F.S.C.M.E. convention in Las Vegas by trimming its representation from five to two delegates, the Contract Action-dominated Mediation Council refused to permit this.

Contract Action continued its opposition role in the 1978 union election. In appeals to members, the slate criticized the retroactive dues increase and the meager raise obtained in the first contract. Contract Action supporters even filed charges with A.F.S.C.M.E.'s Judicial Panel to prevent President Liberles from deducting dues money from the $100 retroactive "lump sum payment" the union had won from the State (*de Pue et al. v. Liberles*). (Contract Action lost the case.) The termination of the I.U.S.S.E.'s credit union due to accounting irregularities was also a point of criticism, as was the decline in the union's membership precipitated by the first contract settlement (Figure 1).

In addition to personal rivalries, criticisms of leader practices, and differences in orientation to A.F.S.C.M.E.'s positions, the split between the leadership and the new opposition faction tapped differences between clerical and caseworker members. When clerical and caseworker negotiators were brought together for the final stage of contract negotiations, "it almost became a battle between the professionals and clerks." The clerks tended to support the stance of the union's president, Max Liberles, and his Executive Board, while many caseworker negotiators were involved in the opposition.

Caseworker dissatisfaction with the union stemmed in part from the effects of the career ladder.

> I . . . couldn't get a promotion. It was not fair for clerical seniority to count as equivalent to caseworker seniority.

While the union continued to support the career ladder, some professionals felt that their position as professionals had been eroded.

> There is resentment of the career ladder by college grads. . . . The motives for the union's position are that seniority is objective and to help minorities, but the union went too far. Employees with talent are not willing to wait twenty years. It is not possible to promote the best new employees to the top.

Dissatisfaction with the career ladder was not the only basis of division between members in lower- and higher-paid occupations. Some activists who had risen to caseworker status from clerical jobs as a result of the career ladder also disagreed with the orientations of clerical activists. The cumulative effect of the flat amount raises negotiated by the union was a particular source of dissatisfaction. Translated into percentage terms, these had amounted to about three to four percent gains for members in the professional unit, while clerks had gained raises of about ten percent. In an inflationary economy, some members in the higher pay grades felt they were being disproportionately penalized. Union staff began to find that clerks were easier to recruit into the union than caseworkers.

In the minds of many union activists in both factions, however, differences in the goals of the two factions were negligible. "They both want higher wages, timely grievance processing. The real issue is, who is in the driver's seat."

The enmity between the two sides found expression in the 1978 election. Calling itself the "Max/Tish Pay Raise Slate" after the first names of its presidential and vice-presidential candidates, the union's leadership found that it had to oppose many of its former supporters in the "Contract Action" slate. Remembered as "a nasty campaign . . . a lot of personal attacks . . . hot and heavy," the election ended with charges of vote fraud directed against the victorious "Max/ Tish" slate. After a "Gilbert and Sullivan scenario" of charges and countercharges, and an unsuccessful hearing before A.F.S.C.M.E.'s Judicial Panel (In re: Local 2000), the Contract Action slate lost by just 908 to 1,134. A third slate comprised of two of the leaders of the former radical opposition secured a total of just 82 votes.

Organizers for the new Contract Action faction were unable to maintain their level of member support. In the 1980 election, they failed to mount an effective campaign, and received only 515 votes to the 1,200 received by the "Max/Tish Pay Raise Slate."

CHANGES AT WORK

As conflict rose and then ebbed again within the union, the organization of public aid work continued to change. Under a fiscally conservative state Republican administration, efforts to control welfare costs heightened (Weatherley, 1983:49). It was not enough to organize public aid in a manner more conducive to efficiency. This efficiency had to be demonstrated. In Illinois, a "Governor's Cost Control Task Force" identified "duplication, overlapping, and functional ineffectiveness" in the organization of public aid (Illinois House of Representatives, 1980). Around the nation, welfare administrators sought to reduce waste and increase productivity (Teare, 1981:7; Weatherley, et al., 1980:557).

Special service units staffed by Caseworkers IV were an early casualty of the cost control emphasis. While separation had routinized work to some extent for income maintenance caseworkers, the less specialized work in service units had defied attempts to set production standards. In addition, several important social service functions had been shifted to other state departments (such as the Department of Aging and the Division of Children and Family Services), and service workers in public aid were soon largely limited to arranging day care, providing information, and referring clients to other agencies. By 1981, there seemed to be little justification for maintaining service units in public aid, and the service side of the separation experiment had ended (Zashin and Summers, 1980).

Concern with cost control led to efforts to automate intake and income maintenance work (Goodsell, 1981; Weatherley, et al., 1980:564; Zashin and Summers, 1980). The agency also attempted to increase the standard of thirty redeterminations per month, contract out the work of Homemakers, and investigate employees who falsified work records, failed to visit clients on "district days," and abused the two-hour leave granted for voting in regular state and national elections. Articles in the union's newspaper warned employees to "Watch Your Step" and "Beware: Investigations" (*Common Sense*, December 1978:1; July 1, 1979:1; August 20, 1979:2).

Among the casework staff, these new policies generated some discontent:

> Formerly, caseworkers had to do case narratives with a written history on each visit. Now, they just check blanks on forms.
> Many college grads are going to Children and Family Services, so they can deal with bigger problems in a more professional light. Public aid is like an assembly line.

Other studies indicated that caseworkers valued the latitude for expression allowed by the traditional narrative forms (Weatherley, et al., 1980:564), and found higher levels of hierarchical control at work to be stressful (Goodsell, 1981).

Efforts were also made to modify the career ladder. It had been a mixed blessing for the agency. The opportunities for upward mobility provided by the career ladder probably helped to mitigate dissatisfaction among employees potentially eligible for it (Doeringer and Piore, 1971; Edwards, 1979:130–47). However, the agency had allowed clerical employees to become eligible for caseworker positions as a result of negotiations with the union. Initially, the caseworker career ladder was to have been open to paraprofessionals only. Union insistence in bargaining that seniority, rather than performance, was to be the primary basis for progression up the ladder had also modified the agency's original plan (*Common Sense*, March 1975:1). Now, at least some administrators felt that some caseworkers were not proficient in written communication, and were making errors in interpreting policy and determining grant levels. New exams were adopted to screen employees seeking to become caseworkers and supervisory caseworkers. The union found itself trying to prevent the agency from hiring caseworkers directly from outside the agency. (*Common Sense*, July 1, 1980:1.)

Another problem also emerged at the Caseworker V level. New employees had probationary status for their first six months, and were subject to termination during this period if they failed to perform acceptably. After this period, union and Civil Service protections made the removal of employees much more difficult. Supervisory caseworkers (Caseworkers V) were responsible for determining whether to terminate probationary employees. However, many Caseworkers V were old union members, and were reluctant to fire new union members. In order to lessen this apparent conflict of interest, the agency sought to have Caseworkers V removed from the bargaining unit. In spite of union arguments that they were being led "Like Lambs to the Slaughter," some Caseworkers V argued for decertification as a means of upgrading their classification (*Common Sense*, October 1, 1979:1).

The Union as a Business

The union responded to these problems without the confrontationist spirit of its earlier days.

> Collective bargaining is a different ball game. The union must be more orderly. There are contractual limits. When you are "in the jungle" [without a contract], anything goes if you have the strength.

Union staff became more skilled in filing grievances, and these and litigation were the preferred tactics. "You didn't go out and organize and have any actions," a former supporter of the radical opposition recalled, "you went and you did a grievance." In spite of complaints that the agency was generating too many grievances, union staff became oriented to processing them (*Common Sense*, November 1979:1; Zashin and Summers, 1980:11).

> I enjoy seeing a group turn on about an issue, seeing the membership increase, and winning grievances for members who are unjustly treated. There is satisfaction in winning. . . . I look on my job as fun and exciting.

Legal action also provided some satisfactions. In an important legal victory, union attorneys persuaded the Illinois Office of Collective Bargaining that the agency had bargained in bad faith in 1977, and had engaged in unfair labor practices when supervisors made anti-union remarks in meetings with employees (*In the Matter of IUSSE and IDPA, IDP*). In February 1983, the U.S. Court of Appeals supported the union's position in its twelve-year-old discrimination suit on behalf of former case aides and trainees, and awarded $15 million in back pay (*Boston Globe*, February 21, 1983:34).

Member involvement declined dramatically after the first contract was signed. In its efforts to reverse this decline, the union's approach was also markedly different from its earlier appeals to employees to join in reforming the welfare system. In 1977, the union gave members a "chance to win your own portable color TV'" for signing up the most new members. In 1979, another "incentive program" was formulated to increase membership: "$5.00 will be awarded to a member in good standing who signs up a new member in accordance with the following rules." Other prizes were also raffled. Three hundred members were recruited as a result. In 1981, members were urged to "sign up your desk mate now and earn yourself some cash while doing so"; the per-member award was increased to ten dollars to compensate for inflation.

As conflict with the Contract Action faction declined after the 1978 election, meetings of the Representative Council became more orderly. "They're not as long, not as wild and crazy." At the same time, the relative influence of the Representative Council on union affairs declined. The role of stewards, charged with handling grievances for members, became more important.

> At one time, Reps played a key role in the union, and stewards were ignored. Now, stewards are on top, and Reps are number two. . . . Reps do not do their homework on issues members are concerned with. They accept the posture of the Executive Board. . . . Now stewards are more important, and answer complaints, and are therefore better informed.

The center of conflict within the union had finally cooled.

CONCLUSIONS

Changes in the union during this last period continued to remove its GIST configuration further from that adopted during its formation. Economic goals were treated as primary for the union, and the union's incumbent president and vice-president campaigned successfully as the "Pay Raise Slate." In practice, increasing attention was given to employment security issues: employee discipline, job classification, and layoffs. Client issues were not at issue, however. Clashes between "bread and butter" and "socially conscious" members were a thing of the past.

Grievances, negotiations, and legal action were the preferred union tactics in this period. Remarkable gains were won as a result of union law suits over promotion opportunities and pay. Staff became increasingly proficient at handling member grievances, and viewed this as a primary activity. Contract negotiations were no longer seen as ensuring achievement of goals, but they continued to be a focus of union strategy. Local work actions rarely occurred, and were viewed by union leaders more with nostalgia than as an effective tactic.

Union structure had continued its bureaucratic trend. Max Liberles, the incumbent president, continued to be reelected. Union business, including most direct membership contact, was increasingly handled by paid staff, and members of the union's Executive Board themselves worked full-time for the union. A professional editor was hired to prepare the union's newspaper, ending the use of member volunteers. The Representative Council played a less significant role in union business, while stewards, the office-level grievance handlers, became the focus of members' attention.

Membership involvement again declined during this period. Economic incentives were used to encourage member recruitment of new employees, but complaints about member inactivity continued. In contrast to the frequent fear in earlier years that the factional battles in the Representative Council disillusioned new members, concern was expressed about the low levels of participation by Representatives to the Council.

The changes in the union's social environment that had begun in the previous period of its development continued in the following years, and were reflected in a new episode of factional conflict. The reorganized caseworker job no longer provided much structural support for caseworker efforts to organize around client issues. Such concerns, which had formerly been most apparent among the college-educated white caseworker staff, were less apparent among those caseworkers previously in clerical and paraprofessional positions. Many of the caseworkers most concerned with service had been promoted to Caseworker IV and V positions, and thus were less directly affected by the routinization of Caseworker III work.

Factional conflict was directly influenced by the career ladder. Members who had experienced upward mobility from clerical to caseworker positions were a particularly conservative force in the union, and their leaders tended to emphasize the value of closer relationships with the Illinois A.F.S.C.M.E. organization. Clerical members continued to provide strong support for the Local's leaders, but were less involved in union politics than other groups. Among college-educated caseworkers, dissatisfaction with the career ladder and with flat-amount raises was voiced for the first time in the union. The new opposition faction's eventual failure to unite the two different groups of caseworkers reflected the depth of this new division in the work force.

The Illinois state government provided a markedly less favorable environment for I.U.S.S.E. Local 2000 even by the end of its first contract negotiations. A more conservative state government allowed state employees only limited economic gains, and began to make changes in the administration of public aid to reduce costs. The union found itself increasingly involved in "defensive" action, and could do little to secure new gains.

Affiliation with a national union had facilitated rapid union growth in the previous period, but a host of problems in interorganizational relations had yet to be overcome. As the largest A.F.S.C.M.E. local in Illinois, I.U.S.S.E. Local 2000 received sufficient dues money to maintain more autonomy from A.F.S.C.M.E. than was traditional in the larger union. Local 2000's leaders tried to prevent any of their responsibilities from being delegated upward to A.F.S.C.M.E. staff, while the members of Local 2000 involved in contract negotiations found that employees in other agencies within the A.F.S.C.M.E. bargaining units tended to have more conservative outlooks than public aid employees. The attempt to combine two established organizational structures and to unify two different types of membership generated clashes for several years.

In this period of diminished availability of resources from the institutional level of its environment, I.U.S.S.E. Local 2000 had difficulty in compensating with greater resources from the social level of its environment. Having adopted a relatively bureaucratic structure, the intense office-level organizing activity that had led members to contribute such substantial resources during the union's formative period rarely occurred. The availability of paid union staff to handle grievances contributed to this situation by decreasing the role of office-level leaders.

As during the years after the second strike, a structure oriented to securing resources from the institutional environment was less capable of securing resources from the social environment. But unlike the earlier period of deficient resources, there were few opposition activists to encourage member involvement in alternative office-level union activities. It was not until relations with A.F.S.C.M.E. improved and the union's staff gained enough experience that the new structure was able to handle union business efficiently, begin to achieve grievance victories from the agency, and draw more employees into the union.

In spite of the decline in availability of resources from the union's institutional environment, the union's structure did not change back toward a more participatory style. Leaders and their staff valued the challenges and variety in their union work, and sought to maintain their positions in the union's structure. Reorganization had increased the difference in the work situations of union leaders and staff compared to that of their membership, and made the thought of returning to public aid work less palatable. Now the internal forces described by Michels and other classic organizational theorists appeared to impede reversal of the transformation process.

CHAPTER ELEVEN

The GIST of Organizational Development

An organization that changes from the style of a social movement to one more like a business travels across familiar territory. The transformation of voluntary organizations from more participatory to more bureaucratic styles occurs with such regularity that variation *from* that pattern is of greater interest than conformance to it. As history, the development of the Independent Union of Public Aid Employees was sufficiently unique to generate some insights into the process of transformation but insufficiently so to be an exception that "proves the rule" (cf. Lipset, Trow, and Coleman, 1962).

It is as a vehicle for the elaboration of organizational theory that the study of the I.U.P.A.E. is of greatest value. The GIST model of organizations and the associated two-dimensional model of their environments provide new conceptual tools for describing the variable configurations of voluntary organizations and their environments. By systematically connecting organizational processes to the features of organizational environments, the resource substitution theory provides a new approach to the explanation of organizational transformation. This approach recasts the problem of organizational transformation from Michels' Iron Law into the greater complexity and variability of social reality.

Evaluation of the new approach in this book has relied on the history of one organization. The Illinois Union of Public Aid Employees was typical of many unions, and in more general respects typical of other voluntary organizations as well. The I.U.P.A.E. was formed in the same turbulent environment of the 1960s that spawned welfare employee unions throughout the nation, as well as a host of other new public and private white-collar unions. In other respects, the story of the I.U.P.A.E./I.U.S.S.E. Local 2000 was more unique. The persistence of factional conflict, the initial participatory democratic structure, the persistent distrust of large unions, and the propensity of some members to mobilize office actions in response to work place problems each distinguished the I.U.P.A.E. from a great many other public employee unions. Application of the new theoretical framework can provide a conclusion to the analysis of the I.U.P.A.E., but only a starting point for attempts to assess the general utility of this framework for the study of other organizations.

The GIST of Union History

Organizational Change

The GIST model yields parsimonious descriptions of voluntary organizations that still capture the essential dimensions of their variation. Distinguishing two organizational dimensions, involvement and tactics, that tie the organization to its environment, the GIST model facilitates development of environmentally centered theory. Throughout the analysis, description of the I.U.P.A.E. in terms of the GIST model has confirmed its utility.

At its emergence in 1965, the I.U.P.A.E.'s GIST configuration consisted of the goal of welfare system reforming, the intense involvement of members, a participatory democratic structure, and tactical militancy. At the new union's first constitutional convention, held before the union was one year old, a modified representative democratic structure was adopted. The I.U.P.A.E. would now have one president, with authority to speak for the organization, and somewhat less direct involvement of the membership in the running of the union. Although a set of four vice-presidential positions suggested some continued allegiance to a collective leadership style, the union's structure had clearly become more hierarchical. Tactical militancy reached its height during the two strikes during this period, and membership involvement continued at a high level until the union's defeat in the 1967 strike. Social reform concerns were still reflected in official union goals, and they were useful in appeals to other organizations and individuals for support during the strikes, as well as in efforts to increase union membership among caseworkers. However, the primary goal of the union's strikes became the internal union concern of securing recognition and a contract, and those most supportive of social reform efforts consistently lost bids for election to the union presidency.

This GIST configuration began to change after the second strike. Membership involvement in the union plummeted, and militant tactics were employed mostly at the office level, without central coordination. Union leaders processed grievances and engaged in some negotiations with agency officials, but generally had little impact on the agency. At the second constitutional convention in 1970, formal union goals and structure were again changed. A more hierarchical structure was adopted, giving the union's representative body somewhat less power, doubling the term of office of the top elected leadership, and ending direct delegate control of the president's salary. The new statement of formal union goals emphasized collective bargaining and economic concerns, and largely dropped commitment to welfare reform.

As the process of institutionalization proceeded, the union's GIST characteristics again changed. Membership involvement rose dramatically, and union leaders successfully employed negotiations and meetings with agency officials to resolve many problems. While the union's formal structure was not altered, the increasing funds received due to affiliation with a national union in 1973 and the associated increase in membership enabled union leaders to hire more staff and increase their influence in meetings of the union's representative body. During this period, union leaders as well as opposition activists emphasized economic gains for members.

Membership involvement declined during the last period studied. At this point, starting in 1977, economic and job security issues were the union's chief concern, and grievances, negotiations, and legal action were the preferred means to achieve them. The union's structure exhibited more bureaucratic features than at any other time in the union's development.

This qualitative description of changes in the union's GIST configuration can be supplemented with results of a content analysis of union literature. A sample of union leaflets and newspaper articles produced throughout its history was coded for references to GIST dimensions (see Appendix). Changes in the proportion of literature with references to three of the four dimensions were apparent (Table 16). In their references to union goals, client issues and service policy declined. However, attention to employee economic goals for pay and benefits did not increase correspondingly. Such economic goals were emphasized during the two periods of rapid union growth, 1965–67 and 1973–76. During the other two periods, economic goals were mentioned less frequently, although still more often than other goals. Emphasis given to other goals changed in tandem with agency policy. Concern with work loads rose into the period of reorganization of public aid (1973–76), and then declined. Concern with layoffs and especially discipline, however, grew in the most recent periods, as the public aid agency felt increasing pressures to cut costs. Throughout the union's history, internal organizational maintenance goals appeared in one-third of the union publications.

There was only a slight decline in references to militant tactics during the union's history, and this decline was primarily accounted

Table 16. Content Analysis of Union Communications, 1965–1980

GIST Dimension/Issue	65–67	Second Strike[a]	68–72	73–76	77–80
Goals					
Hiring, Promotion	8%	15%	8%	17%	40%
Pay, Benefits	76	74	56	69	47
Layoff	8	0	2	23	20
Workload	19	36	34	54	20
Discipline	0	0	11	13	20
Clients	11	2	16	8	0
Union	34	62	31	21	33
Working Conditions	6	2	12	10	0
Other	16	2	11	9	0
Tactics					
Strike	35%	97%	15%	17%	16%
Other Militant Action	26	3	42	41	36
Negotiations	36	10	26	30	14
Legal Action	9	7	25	18	64
Political Action	26	1	29	31	14
Other	7	0	22	19	29
Participation (any reference to)	57%	31%	81%	73%	41%
Structure (any reference to)	14%	20%	9%	43%	47%
Weighted N	66	33	100	139	23
Total unweighted N = 362					

NOTE: Percentages are proportion of union publications.
[a] Literature from the second strike is treated separately because its volume substantially exceeded that produced in any other period.

for by a decline in reference to striking after the second strike. Frequency of mention of other types of tactics did not vary in a systematic historical pattern, except for a marked increase in references to legal action during the final period. Discussion of structural issues increased in the last two periods of union development, while references to member participation first increased, and then declined into the last period.

These findings are generally consistent with the description of organizational development obtained in the historical analysis. Their partial lack of correspondence to that description may be due to the content analysis' lack of sensitivity to the content of messages about particular issues, rather than to its greater sensitivity to underlying patterns. However, the findings do suggest caution in generalizations about several dimensions of the historical description. First, organizational maintenance may be a relatively constant concern of organizations, rather than a goal that begins to displace external concerns as organizations develop. This was apparent in the I.U.P.A.E.'s early concern with securing recognition, and little indication of a slacking of interest in this goal was apparent in the union literature. Second, external goals may be determined largely by the environment confronted by an organization at a particular point, rather than by any tendency toward secular increases or decreases in emphasis on particular types of goals.

Environmental Change

The union's environment changed markedly as the union developed. Changes in public aid influenced the distribution of grievances and resources in the union's social environment. In the mid-1960s, grievances among public aid employees had proliferated as established patterns of agency functioning broke down in the face of the welfare explosion. While public aid had been able to provide few of the rewards of professional social work, patterns of supervision and socialization had facilitated employee adaptation to its more bureaucratic milieu. However, the rapid expansion of case loads required an increase in the proportion of new employees in the public aid work force, while the concomitant growth of the student movement on college campuses ensured that many of these new employees would be unwilling to accommodate to the pressures in public aid. Prior experiences of some new caseworkers in the student movement could be put to work in unionizing public aid, while the diffuse contacts of caseworkers with clients created another source of resources for organizing. A tendency to eschew individually centered professional approaches to social problems in favor of social reform reduced any remaining ideological impediments to unionization.

Reorganization of public aid work lessened the proportion of the casework staff from college backgrounds, and reduced the discretionary authority of most caseworkers in contacts with clients. Both changes reduced the resources available for union organizing, and lessened grievances due to disjunctures between professional orientations and bureaucratic work. Some more experienced caseworkers were able to begin work in more challenging positions. The result again was fewer grievances to motivate union activity, and fewer resources to bring to it. Employees not in the union, its secondary social environment, were clearly now a less fertile source of new members.

Reorganization was followed by increasing efforts to control costs and monitor employee performance. Economic grievances among employees appeared to rise, although the need for resolution of these grievances in the state political arena outside of public aid meant that they produced less conflict within the agency itself. Pressures for a faster work pace renewed grievances over work loads, but these grievances were expressed without the involvement of client groups common in earlier years. The career ladder enabling mobility from the clerical to caseworker level also changed the bases of conflict within the agency. Upwardly mobile clerical members tended to be more satisfied with their work and more committed to employment in the agency than college-trained caseworkers.

Fundamental changes also occurred in the union's institutional environment. State takeover of public aid ended years of ambiguity concerning which agency actually determined work conditions for the Cook County Department of Public Aid's employees. Development of a collective bargaining relationship with the state government brought the union into a more dense matrix of ties to its primary institutional environment. Affiliation with the American Federation of State, County, and Municipal Employees brought another organization into that primary institutional environment. Together, these changes transformed the context of union action.

Union ties to organizations in its secondary institutional environment were important at various times in its development. Community and other political groups were active during the union's emergence, while welfare rights group activity was at its peak during the post-strike years. During the middle period of its history, radical political groups, primarily the Progressive Labor Party, had a significant impact on the union.

An External Interpretation

The theory of resource substitution links these changes in the union's environment to the internal changes in the union's GIST configuration. In its initial period, the I.U.P.A.E.'s GIST configuration reflected a high degree of dependence on its social environment. Member grievances were translated directly into union goals, and a participatory structure relied on substantial contributions of member resources. Militant tactics and high levels of involvement reflected close connections to the social environment, and an absence of established relations in the institutional environment.

Factionalism quickly emerged in this highly participatory environment, and was expressed in sharp divergence in the union goals desired by different groups of members. Due to the union's dependence on its social environment for resources, factions were not at a disadvantage in internal conflict and were able to persist for a long period. Even in the early stages of its development, however, a difference was apparent in the orientations of union leaders and of the opposition faction to the union's environment. The social reform goals associated with the early opposition were generally not accepted as legitimate in the union's institutional environment. Union action over such issues violated established organizational boundaries, and thus was not sanctioned by those within the union primarily concerned with institutional legitimacy. Less likely to be able to secure resources from the institutional environment, members supportive of social reform goals also tended to argue for preservation of the participatory structure that maximized the union's ability to draw resources from its social environment.

The union's first bid for institutional acceptance failed. Although members had experienced a sense of power stemming from their collective efforts, the failure of connection to the institutional environment left the union outside the established matrix of interorganizational relations. Inadequate support for the second strike from the substantial number of nonmembers in the agency's work force left the union without the resources needed to prevail.

Continued grievances felt by workers in the overburdened public aid offices as well as the maintenance of substantial resources among the casework staff enabled the union to continue after its failure in the second strike. The activity of welfare rights groups and of radical political organizations in the union's secondary institutional environment also helped the opposition faction to sustain its activity. In the hope of securing institutional legitimacy, the union's leadership modified union goals and structure in a more traditional direction, but without noticeable impact on the union's success. The union was "becalmed" (Zald and Ash, 1966:329–36).

The advent of collective bargaining rights for state employees created new opportunities for union influence and resource acquisition. Union leaders emphasized the utility of institutionally legitimate tactics, while opposition activists, no longer differing in goal preferences, now made tactical militancy their basic concern. An increasingly bureaucratic structure facilitated union interchange with the institutional environment, and helped to skew the distribution of resources within the union in favor of the leadership. At the same time, changes in the union's social environment due to the reorganization of public aid reduced the ability of the internal opposition to expand its base of support.

As the dependence of the union on its institutional environment increased, membership involvement declined. Union efforts to secure gains for members became more business-like, and relied less on direct member activism. The complexity of the activity of union leaders and staff increased, even while the complexity of work in public aid had declined. The basis for more leader and staff interest in maintaining the current structure was greater than at any previous point in the union's history. In spite of problems of institutional-level resource procurement under a new state administration, efforts to increase member involvement were limited, and no attempt was made to return to a more participatory structure.

This pattern of organization–environment interaction is consistent with the resource substitution theory of organizational transformation. The initial union GIST configuration was highly dependent on resources from the social environment. It was subject to pressures for change due to factional conflict and an inability to achieve goals in the institutional environment. Bureaucratization and institutionalization were viable responses to these problems because of the substitutability of resources. After the union's institutionalization, resources from its institutional environment replaced those previously obtained in its social environment.

The process of translating member grievances into organizational goals is a critical means for external influence on the internal politics of voluntary organizations. But resistance to particular goals in the organization's institutional environment makes continued emphasis on these goals more or less likely. Organizational goals are thus codetermined by the social and institutional levels of the organization's environment. Fluctuating attention to different goals during the I.U.P.A.E.'s history, and even the overall shift from social reform to economic concerns, can be explained in terms of these processes. No "iron law" need apply.

DEVELOPING THEORY

The theoretical perspective used to explain the development of the Illinois welfare services employees' union was tailored to the problem of emergence and change in voluntary organizations. Clarifying the relationship between this perspective and the broader body of research and theory on social movements and organizations will help to identify those aspects of modern theory that are most relevant to the study of voluntary organizations, as well as to indicate the generalizability of the GIST perspective to other types of organizations.

Grievances and Resources

(1) *The Importance of Grievances.* Recognition of the importance of resource availability represented an important advance in the explanation of social movements and associated protest organizations. Both traditional collective behavior and Marxist explanations of protest assumed that grievances were its source. Although they differed in evaluating these grievances as irrational (collective behavior) or rational (Marxist), the neglect of resources by both perspectives impaired their ability to explain much of the variation in organizational emergence.

The new resource dependence approach initially focused solely on the importance of resources, and assumed that grievances were constant or at least always sufficiently high. However, research attempting to confirm the new approach tended merely to *illustrate* the importance of resources, rather than to test for the relative impact of grievances and resources. As empirical researchers turned to more adequately specified models, it became clear that resources and grievances *both* contribute to the emergence of protest (Klandermans, 1984). Moreover, other factors that could be termed constraints also appeared to be important. Thus, activism among local opponents to the Three Mile Island nuclear utility had more of the resources associated with higher socioeconomic status and involvement with others, higher levels of discontent with the nuclear industry, and more liberal and distrustful political attitudes (Walsh and Warland, 1983). The failure of engineers to unionize in response to declining status and security during the 1970s appeared to stem from a professional ideology constraining collective action, as well as from their inadequate bargaining power, job security, and other resources (Latta, 1981). The identification of grievances, resources, and constraints as important in the unionization of public welfare employees thus is consistent with the direction of modern social movement theory.

(2) Grievances and Self-Interest. Mancur Olson (1971) presented another challenge to grievance-based explanations of protest organizations in *The Logic of Collective Action.* Protest organizations, Olson noted, seek to achieve public goods that benefit potential members whether the members actually contribute to the organization or not. The effect of any one member is so slight that it becomes irrational for him or her to make a substantial contribution to the organization. As a result, it is not in the self-interest of any potential member to join or otherwise contribute to the achievement of the public good through the protest organization.

Olson suggested that *selective* incentives made available to individual members could overcome the constraint imposed by the illogic of collective action. The status, income, and other benefits accruing to organizational leaders exemplify the use of selective incentives. Such incentives may also be dispensed to members. In the welfare employees' union, its credit union, group discount vacation trips, and grievance processing all represented the use of selective incentives.

> But we cannot avoid the recognition that many individual
> members cannot be explained in terms of "selective
> incentives" unless we stretch the concept so as to lose any
> distinctive meaning and include sentiments ranging from fairly

unreflective party loyalty to an elaborated set of political beliefs (Barry, 1978:42–43).

Additional factors are needed to explain the contributions of most members to protest organizations.

Feelings of group solidarity may blur the distinction between individual and collective goods (Fireman and Gamson, 1979). Such feelings tend to emerge in groups bound by dense social relations, common orientations, and a shared situation. These feelings may be expressed in ideologies that attribute to the movement a significance going beyond the immediate self-interest of participants (Barry, 1978:36–39). In the welfare employees' union, the association of support for paraprofessional goals with participation by caseworkers, and the relation of identification with clients and distrust of business and government all indicated the importance of group solidarity and ideology.

Belief in the efficacy of participation is also related to the act of participation. When members or potential members feel that the movement/organization is near success and that a final push will achieve spectacular results, they are more likely to contribute (Barry, 1978:29–32, 39). In the welfare employees' union, the rapid rise in recruitment and member activity after the first strike's success and then again after national union affiliation and the advent of collective bargaining confirms this expectation. The rapid decline in membership and participation after the failure of the second strike, and the similar response to the problems in the first contract, are also consistent with the addition of efficacy to the prediction equation for collective action. At the individual level, high rates of participation among upwardly mobile clerks are consistent with the frequent finding of an association between feelings of efficacy and participation (Guterbock and London, 1983).

Whatever its limitations, Mancur Olson's (1971) seminal work focused attention on the role of self-interest calculations in collective action. Throughout the development of the welfare employees' union, there was abundant support for the importance of self-interest calculations. This was most apparent in the course of factional conflict in the union. Caseworker activists tended to focus on the problems in caseloads and welfare policy that affected their jobs, while clerical and other low-paid employees were more concerned with economic rewards. Appeals of the opposition to clerical and other low-paid employees failed to result in radical clerical activism. The greater economic concerns of these employees, and of black employees in professional positions, continued to maintain their support for the union leadership and its primary orientation to economic needs at least until the first contract was negotiated. The radical faction itself was forced to recognize the importance of self-interest and began to emphasize economic issues. When the relative income advantage of union members in professional positions declined after several flat-amount pay increases, the concern of professional employees with economic gains increased. Self-interest differences between employees thus shaped political conflict within the union.

In spite of the manifest importance of self-interest, the union's history fails to confirm Olson's assumption of a narrow, individualistic basis for its calculation. When grievances were high, resources available, and constraints against action low, individuals did not fail to contribute to the achievement of collective goods because they could expect to attain them without much effort. When it appeared that the *sum* of the contributions of individual employees was likely to result in the attainment of the collective good, many were willing to contribute. Stimulated for some by solidary ties and ideological interpretations, and for most by the expectation of success, attention to self-interest became less of a bar to collective action than Olson's formulation allowed. It was in periods when prospects for success were clearly low, and solidary and ideological commitments had ebbed, that selective incentives became critical for maintaining some level of collective commitment among employees.

(3) Self-Interest and Democracy. While cleavages on the basis of self-interest appear to be predictable in a heterogeneous group, such cleavage has been viewed by some as inimical to the maintenance of organizational democracy. Lipset, Trow, and Coleman (1962) concluded that the absence of self-interest cleavages among printers was a primary reason for the persistence of democracy in their union. Since union election outcomes did not differentially affect the self-interests of any groups of printers, incumbent officers and their supporters did not attempt to preserve their power by any means necessary. Differences in support for militant tactics provided a basis for cleavage between the union's two parties that was not threatening to the maintenance of democracy. In a comparative study of union locals, however, Cook (1963) concluded that self-interest cleavages are conducive to democracy. Because they are relatively enduring, Cook reasoned, self-interest-based cleavages could provide a stable basis for democratic conflict.

Neglected in both these approaches are the consequences of differing resources between the groups in conflict. When the array of individual and organizational resources available to groups in conflict are relatively equal, democracy is more likely to persist. When one group has substantially greater resources, organizational goals and tactics will tend to be skewed in its favor, and the chances of its electoral loss to other groups will be minimal. Democratic rule will suffer regardless of the bases of cleavage. It is because cleavages on the basis of self-interest are typically associated with differences in resources between contending groups that Lipset, Trow, and Coleman's (1962) caution is warranted. The homogeneity of income and status among printers equalized resources available to the two parties in the International Typographical Union. Autonomy of the chapel, or shop, from the union's administration increased the ability of chapel leaders to mobilize resources from their social environment, without constraints imposed by the union's administration. However, alternative sources of resources could enable even an economically disadvantaged group to be successful in factional conflict.

External or Internal Influence

The basic weakness in Michels' analysis of the oligarchic transformation of the German Social Democratic Party was his view of that process as "immanent" in organization itself. The GIST approach, in contrast, views interchange with the environment as both inevitable and consequential for organizations. While the goals and structure of an organization set it apart from its environment, involvement and tactics bring both the social and institutional levels of the environment to bear on the organization. The variability of the environment ensures change in organizations, and makes untenable the assumption of inevitability in the particular direction this change takes.

Sociologists have increasingly turned to the environment to explain processes in voluntary organizations. However, the resulting explanations have frequently suffered from only partial conceptions of organizational and environmental variability, and from a tendency to rely on internal explanations without examination of external alternatives. Roomkin (1976), for example, attributed a decline in strike frequency to a growing hierarchical concentration of power in unions on the basis of a simple correlation between these two variables. The possibility that changes in the external environment may have accounted for both of these changes was not studied. Windmuller (1981) also identified a trend toward increasing concentration of power in European and American unions. He speculated that this trend resulted from such environmental factors as changes in the labor force and technology. However, he did not conceive of these factors as lessening resources in the unions' social environments, nor test his interpretation against the traditional internal perspective. McAdam (1983) chronicled the shifting protest tactics employed by the civil rights movement, and identified the motivation for its tactical innovation in the ability of the movement's institutional environment to develop effective control strategies. There was no consideration of variation in support for the movement within its social environment, however, nor analysis of the extent to which institutionalization of the movement decreased the need for noninstitutionalized tactics. Only recently have empirical analyses of the determinants of strike frequency noted the importance of both the grievances and resources available in union social environments and the relations of unions with other organizations (Kaufman, 1982; Skeels, 1982).

The GIST model of organizations, the associated two-dimensional model of their environments, and the principle of resource substitution that links them provide a means for substantially increasing the explanatory power of environmentally centered theory. However, this does not mean that the status advantages of leaders, the attachment of leaders to their positions, or their identification with the social elite are unimportant aspects of organizations (Schwartz, Rosenthal, and Schwartz, 1981). Rather, the source of these internal characteristics can be found in the environment. Institutionalization generates a need for upper-status leaders who can negotiate with leaders of other organizations. This is especially noticeable in those organizations with lower-status memberships, such as many unions and protest groups, whose primary institutional environment consists of organizations with high status leaders. However, the same basic processes are at work in any voluntary organization.

External factors can even reverse the expected pattern of organizational change. For example, in the 1970s the pro-nuclear power movement shifted from traditional lobbying tactics to direct mobilization of citizen support. This reverse transformation was a consequence of the partial "deinstitutionalization" of the movement due to the impact of the anti-nuclear power movement on the government. Faced with a loss of resources in its institutional environment, even the companies supporting nuclear power had to attempt to obtain resources from their social environment. (Useem and Zald, 1982.)

Internal factors do create an inertia that slows organizational change. For example, even as it became increasingly difficult for the union to secure resources from its institutional environment after negotiation of the first collective bargaining contract, union structure did not change to increase the flow of resources from members. The commitment of leaders to their jobs, and the skills in institutional relations they and their staff had developed, slowed modifications of union structure. However, greater efforts *were* made to recruit new members with prizes and competitions. The resource substitution principle was still operating.

While internally-focused explanations of organizational emergence and change are necessarily incomplete, simply recognizing the importance of some aspects of the environment is not sufficient. Analysis of the relations between an organization and just one level of its environment cannot fully explain the process of organizational development nor the variability in organizational configuration. Since resources can be secured from both individuals and other organizations, the absolute level of resources available from only one level can usually predict neither the course of factional conflict nor the likely direction of structural change. The possibility of resource substitution necessarily opens up alternative directions for organizations, and requires analysis of different dimensions of organizational environments. It is only when the supply of resources from one environmental level is invariant at a high enough level (as in the International Typographical Union) that one level of the environment can be neglected to some extent.

The Population Ecology Framework

Population ecology theory provides a general framework within which the behavior of a wide variety of organizations can be explained. Focusing on the environment as the basis of organizational behavior and recognizing resources as the medium for organization-environment interchange, the tenets of population ecology theory are compatible with the theoretical perspective employed in this book. By identifying the similarities between the perspective used to explain the emergence and transformation of the welfare employees' union and the tenets of population ecology theory, this study of one voluntary organization can be more closely integrated into the broader body of research on other types of organizations. At the same time, some of the limitations of population ecology theory as currently formulated can be indicated.

The population ecology explanation of organizational emergence begins with the concept of the niche: "a location in multidimensional space defined by the resources in the environment" (McPherson, 1983:520). Indicators of such a location include available time, space, and a unique, socially defined potential recruitment base that can all be used by an emerging organization (cf. Freeman and Hannan, 1983). The niche concept is thus similar to the concept of untapped resources used to explain the emergence of the welfare employees' union.

Population ecology has not accorded unmet needs, or grievances, a role in organizational emergence. Of course, among the species of biological organisms to which population ecology theory was first applied, needs can be assumed to be constant. Among human beings, however, the variability in perceived needs is too great to maintain this assumption. Variation in human needs and constraints on their expression must be incorporated in the population ecology approach to the explanation of organizational behavior.

Population ecology theory has also been used to explain organizational configurations. This theory presumes that the consequences of particular organizational characteristics vary with the type of environment that organizations confront. Freeman and Hannan (1983) propose that organizations with specialized goals can maximize their success in relatively stable environments, while generalist organizations are more likely to survive in changing environments. This insight is also consistent with the explanation of the welfare employee union's transformation. During its early years, the union was more generalist in character. Its goals were broader and factional activity within the union maintained the responsiveness of the union to the wide range of client and political groups in its environment. As the turbulence in the union's environment subsided, union goals became more limited and the bureaucratization of the union was associated with its specializing on employee economic demands and grievance handling.

The most important contrast between the GIST framework and population ecology theory is in their treatment of the process of organizational change itself. In this respect, as in the explanation of organizational emergence, the population ecology perspective on organizations has not been fully separated from its roots in the study of biology. The capacity of nonhuman biological organisms for adaptation is severely limited by their genetic makeup. Environmental influence operates by affecting birth and death rates, and the object of investigation becomes variation across populations of organisms, rather than variation within organisms, over time. Questions of selection and survival have thus been paramount in ecological theory as applied to organizations, and serve as the key difference between that approach and the "adaptation perspectives" that are "so different it is hard to believe they are talking about the same thing" (Hannan and Freeman, 1977:929–30).

In spite of this difference, the bases for incorporating the explanation of adaptation processes into the population ecology framework have now been established. The concept of invariant organizational characteristics has been replaced by the concept of variable degrees of "structural inertia." The assumption of the primacy of processes of interorganizational selection has given way to a search for the factors that influence the extent of inertia within organizations (Hannan and Freeman, 1984).

Hannan and Freeman (1984) have proposed that organizational environments favor organizations that are reliable and accountable—that have, in other words, high levels of structural inertia. Yet the environmental factors that favor structural inertia are themselves subject to change. Legal constraints, exchange relations with other organizations, political coalitions, and the desire to maintain legitimacy are each subject to variation due to factors beyond the control of any one organization. During the history of the welfare employees' union, legal constraints changed when collective bargaining for state employees was allowed, relations with other organizations changed with the demise of welfare rights groups and the union's affiliation with a national union, and political coalitions shifted as the student movement declined. The union changed in response to each of these environmental changes.

Environmental change cannot result in adaptive organizational change if the environment appears to be highly uncertain to the organization, or if the loose coupling of portions of the organization impairs identification of the appropriate internal changes (Hannan and Freeman, 1984:149–51). The I.U.P.A.E.'s 1965 decision to adopt a more traditional structure initially failed to improve its relations with the agency, for example, when the State of Illinois refused to recognize the new union. The union could not predict the State's response to its efforts—in other words, this uncertainty reduced the fit between the organization and its environment. However, the ultimate acceptance of the union by the State finally resulted in a closer organization-environment fit, and was consistent with the pattern of development of labor relations in most industries. Since the union's internal structure was relatively simple, there was not much "loose coupling" within it. Although at times factional conflict appeared to hinder identification of internal responses to environmental change, major adaptive changes in the union received general support. Factional conflict itself changed along with the transformation of the union.

Ecological theory thus provides a general framework for the interpretation and extension of the resource substitution theory of organizational transformation. While organizations *do* consciously change in response to changes in their environment, the motivation for and consequences of such "autonomous" change stem from the environment itself. Internal organizational processes are ultimately dependent on the external environment.

THE DESIGN OF VOLUNTARY ORGANIZATIONS

To reject the "iron law of oligarchy" is to allow for greater variation in patterns of organizational development. Yet an externally based theory of organizational development cannot, by definition, suggest "one best way" to organize. The inherent tension between the social and institutional levels of organizational environments shapes possibilities for and progress toward particular configurations. The ubiquity of difficulties in organizations due to factional conflict and difficulties in maintenance of leader commitment to their memberships reflect this fundamental tension.

Organizations must accommodate to different needs among their memberships. Pressure to do so increases with the heterogeneity of the social environment, and with the distribution of resources throughout that environment. In organizations that affect critical areas of members' experience, competition among members for organizational attention to their needs, and hence factional conflict, is predictable.

In theory, bureaucratic structures minimize the potential for factional conflict through increasing hierarchical control and separating members' organizational involvements from other areas of their lives. Rather than relying on intense member involvement, bureaucracies reduce their dependence on the social environment. In practice, however, the boundaries within individuals between their "organized" selves and their backgrounds and outside experiences are permeable (Perrow, 1979:4). Bureaucracies are never completely sheltered from their primary social environment. When resources become difficult to obtain in the institutional environment, dependence on the social environment increases and hierarchical structures become even less effective. The bureaucratic solution is thus most likely to succeed in institutional environments that provide a stable source of resources and in social environments that are unlikely to sustain high levels of involvement.

Organizations cannot survive without support from their environment, but such support is most likely to be maintained when there is a balanced dependence on the social and institutional levels of the environment. Exclusive dependence on one level decreases the organization's ability to respond to environmental changes. An organization that becomes too dependent on its institutional environment, for example, may be unable to revive contributions from members if the institutional environment becomes less favorable.

Similarly, the initial relief from overt factionalism provided by bureaucratic structures may work to the disadvantage of organizations. As a result of barriers to factionalism in bureaucratic structures, variation in the social environment is less likely to be expressed in organizational goals. As a result, the conditions for new organization emerge. Grievances, or unmet needs, accumulate. Member resources available for organizing outside of the existing organization are not tapped by the bureaucratic organizational structure, and thus new organization or internal upheaval become more likely (see, for example, Gouldner, 1965).

Democratic organizations have the advantage of maintaining a closer correspondence of leader policies and member beliefs (Handelman, 1977). The conflict in democratic organizations that seems so destructive when it occurs is vital to organizational health. There is no unequivocally "one best way" to proceed in complex, only partially understood environments, and faced with an inability to predict the direction of environmental change. By bringing different groups of members with different needs to the organization's attention, factional conflict sensitizes organizations to particular features of their environment. Internal factional conflict thus generates pressures for alternative policies, and these pressures grow in force as current policies develop discrepancies with the environment. Since the turbulence arising in participatory democratic organizations impairs the translation of these pressures into effective tactics, a representative form of democracy is likely to have a higher probability of success.

Voluntary organizations play a critical role in society, as vehicles for both the expression and satisfaction of needs. In this role, such organizations inevitably experience tensions between pressures to be responsive to their members and to be responsible to other organizations. The theory and findings presented in this book do not provide a prescription for avoidance of these often contrary pressures. However, the book clarifies the nature of these pressures, the options in responding to them, and the means with which to understand them. The central dimensions of voluntary organizations and their environments have been identified and the explanation of organizational emergence has been integrated with the explanation of organizational change. With this theoretical framework, the design of other voluntary organizations can be both evaluated and enhanced.

Appendix I:
Data Collection Procedures

1973 Survey Procedures

Sampling

In March of 1973, there were 3,817 nonadministrative permanent employees in the Cook County Department of Public Aid. At that time, the Illinois Union of Social Service Employees (formerly the Independent Union of Public Aid Employees) had 2,133 members, including a small number from outside the C.C.D.P.A. With the cooperation of the agency and the union, questionnaires were distributed to all employees at work, through regular office distribution procedures. Collection boxes were set up in each C.C.D.P.A. office, and research staff made trips to the offices to pick up questionnaires and encourage employees to respond. As a result of these efforts, 1,218 employees returned completed questionnaires: 654 were union members and 557 were not (seven respondents did not indicate membership

Table A-1. Occupations of Union Membership and Member Survey Respondents, June 1973

Occupation	Union Members	Union Member Survey Respondents
Clerical worker	33%	25%
Case aide	12	9
Caseworker	34	40
Supervisory caseworker	8	13
Other[a]	13	13
	100%	100%
	(2133)	(654)

[a] Including Homemaker, Janitor, and Professional Specialist.

185

status). As indicated in Table A-1, the occupational distribution of union member respondents was similar to that for the union's membership as a whole. However, clerks and case aides were slightly underrepresented in the returns, while caseworkers and supervisory caseworkers were slightly overrepresented.

Measurement

Measures of grievances, resources, and constraints, and of desired union goals, desired union tactics, and union involvement were each developed from questions in the 1973 survey. Many of these concepts were operationalized with indexes constructed from responses to several questions, while several were measured with responses to single questions (Table A-2). Occupation and several demographic variables are used throughout the analysis. (See also, Table A-3.)

Table A-2. Measurement of Variables, 1973 Survey

Grievances/Goals

Job dissatisfaction (JOB); Average dissatisfaction with:
   Authority to do the job well;
   Comparison with the expectations had when took the job;
   Comparison with career expectations;
   Public aid policies enabling doing the job well.
Work load issues (WORK); Average importance of:
   Decreasing employee work loads;
   Hiring more staff.
Service to clients (SERVICE); Average importance of:
   Improving ability to serve recipients;
   More and closer contact with recipients.
General economic benefits (ECON); Average importance of:
   Increasing wages for all employees;
   Increasing employee benefits;
   Increasing opportunities for advancement at all levels.
General employee benefits goal (EMP); Average agreement with*:
   Improving employee conditions as union top priority;
   Increasing wages as major union focus;
   Employee benefits as major union effort.
Client benefits goal (SERVE); Average agreement with*:
   Improving service to recipients as major union goal;
   Organizing recipients as a protest group.
Paraprofessional benefits (PARA); Average importance of:
   Higher salaries for paraprofessionals;
   Opportunities for clerical and case aide advancement.

Resources

Socializing (SCLZE); Average of time spent with types of people on an average day at work (from 1 = "a lot" to 4 = "almost none")*:
  Caseworkers;
  Case aides;
  Clerical staff; and
  How often see coworkers outside of office.
Need for job (JOB NEED); Scored as "1" if:
  Not married;
  Public Aid job main source of support;
  Public Aid job necessary to met financial needs.
Marital status (SINGLE); Scored as "1" if not married.
Education (EDUC); From "0" to "7" for:
  Some elementary school;
  Finished elementary school;
  Some high school;
  Finished high school;
  Business or technical school;
  Some college;
  Finished college;
  Graduate work.

Constraints

Belief in clients (CLIENTS); Average of:
  How much racism in Dept. of Public Aid client policies?;
  How many clients abusing the welfare system?
Institutional alienation (PLTCS); Average agreement with:
  State and federal laws as adequately taking care of the needs of working people;
  Generally speaking, business and industry as carried on in a very satisfactory way in this country;
  Government officials as very concerned about the conditions of working people;
  In general, the profits of business and industry higher than they should be (reverse scored);
  Working people as deserving more say about how things are run at their jobs (reverse scored);
  Management and labor as partners; no reason for unions and companies to fight each other.
Seniority (SNRTY); Years worked for the Dept. of Public Aid.

Union orientation

Work action support (MILTNT); Sum, if "major work-related problem," of "very willing" to:
  Talk to coworkers;
  Petition District Office supervisor;

Join work slowdown;
Have sick call-in;
Picket outside office;
Strike.
Union participation (PART); Sum in past year of:
Union office meetings attended (any = 1);
Voting in union officer election (yes = 1);
Writing for union newspaper, recruiting new members, working on leaflets (any = 1);
Having position in union or on union committee (yes = 1).
Satisfaction with the union (USAT); Average satisfaction with:
Job IUSSE does for client service;
Job IUSSE does for work situation;
Job union does in the agency office;
Way the union is run;
Overall job IUSSE does.
Job attachment (EXIT); Scored from "1" to "6" for plans to leave work in the Department within:
1 year;
2–3 years;
4–5 years;
6–10 years;
11–15 years;
16 years or more.

* Reverse scored so that higher scores indicate more agreement.

Table A-3. Public Aid Occupations and Salaries, Cook County, March 1973

Occupation	Mean Annual Salary	Number	Percent of All Positions
Clerical worker	$5,978	1,510	40%
Homemaker or janitor[a]	6,448	72	2
Case aide (paraprofessional)	7,158	301	8
Caseworker	9,618	1,336	35
Supervisory caseworker	12,675	377	10
Professional specialist	10,826	221	6
Total	$8,299	3,817	101%[b]

SOURCE: Illinois Department of Public Aid. Non-administrative Personal Service—Permanent Positions (Pay Grades 1–14). Mimeographed, March 15, 1973.
[a] Classified as "clerical" for statistical analysis.
[b] Percentages do not total 100% because of rounding.

1976 SURVEY PROCEDURES

Sampling

A stratified random sample of 819 respondents was drawn from a list of the approximately 4,500 paraprofessional and professional union members in the Illinois Department of Public Aid and the Illinois Division of Vocational Rehabilitation (since renamed the Department of Rehabilitation Services). The occupational composition of these categories was determined by the decision of the Illinois Office of Collective Bargaining that established bargaining units for state employees. Homemakers were included in the paraprofessional unit, but clerks and related occupations were in a separate bargaining unit. It was not possible to include members in the clerical bargaining unit in the survey.

Sixty-six percent of the sample returned mailed questionnaires, and some data were obtained on the entire sample from union records. The respondents and the original sample were almost identical in distribution of occupations, and, by occupation, in gender, age, salary, seniority, county of employment, and voting. There were differences between the respondents and the original sample in race and education (whites and more educated members were overrepresented in the respondent group), but even on these characteristics they differed by no more than eight percent.

Measurement

The statistical analyses discussed in chapter 9 identify the impact of the new agency and union environment on the orientations of professional and paraprofessional union members. Independent variables in these analyses are measures of organizational position, occupation, occupational origin, demographic background, and office political context. The dependent variables are measures of union involvement, tactical orientation, and satisfaction with the union and the job. As discussed in the text, extensive tests for interaction effects were also conducted.

Table A-4. Measurement of Variables, 1976 Survey

Organizational Position

Downstate (DWN); Scored as "1" if office outside of Cook County.
Education (EDUC); Formal education completed in year equivalent:
 Grade school (8);
 Some high school (10);
 High school (12);
 Some college (14);
 College degree (16);
 Some graduate work (17);
 Graduate degree (18).
Seniority (SNRTY); Years in agency.

Occupation

Represented in regression analyses with a series of dummy variables:
 Homemaker (HMK);
 Caseworker I, II (formerly Case aide) (CWII);

Caseworker III (CWIII);
Caseworker V (Supervisory Caseworker) (CWV);
Professional specialist (PFL);
Rehabilitation Counselor (VOC).
Mobility experience represented by two dummy variables:
Ex-clerk (CLERK);
Ex-aide (PARA).

Office Political Context

Incumbent Support (PCTMAX); Percentage of votes in office for incumbent.
Office Size (SMALL); Scored "1" if small office (no separate voting statistics).

Union and Job Orientation

Union participation (PART); Sum of:
Voting in election of office representatives (yes = 1);
Attending at least two union office meetings (yes = 1);
Recruiting new members (yes = 1);
Having position in union or on union committee (yes = 1).
Job departure plans (EXIT); Length of time plan to be with agency, scored
from "1" to "5" (reversed) for:
Less than 6 months;
6–11 more months;
1–2 more years;
3–5 more years;
More than 5 years.
Job dissatisfaction (SAT); Average agreement with:
"All things considered, I am satisfied with my job";
"If I could start over again, I would work in another occupation" (reverse
scored);
"If I could start over again, I would work in another agency or firm"
(reverse scored).
Satisfaction with union performance (UPERF); Average rating in terms of
the last two years, from "excellent" to "very poor":
Improving pay;
Improving advancement;
Reducing workloads;
Improving leave provisions;
Effective grievance handling;
Protection against layoffs.
Support for work actions (MILTNT); Number of actions "very likely" to
participate in if "in the future, suppose you felt that there was a major
work-related problem in your office":
Talk to coworkers about it;
Pass a petition around to the office head;
Have a sick-in;
Have a picket line outside work.

Support for a contract strike (STRIKE); Number of issues out of eighteen about which "you would support a strike if this issue was not resolved to your satisfaction in negotiations".

CONTENT ANALYSIS PROCEDURES

A content analysis of I.U.P.A.E./I.U.S.S.E. literature from 1965 to 1980 provides a summary description of changes in the union's GIST configuration. A stratified random sample of documents was selected from the 582 union newspapers and official union leaflets distributed to members.

The analysis focuses on the messages produced through communication (Holsti, 1969). In the process of communication, a source transmits a message through a particular channel to some recipient(s). The messages themselves were coded in the content analysis, but the source, channel and intended recipient of the message were used to define the relevant population of documents. Thus, only general leaflets for the membership and union newspaper articles were coded fully. Documents that did not have the official union as its source, that were not intended for rank and file members, and that were not in the form of a leaflet or newspaper article were not included in the analysis. Documents that explained procedures for discount buying plans or grievance filing were also excluded. These types of documents were distinguished by a preliminary coding prior to sampling. In the detailed coding scheme, references to union goals, structure, involvement and tactics were coded. References to features of the union's environment were also coded.

CONTRACT SURVEY

FOR THE PROFESSIONAL AND PARA-PROFESSIONAL UNITS

NEGOTIATIONS WILL BEGIN SOON FOR STATE EMPLOYEES IN THE PROFESSIONAL AND PARA-PROFESSIONAL UNITS.
The IUSSE/AFSCME Contract Research Committee is sponsoring this survey in order to get a complete, comprehensive picture of the concerns of union members in the professional and para-professional units. Results of the survey will be used in formulating contract demands, in setting priorities in negotiations, in evaluating possible possible actions in support of contract demands, and in seeing how members feel generally about the union and their jobs.

Your responses to the questionnaire will be analyzed by Russ Schutt at the University of Illinois at Chicago Circle, Sociology Department. Mr. Schutt previously (three years ago) conducted a survey in the Cook County DPA and provided the union with a 50 page report.

Your answers in this survey will be completely confidential. Only information on group sentiments, not on individuals, will be available. Questionnaires will be keypunched by trained staff at the University.

PLEASE FILL OUT THE SURVEY COMPLETELY AND RETURN IT QUICKLY IN THE ENCLOSED ENVELOPE.
You are in a scientifically selected representative sample of Local 2000 members. Your response is necessary in order to have a representative picture of union members. (Return envelopes are numbered so that research staff at the University can keep track of who has responded.) Please fill out the questionnaire now so that your opinions will be represented as we formulate contract demands.

THE CONTRACT RESEARCH COMMITTEE
IUSSE/AFSCME LOCAL 2000

Russ Schutt

Russell K. Schutt
Department of Sociology,
Univ. of Ill., Chicago Circle

WORK EXPERIENCE   1/

1a. When did you most recently begin work in the
    agency? (DPA or DVR)

                        ___/___
                        month year   4/

b. Had you worked in a social service agency before
   this?

                        yes.......1
                        no........2   8/

2. At what classification did you start in the
   agency? (Circle one or write in below).
   **Check here if you were in the CCDPA series ___ **

                        Caseworker........1..2..3..4..5
                        Case-aide trainee.............6
                        Case-aide.....................7   9/
   Other (please specify)
   for example: DVR Counselor 3; Clerk 1; ERW 2

3. What is your present classification?
                                                             11/
        ___please specify here___

4. When were you assigned to this classification?

                        ___/___
                        month year   13/

12a. Was a position you were in reallocated in the
     last two years?

                        yes, downward........1
                        yes, upward..........2
                        yes, lateral.........3
                        no...................4   36/

b. If yes, did you remain in this position?

                        yes.....1
                        no......2   37/

13. Generally, have you been satisfied with your
    performance evaluations?

                        yes.......1
                        no........2
            don't know what they have been..3   38/

14a. Have you been subject to any agency disciplinary
     action in the last year?

                        yes.......1
                        no........2   39/

     if no, go to ques. 15

b. Which of the following occurred in the last
   such action? (Circle all that occurred)

                        verbal warning...............1
                        written warning notice.......2
                        pre-suspension hearing.......3   40/

c. Was the disciplinary action......
    reversed......1
    modified......2
    carried out......3
    still pending......4
41/

d. What was the issue involved in this action?
    (for example: tardiness, poor evaluations)

    ――specify here――
42/

15a. How many grievances have you filed (for yourself)
      in the last year? **If no grievances, go to ques. 16**

      ――specify here――
      _____
      no. of grievances
44/

b. Was the last grievance you filed resolved to
    your satisfaction?
    yes......1
    no......2
    still pending......3
45/

c. At what step was this last grievance resolved?
    conference with supervisor......1
    step 1 (assistant office head)......2
    step 2 (office head)......3
    step 3 (CAO or regional director)......4
    step 4 (Director of Personnel)......5
46/

5. Are you presently working...
    (Circle all that apply)
                        Intake......1
                        IM......2
                        Service......3
    Other _____ 4
          specify here
17/

6. What type of cases do you handle regularly?
    (Circle all that apply)
                        ADC......1
                        AABD......2
                        Food stamps......3
                        GA......4
    Other _____ 5
          ――specify here――
19/

7. What is your office?

    _____ | _____
    office name   code no.
21/

8. When did you start working in this office?

    _____ / _____
    month   year
24/

9a. Have you attempted to change your job classi-
     fication within the last year?
                        yes......1
                        no......2
28/

b. If yes, what was the outcome of this attempt?

    got desired job change...............1
    still waiting, expect change soon........2
    still waiting, but have given up hope.....3
    unable to get desired job change.....4
    29/

10. What classification would you ultimately like to have in the agency?
    30/

    --specify here--

11a. Have you worked out of classification in the last year?

    yes, at a higher classification...........1
    yes, at a lower classification............2
    yes, at higher and lower classes..........3
    no.................................4
    32/

b. If yes, how many weeks did you work out of classification in the last year?

    _____ no. of weeks   33/

---

d. What was the issue involved in this grievance?

    the disciplinary action in item 14.........1
    some other issue -- specify below
    47/

16. If something comes up at work that might be a grievance, do you usually talk to somebody about it?

    no, usually don't bring it up.............1
    yes, usually talk first to my steward......2
    yes, usually talk first to my supervisor...3
    no possible grievances have come up........4
    49/

17a. What is the size of your current active caseload?
    _____ no. of cases   50/

    **If not on a caseload, how many applications or cases per month?
    _____ 53/

    If no caseload, go to 18

b. How many of these cases are from uncovered loads?
    _____ no. of uncovered cases   54/

18. How many clients do you talk to in an average day at work?

    in person........... 57/
    on the phone........ 59/
    on district days.... 61/
    (If no district days, check here _____)

19. How many hours of overtime have you worked since January 2, 1976?

_____
no. of hours   63/

20. How long do you plan to be with the agency?

less than 6 months........1
6-11 more months..........2
1-2 more years............3
3-5 more years............4
more than 5 years.........5   66/

****

BACKGROUND INFORMATION

1. What year were you born?   67/

2. What was the usual occupation of the principal breadwinner in your family when you were growing up?

laborer...................1
factory work, truck driver, semiskilled....2
skilled work (craft)......3
clerical, sales worker....4
professional, executive (teacher, engineer, etc.)....5
owned small business......6
farmer....................7
other (_____)........8   69/
--specify here--

3. What is your present marital status?

married living with spouse........1
single, separated/divorced, widow..2   70/

4. How many children under 18 do you have? _____   71/

5. How much of your total family income does your job in the agency provide?

all or almost all.........1
about three-fourths.......2
about half................3
less than half............4   72/

6. How much formal education have you completed?

did not finish high school...1
high school.............2
some college............3
college degree..........4
some graduate work......5
a graduate degree.......6   73/

7. Have you had any training related to your job? (Circle all that apply)

college courses...........1
graduate-level courses....2
agency training...........3
special lectures, etc.....4
other.....................5   74/

CONTRACT ISSUES

1a. Below is a list of issues for negotiation in a contract. Please indicate how important each issue is to you, by circling the number corresponding to your feelings. Then indicate whether you would support a strike if this issue was not resolved to your satisfaction in negotiations. Please respond carefully to each item.

	IMPORTANCE OF THE ISSUE				STRIKE IF IT IS NOT RESOLVED			
	not very	*some-what*	*very*	*extremely*	*yes*	*no*	*not sure*	
A. Improved opportunities for advancement..........	1	2	3	4	1	2	3	75/
B. End working out of classification..............	1	2	3	4	1	2	3	77/
C. Cost of living protection (wage escalator clause).......	1	2	3	4	1	2	3	80/1 1-4/DU:
D. Flexible hours for daily starting time.........	1	2	3	4	1	2	3	5/
E. Extra pay for overtime (more than 37½ hours)...	1	2	3	4	1	2	3	7/
F. More liberal policies for job-related education (excused time, tuition reimbursement).........	1	2	3	4	1	2	3	9/
G. Lower workloads................	1	2	3	4	1	2	3	11/
H. Protection against layoffs..............	1	2	3	4	1	2	3	13/
I. Improving office physical conditions..........	1	2	3	4	1	2	3	15/
J. A large wage increase.................	1	2	3	4	1	2	3	17/
K. Evaluations with only a pass-fail rating.......	1	2	3	4	1	2	3	19/
L. More time for illness, vacation, etc...........	1	2	3	4	1	2	3	21/
M. Automatic steps 6 & 7 (based on seniority).....	1	2	3	4	1	2	3	23/
N. Improved grievance procedure..............	1	2	3	4	1	2	3	25/ 27/

2. Now please compare the issues in each of the following pairs. Circle a number which is closer to the issue you think is more important in each pair. The closer the number is to one issue, the more important it is in relation to the other issue.

ISSUE 1	*Issue 1 most important*				*Issue 2 most important*			ISSUE 2	
Better advancement opportunities.........1	2	3	4	5	6	7	8.........A wage increase		47/
More job security.....1	2	3	4	5	6	7	8.........A wage increase		48/
A wage increase........1	2	3	4	5	6	7	8.........Lower work loads		49/
More sick leave, annual leave, etc...1	2	3	4	5	6	7	8.........A wage increase		50/
Better grievance procedure...........1	2	3	4	5	6	7	8.........Better advancement opportunities		51/

3. How satisfied are you with your present salary?

very satisfied...............1
somewhat satisfied...........2
not very satisfied...........3
not at all satisfied.........4

52/

4. What would be a satisfactory pay raise per month _for you_ in the contract at your current grade and step?

$ _____ amount　　　53/

_____ percent increase　　　56/

5. What do you think promotions in the agency _are_ based on?

	A major factor in promotions	A minor factor in promotions	Not a factor in promotions	
seniority............................	1	2	3	58/
supervisor evaluations.............	1	2	3	59/
education, training.................	1	2	3	60/
favoritism..........................	1	2	3	61/
race................................	1	2	3	62/
sex.................................	1	2	3	63/

6. What _should_ promotions in the agency be based on?

	Should be a major factor	Should be a minor factor	Should not be a factor in promotion	
seniority............................	1	2	3	64/
supervisor evaluations.............	1	2	3	65/
education...........................	1	2	3	66/

7. Please rate union performance in the last two years in the following areas.

| | UNION PERFORMANCE | | | | | |
	excellent	good	mediocre	poor	very poor	
Improving pay........................	1	2	3	4	5	67/
Improving advancement...............	1	2	3	4	5	68/
Reducing workloads..................	1	2	3	4	5	69/
Improving leave provisions..........	1	2	3	4	5	70/
Effective grievance handling........	1	2	3	4	5	71/
Protection against layoffs..........	1	2	3	4	5	72/

UNION ACTIONS

1. How important is a contract for achieving the needs of union members?   73/
   a contract is extremely important........1
   a contract is very important.............2
   a contract is somewhat important.........3
   a contract is not very important.........4
   a contract is not at all important.......5

2. Should the contract permit strikes when negotiations break down?
   yes...........1
   no............2
   not sure......3   74/

3. In the future, suppose you felt there was a major work-related problem in your office.
   How likely is it that you would participate in the following actions if it was not
   resolved?   80/2
   1-4/DUP

	Not at all likely	Not very likely	Somewhat likely	Very likely	
talk to coworkers about it...............	1	2	3	4	5/
have a picket line outside work..........	1	2	3	4	6/
conduct a work stoppage..................	1	2	3	4	7/
pass a petition around to the office head	1	2	3	4	8/
have a sick-in...........................	1	2	3	4	9/

UNION ORGANIZATION

1. How much influence do you think various groups have in setting union policy? How much influence should they have? Circle the numbers that come <u>closest</u> to your feelings.

GROUPS	HOW MUCH INFLUENCE THEY <u>DO</u> HAVE						HOW MUCH INFLUENCE THEY <u>SHOULD</u> HAVE					
	none				a lot	don't know	none				a lot	
International AFSCME......................	1	2	3	4	5	(8)	1	2	3	4	5	10/
Local 2000's president & executive board.	1	2	3	4	5	(8)	1	2	3	4	5	11/
Local 2000's representative council.......	1	2	3	4	5	(8)	1	2	3	4	5	12/
Local committees and their members.......	1	2	3	4	5	(8)	1	2	3	4	5	13/
Members of Local 2000 as a whole.........	1	2	3	4	5	(8)	1	2	3	4	5	14/
Clerical members.........................	1	2	3	4	5	(8)	1	2	3	4	5	15/
Professional and paraprofessional members	1	2	3	4	5	(8)	1	2	3	4	5	16/
DVR members..............................	1	2	3	4	5	(8)	1	2	3	4	5	17/
Members outside of Cook County...........	1	2	3	4	5	(8)	1	2	3	4	5	18/
Some other group --specify-- _____	1	2	3	4	5	(8)	1	2	3	4	5	19/

2. Do you usually agree with Local 2000's policies?

   yes..........1
   no...........2
   not sure.....3   20/

3. Do your elected office union representatives represent <u>your</u> views in the union?

   yes..........1
   no...........2
   don't know..3   22/

23/

4. The Illinois Office of Collective Bargaining set up three separate bargaining units for state employees: clerical; paraprofessional; professional. What set up do you think would have been best for the interests of employees?

    all three groups in separate units........1
    professionals and paraprofessionals in one
        unit, clerks in another........2
    professionals in one unit, clerks and
        paraprofessionals in another........3
    all three groups in one unit within DPA and DVR......4

    24/

INVOLVEMENT IN THE UNION

1. When did you join the union? (AFSCME, IUSSE or IUPAE)   ____/____
                                        month / year   25/

2. How likely is it that you will leave the union within the next year, if you stay in the agency? 29/

    very likely...........1
    somewhat likely..........2
    not very likely..........3
    not at all likely........4

3. IN THE PAST YEAR, DID YOU...
    (Circle all that apply)

	yes	no	
a. hold any office or serve on a union committee......	1	2	30/
b. vote in the election of office union representatives.....	1	2	31/
c. vote in the election for a collective bargaining agent.....	1	2	32/
d. help distribute any union-related petitions or leaflets.....	1	2	33/
e. participate in any office work actions (sick-in, slow-down, etc.).....	1	2	34/
f. recruit any new union members.....	1	2	35/
g. been a member of the credit union.....	1	2	36/

4. How many office meetings of union members have you attended in the past year?

    ____ no. of meetings   37/

5. Have you held any office or union committee position in the past (before last year)? yes.....1   39/
no......2

6. How often do you read the union newspaper, Common Sense?   40/

every issue............1
somewhat regularly.....2
once in a while........3
never..................4

7. How often do you talk with your steward or union representative?   41/

several days a week or more.........1
every week or two...................2
about monthly.......................3
less than monthly...................4
never...............................5
I am a steward or representative....6

8. How often do you get together with union members on an informal basis?   42/

several days a week or more.........1
every week or two...................2
about monthly.......................3
less than monthly...................4
never...............................5

9. What do you think are the three most pressing concerns for the union?

1. _____ 43/

2. _____ 45/

3. _____ 47/

THE JOB

1. (DVR MEMBERS SKIP TO QUESTION 2)
How have the following changes in DPA affected clients and employees? Circle the number that comes closest to your feelings.

	DPA CLIENTS					DPA EMPLOYEES					
	hurt a lot			helped a lot		hurt a lot			helped a lot		
Separation of income maintenance and service.........	1	2	3	4	5	1	2	3	4	5	49/
The flat grant.........	1	2	3	4	5	1	2	3	4	5	51/
Reclassification of case-aides.........	1	2	3	4	5	1	2	3	4	5	53/
The new client grievance procedure.........	1	2	3	4	5	1	2	3	4	5	55/
Redeterminations.........	1	2	3	4	5	1	2	3	4	5	57/
Redistricting in Cook County **only Cook members**.	1	2	3	4	5	1	2	3	4	5	59/
State takeover of CCDPA **answer**.........	1	2	3	4	5	1	2	3	4	5	61/

2. How much do you agree or disagree with the following statements about your job?

	strongly agree	agree	disagree	strongly disagree	
a. If I could start over again, I would work in another occupation.........	1	2	3	4	63/
b. I would like more and closer contact with clients in the job............	1	2	3	4	64/
c. Usually, I can meet the major needs of clients I see in my job..........	1	2	3	4	65/
d. Agency rules should be broken when necessary to help clients...........	1	2	3	4	66/
e. All things considered, I am satisfied with my job......................	1	2	3	4	67/
f. If I could start over again, I would work in another agency or firm....	1	2	3	4	68/
g. Understanding theories of personality and social interaction is important in my job.....	1	2	3	4	69/

3. How much influence do the following groups have on how you are able to carry out your job?

	a great deal of influence	moderate influence	a little influence	no influence	
the government (state and federal)......	1	2	3	4	70/
the agency director and his staff.......	1	2	3	4	71/
your office administrators	1	2	3	4	72/
your immediate supervisor...............	1	2	3	4	73/
yourself................................	1	2	3	4	74/
your clients............................	1	2	3	4	75/
Local 2000..............................	1	2	3	4	76/

4. What are the three most pressing needs on your job?   80/3
                                                                      1-4/DUP
    1. _____   5/

    2. _____   7/

    3. _____   9/

5. What do you think of this survey of union members?

    a very good idea...................1   11/
    a pretty good idea.................2   12/
    a poor idea........................3   80/4

Union Literature Coding Form*

I. *Preliminary Codes*
   1. Document # _____.
   2. Date _____
          mo   yr
   3. Length of text _____pp. (round up to next ¼ page; count legal size as 1.25)
   4. Literature Type
      1. General leaflet for members/employees
      2. Newspaper/Newsletter article
      3. Rep Council motions
      4. Other material for Reps, Stewards, Delegates (e.g. budget, agenda)
      5. Activity reports of officers, President's Report
      6. Technical information—filing grievances, processing forms
      7. Buying plans/Travel packages
      8. Survey Forms, Limited Circulation material (correspondence)
      9. Non-union
      10. Other _____(specify)

   4A. If newspaper article   4B. If Rep Council motion
        Position   Sponsor
        1. Headline story   1. Union leadership
        2. Other front page   2. Office
        3. Editorial   3. Leadership faction
        4. Other   4. Opposition faction
                                      5. Other

   5. Literature content—Special issues
      1. First strike (1966)
      2. Second strike (1967)
      3. Collective bargaining (1977)
      4. Collective bargaining (1979)
      5. Election/campaign literature
      6. Affiliation with AFSCME/SEIU/other national union
      7. Other

II. *Source and Target*
   6. Primary source (code in terms of those who prepared this literature for distribution).
      1. Union—newspaper (Common Sense; IUPAE News)
      2. Union—newsletter (Info and IUPAE Bulletin)
      3. Union—unsigned
      4. Union officers
      5. Union committee
      6. Union faction (the Caucus; Rank-and-Filers; Contract Action, other election slate; PLP News; Black Facts)
      7. Union members in a specific work location/office
      8. Union members—other

---

* Coding instructions available from the author.

9. Dept. of Public Aid/Personnel
10. DVR/DORS
11. Credit Union
12. Am. Buyers' Assoc.
13. Other non-union
7. Secondary source (use for lit. at least in part reprinted from another source, for distribution to members).
   1. Newspaper—general circulation
   2. Literature of other unions, organizations
   3. Correspondence of union leaders
   4. Correspondence from DPA/DVR—DORS/Personnel
   5. Correspondence from national union
   6. Press release
   7. Credit Union, Am. Buyers'
   8. Other _____(specify)
   9. None
8. Primary target (the audience for which the literature is distributed)
   1. Employees—general (if mass-produced and unless otherwise stated)
   2. Employees—DVR/DORS
   3. Union members (if refers *only* to members or if about union elections)
   4. Union stewards, reps, delegates committee
   5. Non-unionized employees (recruitment lit, etc.)
   6. Other _____(specify)
   7. Unclear

III. *Issues*
  A. Goal
   9. Employee conditions/benefits (Circle up to 5)
     1. Criteria for hiring
     2. Promotion
     3. Work out of Classification, Upgrading
     4. Step increases
     5. Cost-of-living, pay raise, overtime pay, "money"
     6. Layoffs (non-disciplinary); position cuts
     7. Workloads, Redeterminations, "30 for 40", GA Review
     8. Office physical conditions, safety
     9. Performance evaluations
     10. Length of workday
     11. Sick Benefits/Leave—holidays, insurance, illness, vacation, voting time
     12. Educational leave
     13. Grievances—change in procedures
     14. Discrimination (race, sex, age, religion, national origin)
     15. Discipline—political (union-related)
     16. Discipline—performance, other
     17. Procedures with clients, at work
     18. Quality of work, "worthwhile jobs"—other than relations with clients

19. Flexible hours
20. Fringe benefits—unspecified
21. Union organizing rights, union perogatives
22. Demands, issues in the agency, type unspecified
23. Other _____(specify)
99. None
10. Occupational Foci (Circle one or two)
     1. General
     2. Homemakers
     3. Clerks/Secretary's/Switchboard; Non-professionals
     4. Caseworker I, II, (after 1/75) Case-Aides, Case-Aides, Case-Aid Trainees—Para-Prof'ls (before 1/75 in Cook County)
     5. Caseworker III (Income Maintenance) (after 1/75); CW I (before 1/75)
     6. Caseworker IV (Service) (after 1/75) (CW II before 1/75 in Cook)
     7. Caseworker V (Supervisory Caseworker—Caseworker III before 1/75 in Cook)
     8. Professional Specialty
     9. DVR/DORS
     10. Other _____(specify)
     99. Unclear
B. Tactics
11. Action at issue—1 (Circle one—see instructions)
     1. Strike—Contract
     2. Strike—Other than contract
     3. *Work action*—Walk out
     4. *Work action*—sick out ("blue flu")
     5. *Work action*—slowdown; "work-to-rule"
     6. Demonstration, picketing of *agency*
     7. Petition to *agency*; call/letters to agency heads, supervisors
     8. Non-contract negotiations, discussions with administrators
     9. Contract Negotiations
     10. Arbitration (binding or not)
     11. Legal action (through lawyers)
     12. *Political action*—telegrams, calls, letters, petition
     13. *Political action*—demonstration, picketing of politicians
     14. *Political action*—voting
     15. *Political action*—contributions
     16. "Militant" action or pressure, type unspecified
     17. "Action," not militant, type unspecified
     18. Other _____(specify)
     19. No action mentioned
12. Orientation to action
     1. Strongly favor action
     2. Somewhat favor action
     3. Neutral—discussion or announcement
     4. Somewhat oppose action
     5. Strongly oppose action

6. Support for *past* action
7. Neutral—*past* action
8. Oppose *past* action
9. Not applicable
13. Action at issue—2 (Circle one—see instructions)
   1. Strike—Contract
   2. Strike—Other than contract
   3. *Work action*—walk out
   4. *Work action*—sick out ("blue flu")
   5. *Work action*—slowdown; "work-to-rule"
   6. Demonstration, picketing of *agency*
   7. Petition to *agency*; call/letters to agency heads, supervisors
   8. Non-contract negotiations, discussions with administrators
   9. Contract Negotiations
  10. Arbitration (binding or not)
  11. Legal action (through lawyers)
  12. *Political action*—telegrams, calls, letters, petitions
  13. *Political action*—demonstration, picketing of *politicians*
  14. *Political action*—voting
  15. *Political action*—contributions
  16. "Militant" action or pressure, type unspecified
  17. "Action," not militant, type unspecified
  18. Other _____(specify)
  19. No action mentioned
14. Orientation to action—2
   1. Strongly favor action
   2. Somewhat favor action
   3. Neutral—discussion or announcement
   4. Somewhat oppose action
   5. Strongly oppose action
   6. Support for *past* action
   7. Neutral—*past* action
   8. Oppose *past* action
   9. Not applicable
C. Organization
15. Participation (Circle up to two)
   1. Membership meeting
   2. Rep/Stewards meeting
   3. Union committee meeting
   4. Office meeting
   5. Faction meeting
   6. Election activity—voting, rallies, etc.
   7. Referenda—voting
   8. Other voting—convention delegates
   9. AFSCME meeting
  10. Survey
  11. "Participate," "Get involved": type unspecified
  12. Other _____(specify)

13. None solicited
16. Structure (Circle up to two)
   1. Contract negotiations—*procedures* for (e.g. bargaining units)
   2. Rep Council, Stewards Council, committee composition, rules
   3. Officers' salaries, expenses
   4. Union elections—procedures
   5. Union dues
   6. Relation of local to national union
   7. Representation of a specific group, or members
   8. Other _____(specify)
   9. No issue of structure mentioned
17. Environmental Focus (if explicitly stated) (up to two)
   1. Agency (or "the Director")
   2. National union
   3. State government
   4. Federal government
   5. Client/community groups
   6. Other unions (not Illinois or national AFSCME)
   7. Other political groups, figures
   8. Other _____(specify)
   9. None mentioned
IV. *Political stance*
18. Factional position
   1. Support for union leadership
   2. Non-partisan
   3. Opposition to union leadership
   7. Other _____(specify)
   8. Unclear

Notes

NOTES TO CHAPTER ONE

1. The fact that an organization's environment may influence its development was explicitly recognized even before the development of formal theories of environmental influence (Lipset, 1960:216). In other areas of organizational theory, the environment has been accorded a critical role (McCarthy and Zald, 1973). In management theory, for example, arguments for "one best way" have been modified to take the environment into account. When the raw materials, tasks, or markets that organizations confront differ, most management theorists now recognize that the relative efficacy of Taylor's "scientific management" approach and Mayo's humanistic style will differ (Tausky, 1978:61–89).

NOTES TO CHAPTER TWO

1. Levels of needs and of resources are not always independent of one another. Levels of need or of felt grievances are not just a product of objective conditions. Since "reality" is known to participants through their perceptions, others' activities to change perceptions (such as "consciousness-raising" by political groups) can alter grievances. Organizers for groups thus expend resources to increase the perceived level of grievances in the population they seek to mobilize (McCarthy and Zald, 1973:23). The result is an indirect as well as a direct effect of resources on the probability of organization.

2. Different types of grievances have been viewed as important in different theories. Smelser's (1962) theory of collective behavior emphasized the importance of both discontent and the generalized beliefs, or "mobilizing myths," about the sources of that discontent. Those adopting a resource-based perspective, on the other hand, have assumed that participants in extremist movements are motivated by the same rational pursuit of self-interest that motivates participants in established organizational settings.

3. Some analysts distinguish an environment that is more immediate than even the primary environment—the "enacted [or perceived] environment"

213

(Pfeffer and Salancik, 1978). This reflects the increasing attention in organizational theory to those factors that affect the flow of information concerning the environment. However, it is potentially misleading to conceive of the perceived environment as a feature of the environment itself, since the organization's perceptions are a result of the interaction of the environment with internal organizational factors.

4. This conception is consistent with Aldrich's (1979:4) definition of organizations as "goal-directed, boundary-maintaining activity systems." Aldrich's definition also recognizes the importance of the organization's links to its environment, through the necessary process of distinguishing between members and nonmembers, i.e., maintaining its boundaries. The definition proposed subsumes this process under the more general "involvement" dimension. While Aldrich's definition is applicable to a wider variety of organizations, this new definition is of greater utility in the description of voluntary organizations.

5. Olson (1971) pointed out that it is not in the self-interest of individuals to contribute to organizations that achieve "collective goods" from which they benefit even without making a contribution. "Free riders" could therefore not be expected to take actions to help achieve group goals, even when these goals reflected their own self-interests. See chapter 11 for a discussion of this issue.

6. Emphasis on degree of centralization reflects the importance of this structural dimension in Michels' and others' statements of the process of organizational transformation. Most theoretical treatments of organizational structure now also distinguish the dimensions of formalization and complexity. Empirical studies indicate that centralization is positively associated with formalization, but inversely associated with complexity (Hage, 1980; Hall, 1982).

7. Within the scope of this definition, Edelstein and Warner (1975:34–53) distinguished ten types of oligarchy. In a "simple official hierarchy," for example, full-time officers are the sole political machine, and a powerful top officer appoints the subordinates. In a "neoclassical federal oligarchy," plutocratic nongoverning oligarchs control a governing oligarchy of full-time officials. For this book, such distinctions need not be maintained.

8. Rather than simply requiring "majority rule with minority rights," this more comprehensive conception of democracy implies that cleavage is a necessary feature of democratic organizations, and that levels of involvement must be high. Though less stringent than Lipset, Trow, and Coleman's (1962) requirements of an "institutionalized opposition," close votes in elections, and high member participation, the conception of democracy proposed here shares their concern with both cleavage and participation.

9. The concept of "technology" rather than tactics is usually employed in analyses of formal organizations (Hall, 1982:63–67).

10. Blau and Scott (1972:173) recognized the crucial role of the environment in organizational change, but formulated only a partial explanation of such change.

11. This theory explains the transformation of voluntary organizations from more to less democratic forms. It begins with a description of initially

democratic organizations, and does not explicitly consider voluntary organizations not formed by their prospective members. Organizations developed and controlled by a charismatic leader share many of the characteristics of participatory democracies (Weber, 1947:358–63). Unlike participatory democracies, however, in such organizations leadership domination is pronounced, and the transformation to more bureaucratic forms involves a less dramatic change in organizational configuration.

12. Zald and Ash (1966) formulated propositions consistent with this expectation, although expressed in terms of "exclusive" and "inclusive" movement organizations. They proposed that exclusive movement organizations are more likely than inclusive ones to participate in coalitions and mergers. Exclusive organizations (which restrict membership) also should be more dependent on their social environment.

NOTES TO CHAPTER THREE

1. This and other quotations without citations or other identification are from interviews with past and present union members.

2. Piven and Cloward (1977:273–74) argued that the increase in the number of individuals in Northern cities eligible for welfare did not immediately lead to an increase in the welfare rolls. Instead, an increase in the percentage of eligible individuals actually applying for welfare precipitated the welfare explosion.

NOTES TO CHAPTER FOUR

1. Union letters, leaflets and other materials are available in the I.U.S.S.E. archives.

NOTES TO CHAPTER SIX

1. The coefficient for each occupation dummy variable shows the deviation of its mean score from that of the excluded occupation, the professional specialties. (When dummy variables are used in regression analysis to represent categorical variables, one category must be excluded to prevent perfect collinearity among the predictors.)

2. Lower levels of job dissatisfaction (JOB) and less institutional alienation (PLTCS) among blacks accounted for a lower level of militancy among black members when these factors were not taken into account (not reported here).

3. These findings contradict Albert O. Hirschman's (1970) basic proposition that members' propensity to leave poorly performing organizations ("exit") would vary inversely with participation ("voice"). In other words, when dissatisfied members were able to express their dissatisfaction verbally, they would be less likely to quit. In the I.U.P.A.E., however, propensity to leave varied directly with participation, and both were associated with dissatisfaction.

Hirschman's failure to anticipate such a relationship may be due to his neglect of the relative opportunities of members outside of the organization, as well as the costs of participation for members. The backgrounds of caseworkers created greater opportunities for alternative employment and greater skills useful in union activity. Clerks and similar workers had fewer outside opportunities and fewer characteristics associated with propensity to participate. Some employees also perceived union participation as potentially hazardous to their future prospects in the agency. Since caseworkers were less dependent on their public aid jobs, they could be less concerned with these consequences. Hirschman's proposition may only be applicable given invariance in characteristics also associated with both "exit" and "voice" other than dissatisfaction, and given a lack of negative consequences of "voice."

NOTES TO CHAPTER NINE

1. Offices in Cook County were redistricted in 1974–75. Several small offices in housing projects were closed, and two larger offices were moved to new locations. Most open offices, however, retained their complement of staff.

2. Context also influences participation in nonunion settings. Zipp, Landerman, and Luebke (1982) found that mobilization efforts by political parties increased participation rates. Cohen and Kapsis (1978) concluded that *group* norms favoring participation increased individual rates of participation. Several studies have found that a supportive political climate in the black community raises participation rates above that expected on the basis of class or social status alone (Danigelis, 1977:39; London and Hearn, 1977; Verba and Nie, 1972:149–73).

3. Multicollinearity prevents simultaneous assessment of the effects of all of the variables determining and representing position in the work place: education, seniority, salary, mobility history, and current occupation. Instead, two specifications of the regression equation are evaluated. The first includes all the occupation and mobility history dummy variables, as well as the dummy variable indicating employment downstate. This specification also indicates the total effects of occupation and mobility history, prior to controlling for the correlated effects of social background variables. Since it is at this zero-order level, with all factors present and operant, that effects are "observed" by participants, this specification complements the impressions reported in interviews. The second specification includes the education and seniority variables, as well as the occupation dummies, but not the mobility history indicators. The measures of education and seniority, social background, and office political context are added to this second equation. Several other specifications were tested for each dependent variable, but none yielded additional information. Salary did not have an independent effect on any variable except evaluation of the union's performance (UPERF). Satisfaction with union performance decreased with higher salary as well as with more education.

4. Interaction terms tested for significant effects in individual-level regression analyses were:

PCTMAX * CLERK, EDUC, SNRTY, SALARY, RACE, AGE, MALE;
DWN * CLERK, EDUC, SNRTY, SALARY, RACE, AGE, MALE;
VOC * CLERK, EDUC, SNRTY, SALARY, RACE, AGE, MALE;
SALARY * RACE; EDUC * RACE; SALARY * CLERK; VOC * DWN

5. Whenever any of these interaction terms had a statistically significant effect ($p \leq .05$), its coefficient was included in the corresponding table. The interaction terms presented thus indicate the instances when the effect of a variable to the right of the multiplication sign varied for different values of the variable it was multiplied with.

Bibliography

Aaron, Henry J.
1973 Why Is Welfare so Hard to Reform? Washington, D.C.: Brookings.
Ad Hoc Committee on Public Welfare
1961 Report to the Secretary of Health, Education and Welfare. Pp. 36–42 in Gilbert Y. Steiner, Social Insecurity: The Politics of Welfare. Chicago: Rand McNally, 1966.
Aiken, Michael and Jerald Hage
1966 "Organizational alienation: A comparative analysis." American Sociological Review, (August):497–507.
Aldrich, Howard E.
1979 Organizations and Environments. Englewood Cliffs, N.J.: Prentice-Hall.
and Jeffrey Pfeffer
1976 "Environments of organizations." Pp. 79–105 in Alex Inkeles, James Coleman and Neil Smelser (eds.), Annual Review of Sociology, vol. 2.
Allutto, Joseph A. and James A. Belasco
1974 "Determinants of attitudinal militancy among nurses and teachers." Industrial and Labor Relations Review, 27:216–27.
American Public Welfare Association
1933–47 Public Welfare News. Chicago: APWA.
Aminzade, Ronald
1984 "Capitalist industrialization and patterns of industrial protest: A comparative urban study of nineteenth-century France." American Sociological Review. 49(August):437–453.
Applebaum, Leon and Harry R. Blaine
1975 "The 'iron law' revisited: Oligarchy in trade union locals." Labor Law Journal, 26(September):597–600.
Aveni, Adrian F.
1978 "Organizational linkages and resource mobilization: The significance of linkage strength and breadth." Sociological Quarterly, 19(Spring):185–202.

Barbash, Jack
  1961 Labor's Grass Roots. New York: Harper.
Barber, Bernard
  1963 "Some problems in the sociology of professions." Daedalus, 92(Fall):669–88.
Barry, Brian
  1978 Sociologists, Economists and Democracy. Chicago: University of Chicago Press.
Becker, Howard S.
  1962 "The nature of a profession." Pp. 27–46 in Education for the Professions, Nelson B. Henry (ed.). Chicago: University of Chicago Press.
Ben-Porat, A.
  1979 "Union democracy: The function of the political parties in the Histadrut." Industrial Relations, 18(Spring):237–43.
Bendix, Reinhard
  1947 "Bureaucracy: The problem and its setting." American Sociological Review, 12:493–507.
Berk, Richard
  1968 "Public welfare workers." Chapter 10 in Between White and Black: The Forces of American Institutions in the Ghetto, by Peter H. Rossi, Richard A. Berk, David P. Boesel, Bettye K. Eidson, and W. Eugene Groves. Published as part 2 of Supplemental Studies for the National Advisory Commission on Civil Disorders. Washington, D.C.: GPO.
Billings, Richard N., and John Greenya
  1974 Power to the Public Workers. Washington, D.C. Fact Research.
Billingsley, Andrew
  1964 "Bureaucratic and professional orientation patterns in social casework." Social Service Review, 38(December):400–7.
Blau, Peter M.
  1956 Bureaucracy in Modern Society. New York: Random House.
  1960 "Orientation toward clients in a public welfare agency." Administrative Science Quarterly, 5:341–61.
  1963 The Dynamics of Bureaucracy. Chicago: University of Chicago Press.
Blau, Peter M., and Richard A. Schoenherr
  1971 The Structure of Organizations. New York: Basic Books.
Blau, Peter M., and Richard W. Scott
  1962 Formal Organizations: A Comparative Approach. San Francisco: Chandler.
  1972 "Organizational development." Pp. 167–76 in Complex Organizations and Their Environments, Merlin B. Brinkerhoff and Phillip R. Kunz (eds.). Dubuque, Iowa: Brown.
Blauner, Robert
  1964 Alienation and Freedom. Chicago: University of Chicago Press.
Boehm, Werner
  1958 "The nature of social work." Social Work, 3:10–18.

Braverman, Harry
1974 Labor and Monopoly Capital: The Degradation of Work in the Twentieth Century. New York: Monthly Review Press.
Brooks, Detan J., Jr.
1963 The Blackboard Curtain: A Study to Determine the Literacy Level of Able-Bodied Persons Receiving Public Assistance. Chicago: Science Research Associates, for the Cook County Department of Public Aid.
Brown, Josephine C.
1940 Public Relief, 1929–1939. New York: Holt.
Bruner, Dick
1957 "Why white-collar workers can't be organized." Harper's Magazine, 215(August):44–50.
Bruno, Frank J.
1957 Trends in Social Work, 1874–1956: A History Based on the Proceedings of the National Conference of Social Work, 2nd ed. New York: Columbia University Press.
Bureau of the Census, U.S. Department of Commerce
1984 Statistical Abstract of the United States, 104th ed. Washington, D.C.: Government Printing Office.
Burnham, James
1943 The Machiavellians, Chicago: Regnery.
Burns, Robert K., and Benjamin Solomon
1963 "Unionization of white-collar workers—extent, potential and implications." Journal of Business, 36:141–65.
Business Week
1963 "Government workers getting organized." February 9: p. 72.

Chapin, F. Stuart, and John E. Tsouderos
1955 "Formalization observed in ten voluntary associations: Concepts, morphology, process." Social Forces, 33(May):306–9.
Child, John, Ray Loveridge, and Malcolm Warner
1973 "Towards an organizational study of trade unions." Sociology, 7:71–91.
Clark, Paul F.
1981 The Miners' Fight for Democracy: Arnold Miller and the Reform of the United Mine Workers. Ithaca: New York State School of Industrial and Labor Relations, Cornell University.
Cohen, Steven Martin, and Robert E. Kapsis
1978 "Participation of blacks, Puerto Ricans, and whites in voluntary associations: A test of current theories." Social Forces, 56(June):1053–71.
Cole, Stephen
1969 The Unionization of Teachers. New York: Praeger.
Coleman, John R.
1956 "The compulsive pressures of democracy in unionism." American Journal of Sociology, 61(May):519–26.

Cook, Alice H.
1963 Union Democracy: Practice and Ideal. Ithaca, N.Y.: Cornell University Press.

Corwin, Ronald G.
1970 Militant Professionalism: A Study of Organizational Conflict in High Schools. New York: Meredith.

Cotgrove, Stephen, and Clive Vamplew
1972 "Technology, class, and politics: The case of the process workers." Sociology, 6:169–85.

Craig, John G., and Edward Gross
1970 "The forum theory of organizational democracy: Structural guarantees as time-related variables." American Sociological Review, 35:19–33.

Curtis, Russell L., and Louis A. Zurcher
1973 "Stable resources of protest movements: The multi-organizational field." Social Forces, 52(September):53–61.

Daniel, John
1978 "Radical resistance in South Africa." Pp. 55–73 in Race and Politics in South Africa, Ian Robertson and Phillip Whitten (eds.). New Brunswick, N.J.: Transaction.

Danigelis, Nicholas L.
1977 "A theory of black political participation in the U.S." Social Forces, 56(September):31–47.

Dean, Lois R.
1954a "Social integration, attitudes, and union activity." Industrial and Labor Relations Review, 8:48–58.
1954b "Union activity and dual loyalty." Industrial and Labor Relations Review, 7:526–36.

Denzin, Norman K.
1970 The Research Act. Chicago: Aldine.

Dill, William R.
1958 "Environment as an influence on managerial autonomy." Administrative Science Quarterly, 2(March):409–43.

DiMaggio, Paul J., and Walter W. Powell
1983 "The iron cage revisited: Institutional isomorphism and collective rationality in organizational fields." American Sociological Review, 48:147–60.

Doeringer, Peter B., and Michael J. Piore
1971 Internal Labor Markets and Manpower Analysis. Lexington, Mass.: Lexington Books.

Dubin, Robert
1956 "Industrial workers' worlds: A study of the central life interests of industrial workers." Social Problems, 3:131–42.

Durkheim, Emile
1951 Suicide. John Spalding and George Simpson (trans). New York: Free Press.

Edelstein, J. David
1967 "An organizational theory of union democracy." American Sociological Review, 32:19–31.
Edelstein, J. David, and Malcolm Warner
1975 Comparative Union Democracy: Organization and Opposition in British and American Unions. London: George Allen and Unwin.
Edwards, Richard
1979 Contested Terrain: The Transformation of the Workplace in the Twentieth Century. New York: Basic Books.
Etzioni, Amitai W.
1969 The Semi-Professions and Their Organization. New York: Free Press.

Feuille, Peter, and James Blandin
1976 "University faculty and attitudinal militancy toward the employment relationship." Sociology of Education, 49(April):139–45.
Fine, Sidney
1958 "The origins of the United Automobile Workers, 1933–1935." Journal of Economic History, 18:249–82.
Fireman, Bruce, and William A. Gamson
1979 "Utilitarian logic in the resource mobilization perspective." Pp. 8–44 in The Dynamics of Social Movements, Mayer N. Zald and John D. McCarthy (eds.). Cambridge, Mass.: Winthrop.
Firey, Walter
1948 "Informal organization and the theory of the schism." American Sociological Review, 13(February):15–24.
Fox, William S., and Michael H. Wince
1976 "The structure and determinants of occupational militancy among public school teachers." Industrial and Labor Relations Review, 30:47–58.
Francis, R.G., and R.C. Stone
1956 Service and Procedure in Bureaucracy: A Case Study. Minneapolis: University of Minnesota Press.
Freeman, Jo
1979 "Resource mobilization and strategy: A model for analyzing social movement organization actions." Pp. 167–89 in The Dynamics of Social Movements, Mayer N. Zald and John D. McCarthy (eds.). Cambridge, Mass.: Winthrop.
Freeman, John, and Michael T. Hannan
1983 "Niche width and the dynamics of organizational populations." American Journal of Sociology, 88(May):1116–45.

Gamson, William A.
1968 Power and Discontent. Homewood, Ill.: Dorsey.
1975 The Strategy of Social Protest. Homewood, Ill.: Dorsey.
Garrett, Annette
1949 "Historical survey of the evolution casework." Journal of Social Casework, 30(June):219–29.

Gaventa, John
  1980 Power and Powerlessness: Acquiescence and Rebellion in an Appalachian Valley. Chicago: University of Illinois Press.
Goldthorpe, John H., David Lockwood, Frank Beckhofer, and Jennifer Platt
  1968 The Affluent Worker: Industrial Attitudes and Behavior. Cambridge: Cambridge University Press.
Goodsell, Charles T.
  1981 "Looking once again at human service bureaucracy." Journal of Politics, 43(August):761–78.
Gottlieb, Naomi
  1974 The Welfare Bind. New York: Columbia University Press.
Gouldner, Alvin W.
  1957 Patterns of Industrial Bureaucracy. New York: Free Press.
  1965 Wildcat Strike. New York: Harper and Row.
Greenleigh Associates, Inc.
  1960 Facts, Fallacies, and Future. New York: Greenleigh Associates.
Gruenberg, Barry
  1980 "The happy worker: An analysis of educational and occupational differences in determinants of job satisfaction." American Journal of Sociology, 86(September):247–71.
Grusky, Oscar
  1968 "Career mobility and organizational commitment." Administrative Science Quarterly, 13(March):488–503.
Guterbock, Thomas M., and Bruce London
  1983 "Race, political orientation, and participation: An empirical test of four competing theories." American Sociological Review, 48:439–53.

Hackman, J. Richard, and Edward E. Lawler III
  1971 "Employee reactions to job characteristics." Journal of Applied Psychology, 55(June):259–86.
Hagburg, Eugene C.
  1966 "Correlates of organizational participation: An examination of factors affecting union membership activity." Pacific Sociological Review, 9(Spring):15–26.
Hagburg, Eugene C., and Harry R. Blaine
  1967 "Union participation: A research note on the development of a scale." Industrial and Labor Relations Review, 21:12–95.
Hage, Jerald
  1965 "An axiomatic theory of organizations." Administrative Science Quarterly, 10(December):289–321.
Hage, Jerald, and Michael Aiken
  1970 Social Change in Complex Organizations. New York: Random House.
Hage, Jerald, and Michael Aiken
  1980 Theories of Organizations: Form, Process, and Transformation. New York: Wiley.

Hall, Richard H.
1968 "Professionalization and bureaucratization." American Sociological Review, 33(February):97–104.
1969 Occupations and the Social Structure. Englewood Cliffs, N.J.: Prentice-Hall.
1982 Organizations: Structure and Process. Englewood Cliffs, N.J.: Prentice-Hall.
Handelman, Howard
1977 "Oligarchy and democracy in two Mexican labor unions: A test of representation theory." Industrial and Labor Relations Review, 30:205–18.
Hannan, Michael T., and John Freeman
1977 "The population ecology of organizations." American Journal of Sociology, 82(March):929–64.
1984 "Structural inertia and organizational change." American Sociological Review, 49:149–64.
Hanushek, Eric A., and John E. Jackson
1977 Statistical Methods for Social Scientists. New York: Academic Press.
Hart, Wilson R.
1964 "The U.S. Civil Service learns to live with Executive Order 10,988: An interim appraisal." Industrial and Labor Relations Review, 17:203–20.
Haug, Marie R.
1973 "Deprofessionalization: An alternative hypothesis for the future." Sociological Review Monograph, 20:195–211.
Hellriegel, Don, Wendell French, and Richard B. Peterson
1970 "Collective negotiations and teachers: A behavioral analysis." Industrial and Labor Relations Review, 23:380–96.
Hilliard, Raymond M.
1964 "The new poverty." Cardinal O'Hara Memorial Lecture, University of Notre Dame, October 7. Mimeographed.
Hirschman, Albert O.
1970 Exit, Voice, and Loyalty: Responses to Decline in Firms, Organizations, and States. Cambridge, Mass.: Harvard University Press.
Holsti, Ole R.
1969 Content Analysis for the Social Sciences. Reading, Mass.: Addison-Wesley.
Hughes, Everett C.
1963 "Professions." Daedalus, 92(Fall):655–68.

Illinois. Department of Personnel
n.d. Class Specification: Public Aid Caseworker Series. Springfield, Ill.: Illinois Department of Personnel.
Illinois. Department of Public Aid (IDPA)
1972 Breakthrough. Springfield.
1973 Non-Administrative Personal Service—Permanent Positions (Pay Grade 1–19). Springfield, Ill.: Illinois Department of Public Aid, March 15, Mimeographed.

Illinois. General Assembly. House of Representatives. House Democratic Staff.
    1980 Public Aid Cost Control. Springfield (April 29).
Illinois Union of Social Service Employees
    1976 In the Matter of the Department of Personnel's Proposed Class
         Specifications: Local 2000's Brief in Opposition to the Proposed
         Job Specifications. Chicago: I.U.S.S.E., Mimeographed.
    1970 Constitution of the Illinois Union of Social Service Employees.
         Chicago: I.U.S.S.E., Mimeographed.
Independent Union of Public Aid Employees
    1966 Constitution of the Independent Union of Public Aid Employees.
         Chicago: I.U.P.A.E., Mimeographed.
    1965 Statement of Goals and Principles of I.U.P.A.E., by the Seventeen
         Founding Members. Chicago: I.U.P.A.E., Mimeographed.

Jacobs, Jerry
    1969 " 'Symbolic bureaucracy': A case study of a social welfare agency."
         Social Force, 47(June):413–21.
Johnstone, Frederick, A.
    1976 Class, Race and Gold: A Study of Class Relations and Racial
         Discrimination in South Africa. London: Routledge and Kegan
         Paul.
Joint Economic Committee. Subcommittee on Fiscal Policy, U.S. Congress
    1972 Studies in Public Welfare Issues in Welfare Administration. Wash-
         ington, D.C.: Government Printing Office.

Kahn, Robert L.
    1972 "The meaning of work." Pp. 159–204 in The Human Meaning of
         Social Change, Angus Campbell and Philip E. Converse (eds.).
         New York: Russell Sage.
Kanter, Rosabeth Moss
    1968 "Commitment and social organization: A study of commitment
         mechanisms in utopian communities. American Sociological Re-
         view, 33:499–517.
    1977 Men and Women of the Corporation. New York: Basic Books.
Katan, Joseph
    1973 "The attitudes of professionals toward the employment of indig-
         enous non-professionals in human service organizations." Socio-
         logical Review Monograph. 20:229–43.
Katzell, Raymond A., Abraham K. Korman, and Edward Levine
    1971 Overview Study of the Dynamics of Worker Job Mobility. National
         Study of Social Welfare and Rehabilitation Workers, Work, and
         Organizational Contexts, Research Report No. 1. Washington, D.C.:
         U.S. Department of Health, Education and Welfare, Social and
         Rehabilitation Services.
Kaufman, Bruce E.
    1982 "The determinants of strikes in the United States, 1900–1977."
         Industrial and Labor Relations Review, 35:473–90.

Klandermans, Bert
1984 "Mobilization and participation: Social-psychological expansions of resource mobilization theory." American Sociological Review, 49:583–600.

Kleingartner, Archie
1967 Professionalism and Salaried Worker Organization. Madison: Industrial Relations Institute, University of Wisconsin.

Knoke, David
1981 "Commitment and detachment in voluntary associations." American Sociological Review, 46:141–58.

Knoke, David, and James R. Wood
1981 Organized for Action: Commitment in Voluntary Associations. New Brunswick, N.J.: Rutgers University Press.

Ladd, Everett Carl, Jr., and Seymour Martin Lipset
1973 Professors, Unions, and American Higher Education. Washington, D.C.: American Enterprise Institute for Public Policy Research.

Larson, Magali Sarfatti
1977 The Rise of Professionalism: A Sociological Analysis. Berkeley and Los Angeles: University of California Press.

Latta, Geoffrey W.
1981 "Union organization among engineers: A current assessment." Industrial and Labor Relations Review, 35:29–42.

Leggett, John C.
1968 Class, Race, and Labor. New York: Oxford University Press.

Leiby, James
1978 A History of Social Welfare and Social Work in the United States. New York: Columbia University Press.

Lester, Richard A.
1958 As Unions Mature. Princeton, N.J.: Princeton University Press.

Lewin, David
1976 "Collective bargaining and the right to strike." Pp. 145–63 in Public Employees Unions, A. Lawrence Chickering (ed.). San Francisco: Institute for Contemporary Studies.

Lipset, Seymour Martin
1960 "The political process in trade unions: A theoretical statement." Pp. 216–22 in Labor and Trade Unionism, Walter Galenson and S.M. Lipset (eds.). New York: Wiley.
1962 "Introduction." Pp. 15–39 in Political Parties by Robert Michels. New York: Free Press.
1963 Political Man: The Social Bases of Politics. Garden City, N.Y.: Doubleday Anchor.
1972 Rebellion in the University. Boston: Little, Brown.

Lipset, Seymour Martin, and Earl Raab
1978 The Politics of Unreason: Right-Wing Extremism in America, 1790–1977, 2nd ed. Chicago: The University of Chicago Press.

Lipset, Seymour Martin, and Mildred A. Schwartz
1966 "The politics of professionals." Pp. 299–310 in Professionalization, Howard M. Vollmer and Donald L. Mills (eds.). Englewood Cliffs, N.J.: Prentice-Hall.
Lipset, Seymour Martin, Martin Trow, and James Coleman
1962 Union Democracy. New York: Doubleday.
Lipsky, Michael
1980 Street-level Bureaucracy. New York: Russell Sage.
London, Bruce, and John Hearn
1977 "Ethnic community theory of black social and political participation: Additional support." Social Science Quarterly, 57 (March):883–91.
Lubove, Roy
1965 The Professional Altruist: The Emergence of Social Work as a Career, 1880–1930. Cambridge, Mass.: Harvard University Press.

McAdam, Doug
1983 "Tactical innovation and the pace of insurgency." American Sociological Review, 48:735–54.
McCarthy, John D., and Mayer N. Zald
1973 The Trend of Social Movements in America: Professionalization and Resource Mobilization. Morristown, N.J.: General Learning Press.
1977 "Resource mobilization and social movements: A partial theory." American Journal of Sociology, 82(May):1212–41.
McKelvey, Jean T.
1967 "Cook County Commissioners' Fact-Finding Board Report on Collective Bargaining and County Public Aid Employees." Industrial and Labor Relations Review, 20:457–77.
McPherson, Miller
1983 "An ecology of affiliation." American Sociological Review, 48:519–32.
McPherson, William H.
1940 Labor Relations in the Automobile Industry. Washington, D.C.: Brookings.
Marcus, Philip M.
1966 "Union conventions and executive boards: A formal analysis of organizational structure." American Sociological Review, 31:61–70.
Marsh, David
1976 "On joining interest groups: An empirical consideration of the work of Mancur Olson, Jr." British Journal of Political Science, 6:257–71.
Martin, Roderick
1968 "Union democracy: An explanatory framework." Sociology, 2:205–20.

Marx, Karl
1961 Economic and Philosophical Manuscripts. T.B. Bottomore (trans.). Pp. 87–196 in Marx's Concept of Man, Erich Fromm (ed.). New York: Unger.
1964 Early Writings. T.B. Bottomore (ed., trans.). New York: McGraw-Hill.
1978 The Poverty of Philosophy. New York: International Publishers. [1847]

Messinger, Sheldon
1955 "Organizational transformation: A case study of a declining social movement." American Sociological Review, 20:3–10.

Meyer, Marshall
1978 Environment and Organizations: Theoretical and Empirical Perspectives. San Francisco: Jossey-Bass.

Meyer, Marshall, and M. Craig Brown
1977 "The process of bureaucratization." American Journal of Sociology, 83(September):364–85.

Michels, Robert
1962 Political Parties: A Sociological Study of the Oligarchical Tendencies of Modern Democracy. Eden and Cedar Paul, (trans.). New York: Free Press.

Moore, Barrington, Jr.
1978 Injustice: The Social Bases of Obedience and Revolt. White Plains, N.Y.: Sharpe.

Morales, Armando, and Bradford W. Sheafor
1977 Social Work: A Profession of Many Faces. Boston: Allyn and Bacon.

Nagi, Mostafa, and Meredith D. Pugh
1973 "Status inconsistency and professional militancy in the teaching profession." Education and Urban Society, 5(August):385–403.

Oberschall, Anthony
1973 Social Conflicts and Social Movements. Englewood Cliffs, N.J.: Prentice-Hall.
1978 "The decline of the 1960s social movements." Pp. 257–89 in Research in Social Movements, Conflicts and Change, I, Louis Kriesberg (ed.). Greenwich, Conn.: JAI Press.

Olmstead, Joseph A., and Harold E. Christensen
1973 Effects of Agency Work Contexts: An Intensive Field Study. National Study of Social Welfare and Rehabilitation Workers, Work, and Organizational Contexts, 1. Research Report No. 2. Washington, D.C.: U.S. Dept. of Health, Education and Welfare, Social and Rehabilitation Services.

Olson, Mancur, Jr.
1971 The Logic of Collective Action: Public Goods and the Theory of Groups. Cambridge, Mass.: Harvard University Press.

Oppenheimer, Martin
  1973 "The proletarianization of the professional." Sociological Review Monograph, 20:213–27.

Pateman, Carole
  1970 Participation and Democratic Theory. London: Cambridge University Press.
Pendleton, Brian F., Richard D. Warren, and H.C. Chang
  1979 "Correlated denominators in multiple regression and change analyses." Sociological Methods and Research, 7(May):451–74.
Perline, M.M., and V.R. Lorenz
  1970 "Factors influencing member participation in trade union activities." American Journal of Economics and Sociology, 29:425–37.
Perrow, Charles
  1961 "Goals in complex organizations." American Sociological Review, 26:854–65.
  1970 "Members as resources in voluntary organizations." Pp. 93–116 in Organizations and Clients, W. Rosengren and M. Lefton (eds.). Columbus, Ohio: Merrill.
  1979 Complex Organizations: A Critical Essay. 2nd ed. Glenview, Ill.: Scott, Foresman.
Pfeffer, Jeffrey, and Gerald R. Salancik
  1978 The External Control of Organizations: A Resource Dependence Perspective. New York: Harper and Row.
Piven, Frances Fox, and Richard A. Cloward
  1971 Regulating the Poor: The Functions of Public Welfare. New York: Vintage.
  1977 Poor People's Movements: Why They Succeed, How They Fail. New York: Pantheon.
Posey, Rollin G.
  1968 "The new militancy of public employees." Public Administrative Review, 28(March):111–17.
Prickett, James R.
  1968 "Communism and factionalism in the United Automobile Workers, 1939–1947." Science and Society, 32(Summer):257–77.
Prottas, Jeffrey
  1979 People-Processing: The Street-Level Bureaucrat in Public Service Bureaucracies. Lexington, Mass.: Lexington Books.

Ragin, Charles C., Shelley Coverman, and Mark Hayward
  1982 "Major labor disputes in Britain, 1902–1938: The relationship between resource expenditure and outcome." American Sociological Review, 47:238–52.
Richmond, Mary E.
  1919 Social Diagnosis. New York: Russell Sage.
Ritti, R.R., and D.W. Hyman
  1977 "The administration of poverty: Lessons from the welfare explosion 1967–1973." Social Problems, 25:157–75.

Ritzer, George
1972 Man and His Work: Conflict and Change. New York: Meredith.
Roomkin, Myron
1976 "Union structure, internal control, and strike activity." Industrial and Labor Relations Review, 29:198–217.
Rosenthal, Alan
1969 Pedagogues and Power. Syracuse, N.Y.: Syracuse University Press.
Ross, Philip
1963 "The role of the government in union growth." The Annals of the American Academy of Political and Social Science, 350(November):74–85.
Rothschild-Whitt, Joyce
1979 "The collectivist organization: An alternative to rational bureaucratic models." American Sociological Review, 44:509–27.
Rudwick, Elliott, and August Meier
1970 "Organizational structure and goal succession: A comparative analysis of the NAACP and CORE, 1964–1968." Social Science Quarterly, 51(June):9–24.

Salamon, Lester M.
1978 Welfare: The Elusive Consensus: Where We Are, How We Got There, and What's Ahead. New York: Praeger.
Salisbury, Robert H.
1975 "Research on political participation." American Journal of Political Science, 19(May):323–41.
Sandbrook, Richard
1975 Proletarians and African Capitalism. Cambridge: Cambridge University Press.
Saucier, Anne
1971 "The qualifications and activities of caseworkers in a county welfare department." Social Service Review, 45(June):184–93.
Sayles, Leonard R., and George Strauss
1953 The Local Union: Its Place in the Industrial Plant. New York: Harper.
Schumpeter, Joseph Alois
1976 Capitalism, Socialism, and Democracy. New York: Harper and Row.
Schutt, Russell K.
1982 "Models of militancy: Support for strikes and work actions among public employees." Industrial and Labor Relations Review, 35:406–22.
Schwartz, Michael, Naomi Rosenthal, and Laura Schwartz
1981 "Leader-member conflict in protest organizations: The case of the Southern Farmers' Alliance." Social Problems, 29:22–36.
Scott, Jerome F., and George C. Homans
1947 "Reflections on the wildcat strikes." American Sociological Review, 12:278–87.

Scott, W. Richard
  1966 "Professionals in bureaucracies—areas of conflict." Pp. 265–75 in Professionalization, Howard M. Vollmer and Donald L. Mills (eds.). Englewood Cliffs, N.J.: Prentice-Hall.
  1969 "Professional employment in a bureaucratic structure: Social work." Pp. 82–140 in The Semi-Professions and Their Organization, Amitai Etzioni (ed.). New York: Free Press.

Seidler, M.
  1961 "The Socialist Party and American unionism." Midwest Journal of Politics and Sociology, 5:207–36.

Seidman, Joel, Jack London, Bernard Karsh, and Daisy L. Tagliacozzo
  1958 The Worker Views His Union. Chicago: University of Chicago Press.

Selznick, Philip
  1943 "An approach to the theory of bureaucracy." American Sociological Review, 8:47–57.
  1948 "Foundations of the theory of organizations." American Sociological Review, 13:23–35.
  1960 The Organizational Weapon: A Study of Bolshevik Strategy and Tactics. Glencoe, Ill.: Free Press.
  1966 TVA and the Grass Roots. New York: Harper and Row.

Shepard, Jon M.
  1973 "Specialization, autonomy, and job satisfaction." Industrial Relations, 12(October):274–81.

Sills, David L.
  1957 The Volunteers: Means and Ends in a National Organization. Glencoe, Ill.: Free Press.

Skeels, Jack W.
  1982 "The economic and organizational basis of early United States strikes, 1900–1948." Industrial and Labor Relations Review, 35:491–503.

Smelser, Neil
  1962 Theory of Collective Behavior. New York: Free Press.

Snyder, David
  1975 "Institutional setting and industrial conflict: Comparative analyses of France, Italy, and the United States." American Sociological Review, 40:259–78.

Spinrad, William
  1960 "Correlates of trade union participation: A summary of the literature." American Sociological Review, 25:237–94.

Starbuck, William H.
  1965 "Organizational growth and development." Pp. 451–533 in Handbook of Organizations, James G. March (ed.). Chicago: Rand McNally.

Stein, Emmanuel
  1963 "The dilemma of union democracy" in "The Crisis in the American Trade Union Movement." The Annals of the American Academy of Political and Social Science, 350(November):46–54.

Steiner, Gilbert Y.
  1966 Social Insecurity: The Politics of Welfare. Chicago: Rand McNally.
  1971 The State of Welfare. Washington, D.C.: Brookings.
Stinchcombe, Arthur L.
  1978 Theoretical Methods in Social History. New York: Academic Press.
Strauss, George
  1954 "The white-collar unions are different." Harvard Business Review, 32(September-October):73–82.
  1963 "Professionalism and occupational associations." Industrial Relations, 2(May):7–31.
Street, David, George T. Martin, Jr., and Laura Kramer Gordon
  1979 The Welfare Industry: Functionaries and Recipients in Public Aid. Beverly Hills, Calif.: Sage.

Taft, Philip
  1944 "Opposition to union officers in elections." Quarterly Journal of Economics, 58(February):246–64.
Takamiya, Makoto
  1978 Union Organization and Militancy: Conclusions from a Study of the United Mine Workers of America, 1940–1974. Meisenham am Glan: Hain.
Tannenbaum, Arnold S.
  1965 "Unions." Pp. 710–43 in Handbook of Organizations, James G. March (ed.). Chicago: Rand McNally.
  1968 Control in Organizations. New York: McGraw-Hill.
Tannenbaum, Arnold S., and Robert L. Kahn
  1958 Participation in Union Locals. Evanston, Ill.: Row, Peterson.
Tausky, Curt
  1978 Work Organizations: Major Theoretical Perspectives. 2nd ed. New York: Peacock.
Taylor, Lee
  1968 Occupational Sociology. New York: Oxford University Press.
Teare, Robert J.
  1981 Social Workers: Their Jobs and Attitudes. New York: Praeger.
Thompson, James D., and William J. McEwen
  1972 "Organizational goals and environments: Goal-setting as an interactive process." Pp. 255–68 in Complex Organizations and Their Environments, by Merlin B. Brinkerhoff and Phillip R. Kunz (eds.). Dubuque, Iowa: Brown.
Tierney, Kathleen J.
  1982 "The battered women movement and the creation of the wife-beating problem." Social Problems, 29:207–20.
Tissue, Thomas
  1970 "Expected turnover among old-age assistance social workers." Welfare in Review, 8(May-June):1–7.

Toren, Nina
  1969 "Semi-professionalism and social work: A theoretical perspective."
       Pp. 141–95 in The Semi-Professions and Their Organization, Ami-
       tai Etzioni (ed.). New York: Free Press.
Trattner, Walter I.
  1979 From Poor Law to Welfare State: A History of Social Welfare in
       America, 2nd ed. New York: Free Press.
Trimberger, Ellen Kay
  1973 "Columbia: The dynamics of a student revolution." Pp. 31–59 in
       Campus Power, 2nd ed., Howard S. Becker (ed.). New Brunswick,
       N.J.: Transaction.

U.S. Bureau of the Census, Department of Commerce
  1984 Statistical Abstract of the United States, 104th ed. Washington,
       D.C.: Government Printing Office.
U.S. Department of Health, Education and Welfare. Social and Rehabilitation
Service
  1974 Overview Study of Employment of Paraprofessionals. National
       Study of Social Welfare and Rehabilitation Workers, Work, and
       Organizational Contexts. Research Report No. 3. Washington, D.C.:
       U.S. Department of Health, Education and Welfare, Social and
       Rehabilitation Service.
U.S. National Advisory Commission on Civil Disorders
  1968 Report. Introduction by Tom Walker. New York Times ed. New
       York: Bantam Books.
Useem, Bert, and Meyer N. Zald
  1982 "From pressure group to social movement: Organizational dilem-
       mas of the effort to promote nuclear power." Social Problems,
       30:144–56.

Verba, Sidney, and Norman H. Nie
  1972 Participation in America: Political Democracy and Social Equality.
       New York: Harper and Row.
Verba, Sidney, Norman H. Nie, and Jae-On Kim
  1978 Participation and Political Equality: A Seven-Nation Comparison.
       New York: Cambridge University Press.

Walsh, Edward J.
  1978 "Mobilization theory vis-à-vis a mobilization process: The case of
       the United Farm Workers' Movement." Pp. 155–77 in Research
       in Social Movements, Conflicts and Change, I, Louis Kriesberg
       (ed.). Greenwich, Conn.: JAI Press.
  1981 "Resource mobilization and citizen protest in communities around
       Three Mile Island." Social Problems, 29:1–21.
Walsh, Edward J., and Rex H. Warland
  1983 "Social movement involvement in the wake of a nuclear accident:
       Activists and free riders in the TMI area." American Sociological
       Review, 48:764–80.

Weatherley, Richard
1983 "Participatory management in public welfare: What are the prospects?" Administration in Social Work, 7(Spring):39–49.
Weatherley, Richard, Claudia Byrum Kottwitz, Denise Lishner, Kelly Reid, Grant Roset, and Karen Wong
1980 "Accountability of social service workers at the front line." Social Service Review, 54(December):556–71.
Weber, Arnold R.
1969 "Paradise lost; or whatever happened to the Chicago social workers?" Industrial and Labor Relations Review, 22:323–38.
Weber, Max
1947 The Theory of Social and Economic Organization. A.M. Henderson and Talcott Parsons (trans.), Talcott Parsons (ed.). New York: Free Press.
Windmuller, John P.
1981 "Concentration trends in union structure: An international comparison." Industrial and Labor Relations Review, 35:43–57.
Wurf, Jerry
1976 "Union leaders and the public sector: AFSCME." Pp. 174–82 in Public Employee Unions, A. Lawrence Chickering (ed.). San Francisco: Institute for Contemporary Studies.

Yuchtman, Ephraim, and Stanley Seashore
1967 "A system-resource approach to organizational effectiveness." American Sociological Review, 32:891–903.

Zald, Mayer N., and Roberta Ash
1966 "Social movement organizations: Growth, decay, and change." Social Forces, 44(March):327–41.
Zald, Mayer N., and Bert Useem
1982 "From pressure group to social movement: Organizational dilemmas of the effort to promote nuclear power." Social Problems, 30:144–56.
Zashin, Elliott, and Scott Summers
1980 "Case processing and error rates in the Illinois AFDC program: A case study of two local offices in Cook County and downstate." For National Academy of Public Administration. Evanston, Ill.: Mimeographed.
Zipp, John F., Richard Landerman, and Paul Luebke
1982 "Political parties and political participation: A reexamination of the standard socioeconomic model." Social Forces, 60(June):1140–53.
Zurcher, Louis A., Jr., Arnold Meadow, and Susan Lee Zurcher
1965 "Value orientation, role conflict, and alienation from work: A cross-cultural study." American Sociological Review, 30:539–48.

SERIALS

Union Newspapers and Newsletters
Black Facts (n.d.)
Common Sense (11/72–12/82)
GA Blues (7/23/72)
Information and Action (6/68–12/68)
IUPAE News (7/66–3/68, 11/68–9/70)
IUSSE Bulletin (5/71–9/72)
IUSSE News (10/70–4/71, 6/71)
Local 73 Union Newsletter (12/8/66, n.d.)
Non-Union Newspapers and Newsletters
Boston Globe (2/21/83)
Chicago's American (5/13/66, 5/27/66)
Chicago Daily News (5/12/66, 5/13/66, 5/21/66, 5/23/66, 5/27/66, 6/ 4/66, 10/22/66)
Chicago Defender (3/5/73)
Chicago Sun-Times (5/12/66, 5/20–27/66, 10/22/66, 8/7/73, 2/25/74)
Chicago Tribune (5/23/66, 5/24/66, 5/26/66, 2/14/73, 8/30/73)
From the State Capitals (1961, 1962, 1967–1969, 1971)
Illinois Welfare News (1/18/73)
PLP News (4/5/76)
Renewal (3/64)

LEGAL CASES

de Pue et al. v. Liberles. A.F.S.C.M.E. Judicial Panel Case #78–51.
In re: Local 2000. A.F.S.C.M.E. Judicial Panel Case #78–52.
In the matter of the Illinois Union of Social Service Employees and the Illinois Department of Public Aid, and Illinois Department of Personnel. October 30, 1979, ULP–69–OCB.
Max Liberles, et al. v. David L. Daniel, et al. September 10, 1979.

UNION LEAFLETS

Collection of leaflets in I.U.S.S.E. archives.

Index